THE AGE OF TRANSITION

BRITAIN IN THE NINETEENTH AND TWENTIETH CENTURIES

THE AGE
OF TRANSITION

BRITAIN IN THE NINETEENTH AND TWENTIETH CENTURIES

D. F. MACDONALD

MACMILLAN
London · Melbourne · Toronto

ST MARTIN'S PRESS
New York
1967

MACMILLAN AND COMPANY LIMITED
Little Essex Street London WC 2
also Bombay Calcutta Madras Melbourne

THE MACMILLAN COMPANY OF CANADA LIMITED
70 Bond Street Toronto 2

ST MARTIN'S PRESS INC
175 Fifth Avenue New York NY 10010

Library of Congress catalog card no. 67–11555

Printed in Great Britain by Richard Clay (The Chaucer Press), Ltd.,
Bungay, Suffolk

Contents

Preface

THIS book derives from a course of lectures on modern
Britain given to undergraduates as part of a wider study of the
political, social and economic structure of the country. Its aim is
not to pack the maximum amount of historical information into a
short compass but to seek to explain and illustrate the process by
which Britain has arrived at its present-day condition and position.
The plan used is to take outstanding developments in different
fields of activity, follow each separately as a theme in its own right,
and at the same time bring out their interrelationships in the overall pattern of change. This is the justification for what may seem
at first sight an odd choice and juxtaposition of subjects like the
linking of industrial growth with foreign policy or population
movements with constitutional reform.

I am fortunate in having in my Department colleagues who
were prepared to suspend their customary tolerance long enough
to make expert criticisms of particular sections, as well as to help in
other ways.

October 1966   D. F. M.

1 The Expansion of Industry

IT has of recent years become generally accepted among historians that the phenomenon known as the Industrial Revolution can be given a starting-point in the last quarter of the eighteenth century and that, as a distinctive phase of economic growth, it lasted for the next fifty years or so. This is a useful convention so long as it is not too strictly interpreted. The fact is that, even if one accepts the nomenclature, an industrial upsurge of any sort cannot be confined within chronological limits in this manner, as anybody aware of the preparatory work involved in introducing new or radically different industrial processes will appreciate. The title Industrial Revolution is, in fact, something of a misnomer and can be misleading. The changes the phrase connotes were spasmodic, piecemeal, unco-ordinated, and were often in the nature of catalysts, precipitating wholesale organic transmutations. They were intensifications of trends under way long before the period specified began and lasting long after it had elapsed. 'The innovations in technique and in the organisation of business, whose result has been called the Industrial Revolution, had been matters of experiment, speculation, and public interest for many decades before they came to maturity.'[1] In a word, this was a period of rapid industrialisation and its genesis can and should be traced back to the sixteenth century at least. Thereafter it gathered momentum, slowing down from time to time for one reason or another, and then accelerating rapidly in the later years of the eighteenth century. The pace was maintained and speeded up

[1] R. Koebner, 'Adam Smith and the Industrial Revolution', *Econ. Hist. Review*, xi. 3 (1959). See also F. Lipson, *Economic History of England*, (1934), iii. 53–55.

further in the early nineteenth century, especially after the end of
the Napoleonic Wars, by which time its repercussions were spreading through the whole of the economy. Nothing short of a
catastrophe could have stopped it by then; it was spreading far
beyond Britain, and the chain-reaction has continued and is
continuing.

It was not an overturn of the established order, as the word
'revolution' suggests; there was a great deal of trial and error,
which was, so to speak, subterranean to the eruption. It was not a
general upheaval: the tremors were felt in different places at
different times and in different degrees. Thus, the linen industry
in Scotland and the woollen industry in England, both of prime
importance in the respective countries, might be expanding faster
in the first three-quarters of the eighteenth century than in the
last quarter and some industries might even show a positive
decline in the period conventionally allotted to the Industrial
Revolution. The fact was that the changes in size and tempo were a
partial thing, which did not operate in all sectors of the economy
simultaneously, and were incomplete in some of those where they
did operate. They did, however, give a new orientation to the
economy by stimulating certain departments of industry which
were to be regarded as staple activities of our modern industrial
society.

The title can be a misnomer in another sense. It suggests that
the Industrial Revolution can be regarded as a purely material
phenomenon, a matter of greater production achieved by new or
improved methods. Material progress was indeed the essence of
the Industrial Revolution, as will be seen; but there were intangible
ingredients. It was a manifestation of human endeavour and therefore cannot be analysed or assessed wholly in terms of 'economics'.
Statistical judgments are proper and useful criteria in its evalua-
tion, but they do not explain the emergence of the many gifted
individuals who, after all, created the Revolution. Human genius,
dedication and self-interest were at the heart of it. In some ways,
it represented a new outlook, a change of attitudes, a quickening
of minds and a widening of horizons. It is not mere academic
speculation to argue that it was in some senses a derivative of the

Renaissance, which transformed the Continent in the sixteenth century and in England and Scotland reached its full flower in the seventeenth and eighteenth centuries.

Scotland, often comparatively ignored in this context, was a good example, for Scotland displayed a remarkable intellectual invigoration in the eighteenth century, which was by no means confined to the 'ivory towers' of pure learning. Francis Home, whose life almost spanned the century (1719–1813) was Professor of Materia Medica in Edinburgh, but, at the invitation of the Scottish Board of Trustees for the promotion of manufactures and fishing, carried out fruitful research into chemical bleaching, and wrote a popular treatise on *The Principles of Agriculture*. There were many more illustrations of science and industry working hand-in-hand, the best known being James Watt, who was mathematical instrument-maker to Glasgow University and gained much from his association with professors there. From a variety of motives, including self-gain, there was engendered a kind of restlessness, a seeking after new things, both in the realm of the mind as well as in the physical spheres, and an impatience with old things — which was often justified, since the old things in many cases formed a part of a closed, claustrophobic economy and had to be got rid of before a new world could be achieved.

'The age is running mad after innovation,' said Dr. Johnson. 'There were infinite numbers daily making machines for shortening labour,' said Josiah Tucker, and 'at Birmingham, Wolverhampton, Sheffield and other Manufacturing Places, almost every Master Manufacturer hath a new Invention of his own, and is daily improving on those of others'. The same sort of thing had been said in the sixteenth and seventeenth centuries and, comparatively speaking, with equal justification. There had been over this long period a disintegration of the traditional tenets and standards, social, economic, religious and political — and often they were intermixed, like the condemnation of 'usury' or interest — which had bound the old order together. In particular there was the clarion call of an ever-larger market beyond the parish, which had long been the basis of social and governmental organisation, and beyond the seas. There was a breaking-down of or escape from the old regimentation, imposed to suit a certain rigid kind of economy, and operated through the guilds, the municipalities and central government.

A recent exhaustive analysis of the growth of modern Britain takes up the study in 1688, mainly as a matter of statistical convenience;[1] but other reasons for this starting-point could be adduced. The political revolution of that year was part of this disintegrating movement. It finally destroyed personal, dynastic government, and replaced it by a form of parliamentary government. It is true that in this latter system the propertied classes, and especially the landed proprietors, were all-powerful; and this, incidentally, had a bearing on much that happened during the Industrial Revolution. Nevertheless, the 'Glorious Revolution' must not be dismissed as merely the substitution of oligarchical government for personal government; it did make possible in the long run a broadening, both in constitutional affairs and in others, which a personal government would have frustrated.

Whatever the causes, in the seventeenth century and even more in the eighteenth, industry was breaking out of its old centres, partly in order to get away from the old-fashioned controls which inhibited free enterprise, and partly in the search for raw materials, sources of power and labour, which were needed. This was one reason for the new growth and distribution of industry. There were many others. England and, after 1745 Scotland, settled down politically to a period of internal stability which made commercial expansion possible. In contrast, France had been set back forty years by the Napoleonic Wars, and Germany was not yet even a geographical expression, any more than was Italy. Britain had the most advanced economy in the world, having thrown off many of the old trammels — serfdom, the stranglehold of guilds and other restrictions — which still permeated industry in the rest of Western Europe. (It is true that, until the end of the eighteenth century, Scottish miners remained bound to their occupation, but this was exceptional.) Britain was more receptive of new ideas and more able to put them into practice. She had a growing and soundly-based trade at home and abroad. Not only had she

[1] Deane and Cole, *British Economic Growth, 1688–1959.*

'cashed in' on the discovery of new trade routes to the west and to the east, but she had by now carved herself a considerable Empire with the accretion of territories and trading privileges wrested from her rivals as a result of the Seven Years War. She had emerged the victor in international struggles, which, while mainly fought in Europe, were largely, from her point of view, wars for colonies, and she had been victorious at the expense of her closest competitor, France. She had become established as the mistress of the seas, commanding all the trade routes through the disposition of her colonial bases and the might of her navy. She had substantial material resources within her own boundaries, both of coal and iron. She had a growing population, providing a reservoir of labour and a market for consumer goods. She was not peculiar in this respect and, even within the frontiers of the United Kingdom there was striking proof in Ireland that increase of population alone was not an 'open sesame' to industrial growth. England and Scotland, however, had other advantages. Thanks to the greatly enhanced productivity of their soil they were better placed to sustain a larger population, with an improving standard of living, while their overseas trade made possible the import of more supplies, for people and machines, as needed. They had the capital to finance the promotion of industry, and this, it has been said, constitutes the greatest single factor in the expansion of an economy. The machinery of money and credit was relatively backward, even in the early nineteenth century, but it was the best in Europe. Some reference will be made later to the sources of capital; it is sufficient here to say that, as the Industrial Revolution progressed, and as the investment habit spread, sound projects—and many that were not—seem to have had little difficulty in attracting the necessary funds.

These are some of the reasons why Britain was ripe for the Industrial Revolution. There were other factors which helped to explain its success, although with them it is sometimes difficult to separate cause from effect. The country's very smallness in one way helped in that, unlike, say, Russia or America, raw materials, labour and markets, were all close together, while nature had provided the country with good natural outlets. Even so, the improvement of transport and connections played a vital part. Here striking advances were being made, by dint of private capital, for instance, through the formation of turnpike trusts for road-making and maintenance. (While this method was much criticised then and later, it is interesting to note that today Britain is returning to the idea of charging tolls, in addition to taxes, for the construction of roads and bridges, and that the practice has long been accepted in the United States.) New skills were emerging in the realm of civil engineering, pioneered by brilliant individuals such as Thomas Telford, John McAdam and James Brindley. The canals were regarded as miracles of progress in the later eighteenth century, as indeed they were, for they made possible for the first time the carriage of heavy or delicate goods when other means did not exist. Then there was the development of shipping, including coastwise shipping, and of ports, essential to an island economy relying on foreign trade. Finally there was the application of man's ingenuity to the technology of manufacture.

The inventions were not the work of professional 'technologists', in the modern sense: there were none. They might come from men working with their hands seeking working improvements, or from amateurs with a scientific bent, such as the Reverend Edmund Cartwright, pursuing likely ideas. Generally speaking, however, they had one thing in common: they were the direct response to practical requirements. The inventors, in other words, were working on the solution of specific and urgent problems, in close co-operation with industrialists, and with an eye on the financial exploitation of their discoveries, even if, in some cases, their business acumen proved not to be equal to their ingeniousness. The spectacular successes of the Industrial Revolution in this field were usually the consummation of work done by a multitude of comparatively unknown men who had gone before. A high proportion of the inventors were Scots. This was no accident. It may be that the Scots are mechanically-minded and have a natural proclivity to seize 'the main chance'; but their outstanding work in the field of what might be called applied science, as in medicine and other skills, was probably due more to their superior system of education, both in schools and universities. It was much easier for the ordinary

man to get a grounding in elementary knowledge than it was in
England. In the eighteenth century there were no less than five
fully-fledged universities in Scotland, when there were only two —
and those two open only to the few — in England.

The times produced their philosophies to reinforce the logic
of events. Adam Smith laid the foundations of modern political
economy with the publication in 1776 of *An Inquiry into the Nature
and Causes of the Wealth of Nations*. It is doubtful if he appreciated
the scale or momentousness of what was happening around him in
British industry, nor was he indeed very sympathetic to certain of
the influences at work. While he was not, as is sometimes said, the
prophet of the Industrial Revolution, he was a product of his time,
in that he translated into what many regarded as unassailable
doctrines sentiments in regard to freedom of trade in particular
which were already affecting the outlook of the more far-sighted
industrialists and reformers. There was little, however, of the
theorist about James Watt (1736–1819) — who did *not* invent the
steam-engine; Newcomen had used steam-power to pump water
out of mines as far back as 1712. In passing it might be said that
the development of steam-power in the eighteenth century was
largely motivated by the needs of the mining industry. Watt,
working on a model of Newcomen's engine used for demonstration purposes in Glasgow University — and with encouragement
from Roebuck of the Carron Iron Works in Scotland and later
from Boulton of the Soho Works in Birmingham, with whom he
entered into partnership — made the vital improvements, first by
the introduction of a separate condenser (patented in 1769) and
later by evolving the rotative steam-engine (1781) which enabled
steam-power to be applied to manufacturing processes.

The harnessing of steam marked the beginning of a new era
for industry and, it is no exaggeration to say, for civilisation as we
know it. Here at last was a source of unlimited power, and all else
flowed from it. The clue to what happened in the Industrial
Revolution, and in the evolution of industry since then, was to be
found in this. Boulton spoke no more than the truth when he said
to Boswell, 'I sell what all the world desires, power.'

It was a comparatively slow business. By 1800, when Watt's

patent for the steam-engine expired, there were only about 250 of
them in operation. There had been startling improvements in the
technology of production in the eighteenth century. There was
Hargreaves's spinning-jenny, designed about 1765 although not
patented until five years later. This speeded up cotton-spinning
enormously, but it did not dispense with hand-power. Perhaps a
more important step was Arkwright's water-frame (1769) and
Crompton's mule, which came ten years later, and which combined
the best features of the spinning-jenny and the water-frame. These
discoveries set off a never-ending series of other inventions.
Machine-spinning became the norm, but the application of steam
was a slow and difficult matter. Crompton's mule was first operated
by hand, then adapted to water-power, in David Dale's New
Lanark Mill, in 1792, and thereafter to steam-power.

With power-spinning, power-weaving could not be far behind,
unless the advantages of the former were to be largely nullified.
Here the same fits and starts were found. Cartwright's power-loom,
invented in 1784, was first horse-driven, and it was not until five
years later that steam-power was invoked. In the intermediate
phase, after the advent of power-spinning, and before the various
snags in changing to power-weaving were overcome, there was an
interlude of unparalleled but brief prosperity for the hand-loom
weavers. Some mills used both machine and hand-weaving, like
New Lanark. Even in 1817 there were a hundred times as many
hand-looms as power-looms (which then numbered between two
and three thousand), and in the middle of the nineteenth century,
in the cotton industry, which was the prime example of industrialisation, one-third of the cotton-weavers were outside factories.
By then, however, they were a rapidly diminishing and miserable
survival.

Delays and interruptions were, in the nature of things, una-
voidable. The early machines were clumsy and costly, with each
part fashioned singly and by hand. They broke down easily and
there were no trained engineers to provide repairs and maintenance.
The experience of one manager must have been a common one:
he records that, in a Scottish mill erected in 1799, 'the steam
engine was constructed by the celebrated Watt and Boulton of

Birmingham, and the spinning machinery for the most part made at the mill ... spinning machinery was but ill-installed and ill-managed, and for the steam-engine nobody could lay a hand on it but English engineers who had often to be sent for though little was the matter, and who created an immense deal of stoppage and expense'.[1] There was a reluctance on the part of many employers to spend a great deal of money on new and untried machinery, and there was the more commonly known reluctance on the part of labour to accept devices which threatened their livelihood — their sole livelihood in many instances, as textile work became a full-time occupation. The weavers in Manchester threatened to destroy the mill housing Cartwright's power-loom and it was, in fact, burnt down. Hargreaves's loom was broken, and Arkwright's works went up in flames. One of the partners in the Catrine Mill in Ayrshire said in 1812, 'the weavers are resolved to destroy the power-looms in all places', and at Deanston in Perthshire, in the same year, an attempt was made to wreck the machinery.

The whole gamut of processes in the cotton industry was affected by the pressure of machine-production. Printing came to be done by machinery with the introduction of cylindrical printing in 1784. Chemical bleaching was begun by James Watt in 1786, and, almost at the same time, and quite independently, was started elsewhere in Scotland. This is an interesting instance of how knowledge spread in spite of efforts in some quarters to keep it exclusive to the firm. Watt had acquired the secret during a visit to the Continent. In 1787 a Professor Coupland, occupying the Chair of Natural Philosophy in Aberdeen, was touring the Continent with the Duke of Gordon and he duly noted the process and passed on the information, when he got home, to the Aberdeen firm of Messrs. Gordon Barron & Company, which had introduced the cotton industry into Aberdeen eight years before and which, incidentally, was the only firm in Scotland to import, spin, weave and print the material. This kind of thing marked the beginning of mass-production, as the interrelationship between different processes and stages became even more apparent. This prompted

[1] D. Chapman, 'William Brown of Dundee, 1791–1864', *Explorations*, iv. 3 (Harvard, 1952).

their closer association, preferably under one control, both for the sake of economy and efficiency, to eliminate competition, and to prevent any hiatus between the making of the unfinished article and the final marketing.

The same progression of events was taking place in other branches of industry. Cotton has been singled out because it became pre-eminent among textiles and set the pattern for the factory era. It brought cheap, easily-washable clothing to the masses, and commanded a market of seemingly inexhaustible proportions at home and overseas. It made fortunes and altered social habits. It built up groupings of population. At the beginning of the eighteenth century perhaps 2 million lb. of cotton were imported; at the beginning of the nineteenth, the figure was around 56 million lb., and by mid-century it was well over 600 million lb. By then it was the biggest occupation next to agriculture and employed half a million operatives. Much the greater part of cotton production was for export; by the end of the century, cotton constituted about one-quarter of British exports. The industry flourished at first both in Lancashire and Cheshire, but Scotland — especially West Scotland — claimed about 20% of the total production in the early nineteenth century. It declined there rapidly as the century wore on, for reasons which are not entirely clear; but a contributory factor was the diversion of capital to the expanding heavy industries, particularly shipbuilding and engineering.

The linen industry, which had been Scotland's staple manufacture in the eighteenth century, survived the competition of cotton and even flourished. In 1835 there were a little over 200 power-looms in the linen industry, of which 168 were in Scotland; Ireland was the main producer. It was said that Baxters of Dundee, which had started power-loom weaving of linen in 1828, were forty years later using more power-looms than any comparable undertaking in Britain. Linen, however, was soon surpassed in its main habitat, East Scotland, by the jute industry which, starting in 1832, was well established by 1850 and quickly took over the primacy from linen even in its main centre, the county of Forfar.

Wool had been the biggest industry in England, next to agriculture, and up to the end of the eighteenth century it remained cotton's chief rival. It was also the first industry, except agriculture, to feel the impact of capitalism. Even after it began to be overtaken by cotton, it continued to grow, but the old methods, especially in weaving, survived longer, as was natural with an old-established craft. The same trend was, however, evident; indeed, wool exemplified very well both the long process of change and the resistance to change. There had been attempts as early as the thirteenth century to apply mechanical methods, in the shape of gig-mills to raise the nap on cloth, and this provoked a reaction from labour and from officialdom, being finally forbidden by statute in the sixteenth century. Like other prohibitions of the kind, it was ineffective, and even government connived at its evasion by the issue of special exemptions. Yet for one hundred years or so, government, while willing to encourage new techniques, tried to inhibit the development of labour-saving devices, on the grounds that these were anti-social, as making for unemployment and unrest.[1]

Machine-spinning in wool began in the 1780s and wool and worsted spinning was a factory industry by 1830. Power-loom weaving made headway also in the 1830s, after the large Australian wool supplies became available. The introduction of machinery on a large scale, in both cotton and wool, took something like seventy years to achieve (1771–1840) and the changeover was by no means complete until the 1870s. In the middle of the nineteenth century about 40% of the workpeople in the woollen industries were still outside factories, and as late as the 1880s hand-loom weaving was of some significance, but thereafter it was practically finished.

The woollen industry also expanded as a whole, although on a much smaller scale — relatively to cotton it lost ground — and it soon outgrew the native resources, although wool continued to be exported as well as imported. As late as the mid-nineteenth century about 12 million lb. of wool were exported out of a total production of 130 million lb. but at this stage over 70 million lb.

[1] Lipson, op. cit., pp. 50–53 and 352–4.

were imported, and by 1870 the figure had risen to 266 million lb. as against 150 million lb. home-produced. The great source of the raw material was Australia, which had started sheep-farming in New South Wales in 1788, with twenty-nine sheep sent from the United Kingdom. The industry was concentrated mainly in the West Riding, where it maintained itself at the expense of the old centres in the south-west and east. It is again a little difficult to say why the industry flourished here and not in other places. Partly, however, it must have been due to the ingrained conservatism of the older practitioners of the trade, and the better response to the challenge of innovation from new men in new places. Scotland retained a small part, especially in the making of tweed cloth.

The most conspicuous example of the manner and effects of industrialisation other than cotton is to be found in the iron industry. The use of steam-power would obviously mean a demand for a stronger and safer medium than wood. Before the Industrial Revolution the industry was not a large one and pig-iron, so called because of its shape, was largely imported. Iron was limited in its uses — for example, ships were still made of wood — but in any case it was strictly limited in output, both because of the techniques employed and the limitations on the supply of fuel. It was smelted with charcoal, and the industry's location was to a great extent determined by the availability of woodlands. Thus one finds ironworks in such unlikely places as Wester Ross and Argyllshire, despite the fact that manufacture there presented quite extraordinary transport and other difficulties. Abraham Darby, of Coalbrookdale, began to use coke for smelting in 1709, although the method was not widely adopted for a good many years thereafter. This clearly meant, in time, the bringing of the iron producers to the coalfields, and the publication in 1783 of Henry Cort's process of puddling and rolling finally completed the switch by ending for ever the reliance on charcoal. It also meant that the aggregation of the different processes in the industry was immensely facilitated. Strong, 'integrated' groups settled in Staffordshire, South Wales and the Clyde Valley. The steam-engine, which had started by being used to work the blast furnaces not later than 1776, came thereafter to be applied to forge hammers, then to rolling and slitting mills. Production of pig-iron rose more than eight times between 1770 and 1805, to about one-quarter of a million tons, of which approximately one-fifth was being exported. Around 1740, Huntsman of Sheffield — like Darby and other notable entrepreneurs, a Quaker — had perfected a steel-making process, which was to make Sheffield famous in this sphere. In 1779 Abraham Darby III (1750–91), built the first iron bridge, which still exists, over the Severn. John Wilkinson (1728–1808), a great ironmaster and colliery owner, had extensive operations in Shropshire, Staffordshire and South Wales. He had four steam-engines to work his blast furnaces by 1780, and by 1806 there were thirty Boulton and Watt steam-engines at work in the industry.

In Scotland the Carron Iron Works, near Falkirk, were established by John Roebuck in 1759–60; he lost control in 1773 when the Carron Company took over. The Seven Years War gave a fillip to the iron industry, and both Wilkinson and Roebuck benefited from the demand for armaments: the word 'carronade' was derived from the Carron Iron Works. The discovery of blackband ironstone in Lanarkshire in 1801 put Scotland in a fine strategic position to take full advantage of the 'iron age' in the early nineteenth century. This kind of ore, however, was not easily worked, and it awaited full exploitation until Neilson, the manager of Glasgow Gas Works, introduced the 'hot blast' in 1828 (patented in 1829), which reduced coal consumption in the furnaces to one-quarter of its former volume. It was first tried out in the Clyde Iron Works. Scotland's output of pig-iron rose from 37,000 tons in 1830 to 195,000 tons in 1839, and to well over half a million tons in 1847, by which time it constituted over one-quarter of the total British output.

The improvements in production meant more and cheaper iron and steel, the material for rails, engines, machines, ships and all the other manifold instruments of the iron age. With this went, of course, the exploitation of the coalfields, in which Britain, fortunately for herself, was rich. In the first half of the nineteenth century coal production rose from 10 to 50 million tons. There were, too, promising by-products. For instance, one of those landowners who had the wit and the capital to exploit the opportunities of the new age, the Earl of Dundonald, author of *The Connection Between Agriculture and Chemistry* (1795), in 1782 established works at Culross to extract tar from coal. Tar was needed for wooden ships and a multitude of other things, and previously had been imported from the Baltic countries.

Coal and iron were Siamese twins; they were interdependent and grew together. From coal was derived another source of heat and light as well as power — that is, gas, which was first used for lighting about 1800 by a Scotsman, William Murdoch, in the Soho Works of Boulton and Watt. It was increasingly used for street-lighting and for domestic purposes. Then in the 1860s its potentialities were realised as a fuel for the internal-combustion engine, which was very suitable for the needs of the small manufacturer. Electricity was already being experimented with by the end of the eighteenth century, but its day as a source of power was not yet, although by the 1830s it was identified with telegraphy. The turn of electricity and oil was still to come.

Coal was needed at home and abroad, as was iron. At the end of the eighteenth century the total output of coal in Britain was perhaps 10 million tons. By the 1850s it was 60 million tons, and by the end of the century 225 million tons. One of the chief reasons for the industry's prosperity in the nineteenth century was that it was a large and increasingly valuable constituent in foreign trade. Ships lacking other export cargo, instead of going in ballast, could go out carrying coal, with the certainty of a market abroad, and come back bringing the raw materials which Britain needed for her manufactures. The export of coal was under half a million tons in 1831; by 1861 it had increased to 8 million tons; and by 1913 not far short of one-third of home production, well over 90 million tons, went overseas. The story here is essentially one of increased production achieved mainly through run-of-the-mill expansion by conventional methods. In the middle of the nineteenth century perhaps 200,000 people were employed in the industry in its various ramifications, while by 1913 about 1 million were employed. Partly the higher output was achieved through better winding-gear, better ventilation, better transport, and safer and faster methods of winning coal. In this second causation, however, there was nothing particularly revolutionary in the way of innovation, apart from the Davy lamp, invented in 1815.

The new forms of transport created boom conditions for the industry. Railway construction went on at, for a small country, a fantastic rate. The development of transport will be referred to elsewhere, but in this context it might be mentioned that in 1838 there were 500 miles of railway, and at this stage the expenditure on tracks and rolling-stock was believed to be running at an average of £10 million a year. In the following ten years the 'railway mania' mounted to a feverish pitch, until, in the later forties, 1,000 miles of railway was being opened annually. This intensity could not be maintained — indeed, it was almost bound to provoke a relapse — but, as it abated, the large home demand was supplemented by demands from overseas. Iron was being used in machines, steam-engines, boilers, bridges and, as the century advanced, ships. Its use in shipbuilding was a slower development; the suspicions of the Admiralty and other ship-owners needed time to dissipate; but between 1850 and 1870 the net tonnage of iron ships rose from about 1,300 tons to $\frac{1}{4}$ million.

Iron manufacture, unlike coal production, was susceptible to all sorts of improvements. True, as in coal-mining, more people were employed as the century advanced; there were perhaps 80,000 in 1850 and more than three times as many seventy years later. Much more was being produced. In 1850 the output of pig-iron was in the region of 3 million tons, having quadrupled in the last twenty years. By the end of the century the figure was 8 million tons, after which progress was much slower, until by 1913 it had risen to its peak of over 10 million tons.

Iron, as well as iron goods, was exported in huge quantities. It was in demand in the United States, Germany, Russia and other continental countries. Exports reached nearly $3\frac{1}{2}$ million tons in the early seventies, after which there was a slump. Later, with the industry adapting itself to new techniques, as it had to do or perish, there was a partial recovery, and in 1882 the total had more than recovered to over $5\frac{1}{2}$ million tons. The increase of production was the result not merely of growth as such, but of new processes, and was accompanied by a greater reliance on foreign ores. In the 1870s imported ore was equal to perhaps one-thirteenth of home production, whereas by 1913 it was about one-half. This increasing dependence on imports was not peculiar to the iron industry, and was reflected in the balance of trade.

In the 1850s — and it is not without significance that again there was a war in progress — Bessemer devised a process revealed in 1856, of making steel by forcing air through the molten iron to eliminate the carbon impurities and produce wrought iron or steel. This meant a great saving in fuel and a much cheaper product. Then came William Siemens, with his open-hearth process (1866), which in time almost superseded Bessemer's process. These two methods required haematite ore, found in Britain only in Cumberland — with obvious consequences for the development of that area — but they were so much cheaper that it paid handsomely to import ores, mainly from Spain. There followed Gilchrist and Thomas's process in the late seventies, which allowed, as Bessemer's and Siemens's did not, for the use of phosphorus-bearing ores. It gave a great advantage to Germany, which had this kind of ore in quantity, and to the United States of America, where supplies were also abundant. As a consequence of this development, steel production overhauled that of iron. It was stronger and cheaper, and was increasingly used in such things as the making of rails and ships, even if as late as 1880 there were nine iron ships for every one of steel.

In the 1870s the production of steel ran at half a million tons, in 1914 it was fifteen times as much, and yet, at this latter point, British production represented only one-tenth of world production. Britain's proportion of pig-iron also fell in the same period from one-half to one-eighth. Before the end of the century Germany had outstripped Britain in steel production — and was shortly to do the same as regards pig-iron — and before 1914 it was showing double the output, much of it being sold to Britain. This advantage 'played a very important part in pre-disposing Germany to aggressive war and enabling her after 1914 to sustain and prolong it'.[1] One of the reasons for Britain's relative decline was the

[1] R. C. K. Ensor, *England 1870–1914*, p. 106.

interruption which the imperative need to adapt itself to new processes imposed on an old industry; it meant, in the eighties, 'the scrapping on a wholesale scale of the greatest iron industry in the world'. Germany and the United States were able to start where Britain left off, a fact which contributed largely to what has been called, with some exaggeration, the 'great depression' in Britain in the seventies. Britain was, in a sense, paying the price of being the pioneer and of resting over-long on her laurels. The 'depression' was partly a natural, and in some ways an inevitable slowing-down.

These developments resulted in a shifting of the iron industry's distribution. With the Industrial Revolution it had been brought within the area of the coalfields, but native coal was coming to be a less important factor. Then the amount of phosphoric ores available locally was limited and the quantity of imported ore was increased, so that the steel industry tended to move to the north-east, with good and handily-situated ports, and the north-west of England. South Wales and Staffordshire, which in 1830 had been responsible for four-fifths of Britain's pig-iron production, were by 1880 down to one-fifth and by 1913 to one-sixth, while the north-east's share rose from a negligible quantity to be almost one-third of the total. Cumberland and Lancashire rose from minute proportions to one-fifth. Scotland, which had advanced fairly rapidly in the forties and fifties, from about 15% to nearly 25% of the national output, declined comparatively until by the eighties it was about 13%.

As the century advanced, engineering became of paramount importance. The prototypes of the engineers were the millwrights. Mechanics of a sort soon appeared, and quite early in the nineteenth century one hears, as in the case already mentioned, of men attached to textile mills whose business it was to make and mend machinery and nothing else. The new age required above all, however, precision tools to turn out uniform components, if machines were to be produced, maintained and repaired fairly easily. Boulton and Watt's Soho Foundry set an example to the world. On a carefully-selected site (by a canal, for obvious reasons), the new works were planned and operated in a manner which could have been profitably emulated a century and a half later. It is not surprising that the techniques of management should have attained an extraordinary excellence there, for Boulton, before ever he teamed up with Watt, had been an exponent of some of them in his earlier venture as a maker and seller of fine wares. So had his acquaintance Wedgwood, who in the later eighteenth century built up from the humblest beginnings an international business by concentrating on quality production and, above all, marketing. Boulton and Watt until then (1785) had put the emphasis more on consultancy and designing than on production; but the imminent expiry of their patent for the improved steam-engine with a separate condenser, and Watt's evolution of the rotary-engine, decided them to concentrate on production. Mechanics had to be trained in the works; and this became the normal procedure.

Henry Maudslay (1771–1831) in 1797 started his workshop for making machine tools and produced, among other useful instruments, the slide rest. Maudslay had been for a time in the employment of another remarkable man, Joseph Bramah (1748–1814). Bramah produced all sorts of new and intensely practical things, ranging from the water-closet to the beer-handle tap. The two worked together on new ideas; for instance, Maudslay perfected Bramah's hydraulic press by devising a self-adjusting collar. He also evolved the heavy screw-cutting lathe. After he set up on his own, James Nasmyth was one of his pupils, as were Joseph Whitworth and Richard Roberts, the inventor of the self-acting mule. James Cook, in Glasgow, manufactured steam-engines, and his works turned out so many mechanics that it became known as 'The College'. This proliferation of workshops was a necessity forced on the producers. James Nasmyth, who in 1830 invented the steam-hammer (first used in the Schneider Works at Le Creusot, in which there was a strong British interest), established his own place, as did Joseph Whitworth and Joseph Clement. They trained others, and the industry progressed rapidly until British engineers were training the world. It was no accident that the first of the 'model' trade unions was the Amalgamated Society of Engineers (1851) and significant that, in its formation, it embraced the

Journeymen, Steam Engine and Machine Makers' Friendly Society.

A feature of the spread of industrialism was the multiplication of larger units of enterprise. This development, like other features of capitalism, had begun before the Industrial Revolution and had affected agriculture as well as industry; but as manufacture became more complicated, requiring the installation of costly machinery and its proper utilisation, the tendency was bound to become more marked. Different processes in the one industry were brought together for reasons of convenience, efficiency and economy, and there was a growing interdependence of different branches and different industries.

There were impediments to the formation of large entities, both psychological and physical. A great many of the new industrialists were 'self-made men' and cherished their independence. The virtues of free competition were extolled by the political economists, and individualism and self-help were elevated to be the gospel of material and moral success. The fear of monopoly, as a threat to the public interest, was a cardinal point in the Liberal philosophy, and combination in any form, whether of employers or workers, tended to be regarded by the pundits as an alliance for selfish, mercenary ends — which it usually was. Nevertheless, the very forces of competition made integration and combination, including loose forms of association to control output and price, inevitable, and, from an early stage of industrial development, there were manifestations of the desire to soften the impact of competition, as a matter of self-preservation, for both labour and capital. The State grudgingly recognised this. It repealed the Anti-Combination Laws and so promoted the emergence of trade unions. As regards business it was, if anything, more cautious, but it made considerable concessions. The joint-stock principle — by which individuals willing to venture their capital, but anxious to minimise the risks, pooled their resources and were accorded certain privileges — had long been accepted, but under the sanction and, in theory at least, the surveillance of the State. There still remained at the end of the Industrial Revolution the deterrent of unlimited liability, which greatly inhibited this form of organisation. This kind of restriction, too, was under attack and could not long survive.

Some industries lent themselves more easily to concentration or consolidation. Thus the iron industry, with its heavy capital costs, clearly was one where grouping would eliminate not merely competition, but waste and delay, while it also offered a natural partnership with coal-mining. Perhaps the most outstanding name was Crawshay of Cyfartha, who was largely responsible for turning South Wales into a great iron-making area. In the early part of the nineteenth century, he employed a total of 1,500 men. Cotton manufacture, on the other hand, remained an industry of specialisation, but this did not prevent the creation or evolution of large firms.

The small enterprise, however, remained — and still remains — an important element in the industrial structure. This was not inconsistent with an element of co-operation between employers, in one guise or another, as with some of the early woollen clothiers. Even in mid-nineteenth century, about one-third of all employers were self-employers and most of the remaining firms were small, having less than ten workers apiece; only 228 had a labour force of 350 or more. In the cotton industry, over half the firms had less than fifty employees. At the same stage, out of 677 'engine and machine makers', roughly two-thirds employed no more than ten men each. Perhaps it is more remarkable that already fourteen employed 350 or over apiece.

The vast expansion of material wealth was welcomed and generally attributed to the working of free enterprise. Although there was as yet no suggestion, except among a few extremists, that there should be any systematic attempt at a more equitable distribution of property — this would, as Pitt had said, be 'a presumptuous attempt to derange the order of society' — some of the benefits of industrialisation nevertheless accrued to the working classes. Industrialisation, with all its excesses and abuses, offered the workers certain advantages over the old system. Some of them were indirect. Thus the greater production of coal for industry meant also more fuel for domestic uses, warmer houses, more efficient cooking and greater cleanliness. Sugar and tea were ceasing to be considered luxuries; the import of sugar in the eighteenth century rose from 10,000 to 150,000 tons.

It can be argued that there were many who could not afford such things, and certainly this is true. Yet it remains that industrialisation opened up more avenues of employment than had ever existed before, and that the towns, with all their shortcomings, offered the wage-earner the promise of better prospects of a livelihood and even of advancement, and better amenities. Wages and conditions were shockingly depressed, and exploitation of workers was rampant; but this was nothing new. It had been, and continued to be, a feature of the domestic system, under which work was on offer by fits and starts, the financial rewards were to a peculiar degree within the employers' control, and whole families lived in miserable surroundings, depending for a meagre and precarious living on the labour of men, women and children, whose hours of work were subject to no sort of scrutiny. This state of affairs was still the rule in agriculture, where the workers were traditionally weak in their relationship with their masters and, being mainly scattered, were unable to exert their strength collectively to resist oppression, except through occasional riots.

This is not to say that conditions of employment in the mills and the mines were by any standard reasonable. On the contrary, there is ample evidence that they were generally bad and frequently quite vicious. Children were employed from a tender age, and a high proportion of the workers in the early factories were children or juveniles; it has been estimated that at one stage in the Industrial Revolution they constituted between 40% and 50% of the labour force. Hours were unbelievably long, while brutality and degradation were common. Yet from the outset there were forces at work which promised reform. It would be foolish to try to absolve employers as a class from their responsibilities; but equally it would be wrong to charge them with systematic cruelty. 'Sweated labour and cellar dwellings were not invented by the men who made the Industrial Revolution; they were discovered by them, discussed by them, and in the end partially remedied by them.'[1] The writer might have added that they also helped to create them;

[1] D. Thomson, *England in the Nineteenth Century*, p. 19.

but the creation of slums and the abuse of workers was not so much a matter of deliberate policy as one engendered by unregulated self-interest, ignorance, — as with the belief supported by eminent economists, that the shortening of hours would involve a more than proportionate loss in output, — and, finally, the callousness of the age. The landowners might accuse the mill-owners of depravity, but there is little evidence of any tenderness on their part to their own farm-labourers.

Ignorance was a large factor. There were progressive employers, usually the bigger ones, who, while they did not hesitate to employ children in large numbers and often believed they had no alternative, at the same time were conscious of the defects of the practice and sought to make the factory atmosphere less repellent. They acted from a variety of motives; it might be the dictates of humanitarianism but more often those of expediency. It was in the early stages very difficult to secure labour at all, especially in the new centres. The regimentation of the factory was intensely disliked by people who had been accustomed to casual working. It was said ruefully of Scottish mills that to put a Highlander in charge of a machine was like yoking a deer to a plough. David Dale, Richard Arkwright, the Strutts and many others were hard put to it to find recruits. They did so by advertising through the use of agents and so on; they also built whole villages which, for the times, were very advanced in design. It was David Dale, the capitalist, who built New Lanark, not Robert Owen the socialist. They frequently thought out what today would be dubbed 'fringe' benefits, including holidays, and education for the factory children. Bonuses were given for good performance, and piece-work was common (too common, according to many trade-union leaders), as were long-term contracts — the latter being, in some instances at least, not a survival from an earlier age, but a way of assuring the retention of good workers.

Absenteeism, nevertheless, remained a constant problem, and there was a high labour turnover, which in the factory of an enlightened employer might be 100% over the year. Dismissal, or the threat of it, was the chief means of enforcing discipline, but this had to be used guardedly where skilled labour was involved, as in the Soho Foundry, and most employers preferred a system of fines. A good deal of exploitation of workers derived from the system which some employers adopted, of leaving it to contractors to engage and pay labour. 'In some English Mills the overseers of rooms find hands for themselves, paying them out of their own pockets and making the best bargain they can with them. On this plan they drive economy of hands to the utmost pitch, employing and teaching many new cheap ones, squeezing down wages to the lowest fraction and giving each hand as much work as she can possibly do and enforcing the most rigorous attendance and attention; thereby doing the business of a room not only at lower rates of wages, but also with a considerably less number of hands. On this plan masters have much less trouble themselves and nothing can more effectually tend to keep down the rates of wages in general.'[1]

Many of the faults of the factory system were a corollary of sheer inefficiency and since even the most enlightened employers believed that the first essential of management was to make profits some of the malpractices would disappear as managerial expertise improved. It was no accident that certain employers helped to focus public attention on conditions in the factories. The first Robert Peel, who used a large proportion of children in his mills, was only one of those who helped to force the attention of the Government to the miserable conditions of the apprentices in the cotton industry and, from the almost contemptuous beginning of the first Factory Act in 1802, the long, if slow, stream of State regulation flowed.

The Marxist interpretation of history has found in the shortcomings of the factory system proof of the inherent failings of capitalism. Certainly it quickly became all too clear during the Industrial Revolution that unbridled self-interest meant exploitation of wage-earners, and that it would have to be restrained. At the same time it should be remembered that the Industrial Revolution in Britain marked an early stage in industrialisation. This meant, among other things, that the well-being of the workers

[1] Chapman, op. cit.; S. Pollard, *The Genesis of Modern Management*, ch. 5.

was subordinated to the needs of capital investment. This is also
to be found in modern 'socialist' economies, with the difference
that in the latter it has been part of a deliberate State policy. In
Britain, by contrast, industrialisation was the product of a free,
'unmanaged' economy.

There seems little doubt that, after allowing for the fact that the
expansion in output was to some extent offset by the increase in
population, the standard of living for the working classes was
advancing. It rose steadily in the early part of the Industrial
Revolution, but came almost to a standstill during the French
wars, for several reasons: economic dislocation, inflation, war-time
stringencies and Government inertia or reaction. Thereafter it
resumed its upward course, although in fluctuating fashion, up to
1840, after which it gathered pace and maintained its momentum
until the close of the nineteenth century.

A number of striking social gains have been credited to economic
expansion, including, paradoxically, the reduction in child labour
and the raising of the social and economic status of women, as well
as the growth of trade unions and co-operative societies, the spread
of education, and the less violent character of society. Whether these
things could be said directly to result from, or to be rather a
natural accompaniment to, industrial progress may be argued; but
there can be no doubt that industrialisation provided the raw
materials and the furnace for the forging of a new and better
society.[1]

[1] See Hobsbawm and Hartwell, 'The Standard of Living in the Industrial Revolution: a Discussion', *Economic History Review*, xvi. 1 (1963),
and A. J. Taylor, *Progress and Poverty in Britain, 1780–1850*, reprinted
in E. M. Carus Wilson (ed.), *Essays in Economic History*, iii (1962).

2 Population

A RECENT writer, in a searching examination of the evolution of Victorian England, has singled out two 'blind forces', as he terms them — that is, forces not actuated by conscious aims — which were of paramount importance in the process of change.[1] The first was the dramatic increase in productive capacity; in regard to this the only possible quibble might be about the precise description, since, even as defined by the author, it could be taken to support the facile assumption, too often made, that this happened in Britain, and happened when it did, more or less by accident. The other 'blind force' was the great increase in population, and here both the phrase and the assessment are apt.

As with all the major developments that transformed the nineteenth century, population growth was in the nature of a trend, not a sudden occurrence, and had its beginnings in an earlier period. It was not, however, until the late eighteenth century that it came to bulk large, as a phenomenon and a problem, although demographical issues had been discussed — as what issues were not? — in the previous century. There were various reasons for this. One was that, before this time, the country had been deemed to be self-supporting so far as food supply was concerned. The export of grain, like that of other marketable commodities, was officially approved and even artificially fostered by a system of bounties, until 1773, by which time grain exports had, in any case, practically ceased because of high home demand and prices.

Another was the persistence of the belief among political economists and politicians that the nation must maintain a full complement of people, as of other natural resources, both for military

[1] G. Kitson Clark, *The Making of Victorian England*, chs. iii and iv.

25

strength and for economic viability. Government went so far as to
discourage the emigration of artisans as a loss of skill to England
and a corresponding gain to her international rivals. In this connection, it is interesting to find that some intelligent contemporary
commentators were apprehensive because they thought that the
increasing reliance on machinery was making the country internationally more vulnerable, since the new technical knowledge
'was capable of being conveyed away' — that is, of being passed
on by informers to foreigners.

Besides, there was no over-population, rather the contrary. In
the seventeenth and eighteenth centuries industry was on the
move, in more ways than one, and labour was increasingly in
short supply, a situation which elicited repeated complaints from
both agriculturalists and industrialists. The 'abridgement of
labour', in Dean Tucker's expression, was one of the chief incen-
tives to the greater use of machinery, and was to be a recurring
theme in the transition from a semi-rural domestic economy to
one where the 'motif' was mass-production.

This attitude survived into the nineteenth century. It has, in
fact, never been entirely abandoned. In the eighteenth century,
however, there was an increasing awareness of the realities of
population growth, more actual knowledge of its extent, and more
inquiry into the possible implications. There were various more or
less unofficial attempts, in both Scotland and England, to make
comprehensive estimates of the total population. These provided
material for students of the subject. Then in 1798 Thomas Malthus
propounded his famous theory in the *Essay on the Principle of
Population as it affects the Future Improvement of Society*. Like so
much else in this age, it was not particularly original in its thesis,
but it was an impressive synthesis of older propositions. Briefly, it
was that population increases in geometric ratio as against an
arithmetic ratio for food supply. The human species, in common
with others, must therefore always be pressing inexorably on the
means of subsistence, and it must perforce be kept in bounds by
positive checks — war, pestilence, vice and famine, or (a qualification he added in a later edition) moral restraint to limit the birth-
rate.

It was a kind of 'iron law' of population and detested by the idealists, who held that want was entirely due to the maldistribution of wealth; but it was plausible reasoning in the circumstances then prevailing. William Beveridge, much later, echoed it when he said that 'the idea that mankind can control death by art and leave birth to nature is biologically absurd'. As it turned out, Malthus's conclusions, if not his premise, were to be invalidated at least so far as much of Europe and the 'new' countries such as North America were concerned, by the unprecedented expansion in food supplies at home and overseas, resulting, in some quarters, in vast exportable surpluses. It was, however, to have a powerful influence on thinking in the early nineteenth century, when the doctrine of the free play of economic forces achieved considerable respectability, and when the size of the problem was appreciated, with some accuracy, for the first time with the institution in 1801 of authoritative Census Reports.

What statistics there are for the eighteenth century demonstrate that population was increasing very slowly in the first half and much more quickly in the second half, especially in the last twenty years. The population of Great Britain is thought to have increased from under 7 million in 1701 to 7·4 million in 1751 and then to have shot up to 10·7 million by 1801. The acceleration was maintained in the nineteenth century: between 1801 and 1851 the figure almost doubled (10·7 million to 20·9 million) and between 1851 and 1901 it increased from just under 21 million to 37 million.

In Ireland, where the first census was held in 1821, the advance was also rapid, and much more ominous to anyone interested enough to read the signs. In a country which, unlike Britain, was showing little corresponding rise in economic capacity, the total rose from 2½ million at the beginning of the eighteenth century to over 3 million in 1751 and to over 5 million in 1801. By 1841 it was over 8 million, three times that of Scotland. Then, in the mid-forties, the prognostications of the Malthusians were tragically fulfilled. The failure of the potato crop, the staple food of the mass of the people, removed the fragile barrier between subsistence and starvation, and the shock not only decimated population immediately but also created wave-effects continuing throughout the

century. At a 'normal' rate of increase the population would have
become 9 million in 1851; in fact, in that year it was down to
6½ million. By 1901 the population of Ireland was actually lower
than that of Scotland and falling further behind, despite a comparatively high standard of living.

It is important to bear in mind that the phenomenon of rapidly
expanding population was not peculiar to Britain or Ireland. It is
estimated that the population of Europe rose from 140 million in
1750 to over 400 million in 1901. It was also true, however, that
Britain led in this as in other fields; in the nineteenth century her
proportion of Europe's population rose from 5·7% to 9%. The
increase in Europe was not uniformly spread. The rise in France,
in particular, was much below the average. Whereas Britain's
population multiplied well over three times in the nineteenth
century, France's population only increased from above 28 million
in 1801 to 39 million in 1900 and ten years later it was less than the
total for Britain.

A slowing-down in Britain, as in most of Europe, set in during
the 1870s due to a falling-away in the rate of natural increase —
that is, a decline in fertility, with later marriages and smaller families — which was not compensated for by the higher survival rate.
By the 1940s the average number of children per family was 40%
of the average in mid-Victorian times, while the expectation of life
was sixty-five years of age, compared with forty-three. It was
generally accepted by the twentieth century that the slowing-
down was healthy; a Royal Commission on Population, reporting
in 1949, welcomed it as necessary and inevitable if the forces of
Malthusianism were to be averted. By then Britain, having experienced a sevenfold increase, had the largest population in
Europe, bar Germany and the Soviet Union, and the eighth
largest in the world. With one exception, she was also the most
densely populated country in Europe. Since the Second World
War there has been a renewed acceleration in the birth-rate,
attributed to earlier marriages, as well as a sharp rise in immigration.

What lay behind this tremendous upsurge of population in the
late eighteenth and early nineteenth centuries? There has been,

and is, a vast amount of argument about this, much of it speculative and inconclusive, partly because the facts for the earlier periods are so scanty, and partly because they are capable of different interpretations. Even, however, if the data were much more exhaustive than they are, some doubts would remain, since this is a matter of human behaviour, which can never be explained wholly in terms of economics and statistics. Queen Victoria protested at the very idea of her becoming the '*maman d'une nombreuse famille*', but the protest was addressed to the wrong quarter and she bore nine children. There seems to be fashions even in procreation. And there are other imponderables. For instance, it appears that some epidemical diseases can alter in character and virulence without any identifiable cause.

Malthus, in the second edition of his work, asserted that 'the more rapid increase of population supposed to have taken place since the year 1780 has arisen from the diminution of deaths and the increase of births'. This simple statement is perhaps as near the truth as can be expected. It is not denied by most recent scholars, the crux of whose disputation has been the relative importance of each of those factors. It is accepted that the death-rate declined sharply in the later eighteenth century, and, despite temporary aberrations, continued to do so. The fall in infant mortality was the chief feature, and seems to have intensified to a spectacular degree in the last twenty years of the century. This was a more effective factor than a mere rise in the birth-rate, because it meant a higher rate of survival, with, one might expect, cumulative effects in reproduction in due course. It has been estimated that, up to 1750, three-quarters of all the children born in England died before they were five, and that the proportion had by 1830 fallen to one-third.

There still remains the problem of explaining the fall in mortality-rates. The advance in the practice of medicine has been adduced as a contributory element. Plagues had been common. Smallpox, for instance, had been a scourge, and there is good evidence that the introduction of inoculation, from Turkey, by Lady Mary Wortley Montagu in 1721 and of vaccination by Edward Jenner in 1798, did much to check the disease, especially

among children. Inoculation was widespread in the latter part of
the eighteenth century, and its effectiveness was unquestionably
an important factor. Smallpox, nevertheless, remained a recurrent
menace well into the nineteenth century, as did other epidemical
sicknesses, notably typhus, cholera, and scurvy, which ravaged
town and country alike. Cholera, in fact, was said to have become
much more prevalent in the 1830s and 1840s; it was said that in
the forties a quarter of a million of the population of the United
Kingdom died from cholera and diarrhoea. Typhus was perhaps
even more deadly, and there were severe outbreaks in Scotland
in mid-nineteenth century. There are therefore good grounds for
the scepticism voiced by certain investigators about the effect of
improved medical therapy on population growth: but, while this
may have been exaggerated in the past, it may also now be over-
discounted, because of the failure to find an immediate correlation
between remedies and diseases. It was a slow business, requiring
the wide dissemination of information and precepts. The medical
advances were important in themselves, but were also significant
as manifestations of more diffused and more intelligent concern
about public health, aroused by the urgency of the perils which
industrialisation had in some ways accentuated.[1]

To the credit of the medical profession and of the philanthropists
who backed it, much work was done in the town slums, where dirt
and poverty made disease endemic. The University of Edinburgh
started a Faculty of Medicine in 1726, and the co-operation
between it and the Royal Infirmary, founded three years later,
marked the beginnings of institutional medicine. Scotland was in
the lead — ironically enough her own health record was notori-
ously bad — and many of the most illustrious pioneers in medicine received their initial training there, although, like many of the
practitioners of the new skills, they might make their reputation in
England. Two might be singled out, namely James Lind and Sir
John Pringle, since they are acknowledged to be the precursors of
the public health service.

There was an outburst of private philanthropy, in the absence of

[1] See P. E. Razzell, 'Population Change in Eighteenth Century England: A Re-interpretation', *Economic History Review*, xviii. 1 (1965).

any state interest, throughout England as well as Scotland. Wealth was concentrated among a comparative few, but their numbers were being increased from the ranks of merchants and manufacturers; and large-scale charity went a little way to meet the urgent social needs of the period as well as to procure memorials for individuals.

Many hospitals were erected or reformed in the eighteenth century; the list included Guys', St. Bartholomew's, the Westminster and St. Thomas's. The importance attached to lying-in hospitals and knowledge of midwifery was also a sign of the better appreciation of the situation, while the recognition in medical circles that the root cause of disease lay in dirt and malnutrition, and the fact that elementary rules of health were getting through to a surprisingly wide public, held a promise for the future.

With all this, treatment of sickness, whether in or out of hospital, remained dismal, and hospitals themselves were often death-traps because of infection, as Florence Nightingale was to demonstrate during and after the Crimean War. The first operation under anæsthetic was not until 1846 and antiseptic — and later aseptic — surgery were little thought of before Lister (1827–1912) made it his life-work. There was a fair amount of progress in the practice, if not the science, of public health, in the eighteenth century, but the new towns — and, even worse, old towns subjected to new pressures — were hot-beds of disease. Old towns and old villages had been, and remained, unhealthy enough in all conscience, but the expansion of population and the headlong increase in urbanisation were bound to make matters even worse for a time.

Yet there was evidence in many places of progress and, even more, of sustained efforts in search of progress. There were elementary but useful improvements even in the second half of the eighteenth century. In house-building the use of bricks instead of timber was a great help to safety and cleanliness, while progress was also made in the paving of streets, drainage, water supply, and hospital management. The improvers had to learn by experience, for they had nothing else to teach them.

Personal habits were changing, too, and for the better. There was less of the debauchery associated particularly with

gin-drinking, which had been discouraged by a heavy tax in 1751.
Tea was becoming a substitute beverage in both England and
Scotland and to this Rickman, in his census reports of 1827,
mainly attributed the fall in the death-rate. There were more and
cheaper goods, including cheaper and more hygienic cotton
garments. This, with the more common use of cheap soap, greatly
helped the fight against germs. The availability of inexpensive
pottery encouraged cleaner eating habits.

Malthus agreed that the 'Speenhamland' system of poor-relief,
by which allowances were graduated in relation to the size of the
family, encouraged large families; but the Speenhamland system
did not apply to parts of England and not at all in Scotland and
Ireland, where large families were equally the rule. Some modern
writers have continued to hold that the demand for child labour in
factories was a stimulus and that, conversely, the birth-rate fell in
the forties because of the tightening-up of the Poor Law in 1834
and the limitations on the use of child labour imposed by the
Factory Act of the previous year. It is doubtful if such factors
can have had more than a marginal and local effect at most.
Clapham points out, in this connection, that as late as 1830 the
cotton-mill population of Great Britain was perhaps no more than
one-eightieth of the whole. Certainly, there was a demand in the
new mills for large families. David Dale, who had to build up a
labour force for his New Lanark operations from almost nothing,
recruited from far afield, especially in the Highlands and Ireland,
and offered a special welcome to 'families from any quarter,
possessed of a good moral character, and having three children
fit for work'. Arkwright and others did the same. Contemporary
accounts record that 'the benefits of a family are obvious'. This
attitude undoubtedly was an incentive to the redistribution of
population, but its effect on the birth-rate is a matter of speculation.

At the same time, it cannot be doubted that industrialisation
must have had a profound influence on population growth,
although one not so direct as contemporary writers contended.
The greater opportunities of gainful employment, and especially
employment outside agriculture, made for earlier independence

and marriages. But almost certainly the most potent of all economic causes was to be found in the simple fact that it was easier to make a living, in the literal sense of the phrase. The greater food supply allowed more people to survive. Conversely, in an economy at bare subsistence-level famines were positively lethal and had side-effects in the encouragement of disease.

There was an Agricultural Revolution as well as an Industrial Revolution in Britain in roughly the same period, between 1770 and 1830, and here, too, the phenomenon was really an intensification of a process of evolution already well under way. The introduction of improved methods of arable farming, and even more the conversion to pastoral farming on a large scale, which were the main elements in the change, necessitated the break-up of the old and wasteful type of communal peasant farming which had survived since medieval times. The Revolution involved the absorption of the common lands and the consolidation of small-holdings, accompanied by 'enclosure', for the creation of larger, self-sufficient units. The degree of dislocation which resulted depended, to a certain degree, on what was the purpose of the change; enclosure for arable was bound to displace the small 'marginal' tenant and the cottager with customary rights, whose only recourse was to become a landless labourer or to seek work in the towns. A sheep farm, on the other hand, obviously meant a wholesale clearance of all the tenants, and in Scotland the word 'clearance' to describe the expulsion of crofters from their little holdings became accepted currency.

Enclosure had been a source of rural unrest and of concern to government even in Tudor England. It was the response to the demands and profits of a growing market, in the first instance for wool; and this was in a sense an extension of capitalism in the woollen industry. In the second half of the eighteenth century the pressure on the market increased with the growth of population, which meant a rise in the price of meat and grain. The immediate reaction of the farmers who could afford it — and many could not — was to invest capital in expanded production. Over 500 Enclosure Acts were passed between 1765 and 1774, and the French Wars gave added encouragement to the movement. Scotland vied with

England and sometimes surpassed her in the race to introduce new techniques, which were often borrowed from the Continent. Cobbett in 1832 remarked, of farms in Berwickshire and the Lothians, that they were 'factories for making grain and meat, carried on by means of horses and machinery'.

The new methods included better drainage and fertilisation, new ways of planting and irrigation of crops, better feeding and breeding of livestock. All this enormously increased the quantity and quality of the product. A great deal of land hitherto uncultivated was brought into use; one estimate suggests the addition of 2 million acres between 1790 and 1810. Taking the eighteenth century as a whole, the acreage under cultivation rose by about one-third and the yield per acre by one-tenth. In some parts of the country, and notably in the Highlands of Scotland, there was what was nothing short of a craze for sheep-farming. While this meant that many straths were almost stripped clean of their human inhabitants, those who were left could enjoy the benefits of the Agricultural Revolution in the shape of the easily-grown potato crop.

The growth of population was uneven, and the increased density in certain regions was one of its chief characteristics. This was caused not only by natural increase; migration played a most important part. There had always been some movement from country to town, but it had been discouraged by the authorities, since the administration of government, and especially of the Poor Laws, was on a parish basis. Difficulties of transport had also militated against movement, as had the tight regulation of industry, and indeed the whole conception of community living.

The Agricultural Revolution forced many to leave the countryside, and to make for the towns. Alongside this, there was the positive attraction of the new centres of industry — the pull of higher wages and a better standard of living. The net result was a widespread and usually short-distance movement. In 1851, in almost all the great towns in England, the migrants from beyond the town boundaries outnumbered the people born within them. In Scotland a similar situation obtained; in Dundee in the same year 54% of the population had come from outside.

The reorientation of industry that was taking place was bound to bring about a shifting of population. The old woollen and worsted manufacture, previously the staple industry of England, had been strongly entrenched in the south-west and in Norfolk. At the beginning of the eighteenth century, the most populous counties were Middlesex (including London), Somerset, Gloucester, Wiltshire and Northamptonshire. Lancashire was less well populated than Worcester, Somerset or Devon. As the century advanced, the woollen and worsted industry developed fast in the West Riding of Yorkshire. The iron industry, which had been widely dispersed in its search for fuel, gravitated to the coalfields of the Midlands in both England and Scotland — Warwickshire and Staffordshire in England, and the Clyde valley in Scotland. The new cotton industry had its chief seat in the north-west of England (Lancashire and Cheshire) and in Lanarkshire and Renfrewshire, although in Scotland it was fairly scattered. After 1750 only Middlesex and Surrey exceeded Lancashire in terms of population density. During the century Lancashire's population rose from 160,000 to well over 670,000; between 1801 and 1831 it almost doubled again. The north-east, too, was affected; during this latter period, Durham's population rose by 58%. Overall, the shift was to the Midlands, Lancashire and the West Riding, Northumberland and Durham, and South Wales.

Scotland was experiencing a similar development, and for the same reasons. Here the movement was from north and south to the midland belt, especially Renfrewshire and Lanarkshire, where the allied coal and iron industries and cotton manufacture were the attraction. By 1850 one-third of Scotland's population was grouped in the narrow strip of country which included Renfrewshire, Lanarkshire and Edinburgh. In 1801, seven regions, in area roughly one-quarter of Britain's, contained slightly less than one-half the population; by 1931 they held nearly three-quarters of a population four times the size.

With this regional concentration went concentration in towns, the growth of urban population. In 1763 Glasgow, which had begun to flourish on the colonial trade after the Union of 1707, held 28,300 people; but Scotland's centre of gravity was now moving quickly from east to west, and by the end of the century Glasgow held about 80,000, and thirty years later in the region of 200,000. The concentration in Glasgow increased even faster, proportionately, than that in London. In 1801 its share of Scotland's growing population was about 5%; in 1851 it was between 10% and 11%.

London was exceptional; its population in 1801 was not far short of 1 million or about 11% of the total population of England and Wales; but there was no other city in Britain one-tenth of its size. It rose in the first thirty years of the nineteenth century to 1,400,000; but other places were growing even faster. Liverpool in the same period more than doubled, from 78,000 to nearly 166,000; Manchester and Salford increased from 84,000 to nearly 183,000. In 1811 Britain had nineteen towns, excluding London, with more than 20,000 inhabitants; twenty years later it had forty-nine, and six 'conurbations', again excluding London, had over 100,000 inhabitants each.

The urban population caught up with the rural population in the mid-nineteenth century, and by the end of the century the proportions were three-quarters urban to one-quarter rural, at which ratio they have, roughly speaking, remained. It has been calculated that in England and Wales between 1841 and 1901 3 million people moved into the towns, while the country districts lost 4 million.

The internal currents were swollen by an influx from Ireland, which was on a considerable scale in the latter part of the eighteenth century, and in the early nineteenth century reached such proportions, in both England and Scotland, as to constitute a grave social problem in certain areas. The Irish were a very useful supply of labour, especially for the less skilled employments — for example navvying (that is, work on 'navigations', inland rivers and canals, in the first place), which was essential to the heavy constructional engineering of the period. The new cotton mills found the Irish very useful, as did the linen factories, and the coal- and iron-mines. They brought, however, from their poverty-stricken origins, a very low standard of living wherever they settled, and, not infrequently, disease. In the 1830s perhaps one-fifth of Manchester's population was Irish-born, and Glasgow's proportion was little less. The 'Great Famine' in Ireland made the stream a flood: in that grim decade the total of Irish-born in Britain rose from 419,000 to 727,000. After 1851 the current slackened, the New World exercising a superior attraction, but by 1861 there were over 600,000 in England, settled mainly in Lancashire and Cheshire, and 204,000 in Scotland, where they represented 6·6% of the total population, or 15·6% of the population of Glasgow and Dundee.

There was also a movement from Scotland to England and overseas, so intense as to warrant particular mention. It went on steadily after the Jacobite Rising of 1745, and was so heavy in the 1770s, especially in the direction of America, that Dr. Johnson called it 'a fever of emigration'. It was largely due in the Highlands to the collapse of the old clan system and of the close-knit communal society which had been part of it. In the Lowlands the main cause was the expansion of sheep-farming, the 'enclosure' of arable, and industrial depression, especially among hand-loom weavers. The drain continued throughout the nineteenth century, and indeed throughout the twentieth. In 1801 the Northern Division (as distinct from the Central and Southern Divisions) held nearly one-half of Scotland's population (46%), and the Southern Division one-tenth; in 1951 they held respectively one-fifth and one-twentieth. After 1831 actual decreases of population were recorded in various Scottish counties: Perth, Kinross and Argyll each reached their 'all-time' maximum in that year, Inverness in 1841, Ross and Cromarty, Dumfries, Kirkcudbrightshire and Wigtown in 1851. In 1961 the population of Scotland was more than three times as great as in 1801 — 5 million as compared with 1½ million — but seven counties had absolutely smaller populations.

Between 1871 and 1931 Scotland recorded a net loss of population of 1¼ million, greater than that of any other European country. Between 1921 and 1931 her population actually fell for the first time, so great was the drain of emigration. And the increase between 1951 and 1961 was the lowest ever recorded, 1·6% as compared with 5·2% in 1931–51, which meant that Scotland sustained a net loss of well over a quarter of a million people

in those ten years, of whom perhaps one-half went to England and
one-half overseas.

In England and Wales there was a marked change of direction in
migration in the 1930s, which has continued up to the present.
This shift, initiated by the inter-war depression, and especially
by the decline of textiles and the heavy industries, took the form
of a flow from the rest of England and Wales to London and the
Home Counties and the Midlands. The last Census (1961) showed
that this drift was being maintained.

One other important feature of the movement can be only briefly
noted, that is, changes in the make-up of the occupied population.
There was in the first half of the nineteenth century a change of
emphasis in the balance of employment. At the beginning of the
century, the group comprising agriculture, forestry and fishing
claimed well over one-third of the labour force, while industry
(manufacture, mining, etc.) took under 30%. By mid-nineteenth
century, the latter claimed almost twice the proportion of the
former (43% as against 22%). At that latter stage a substantial
element (13%) was engaged in domestic service, which throws a
light on the nature of society at the time. Thereafter the growing
sophistication of the economy was reflected in the needs of
distribution — taken in a broad connotation to include trade and
transport — and of the public and professional services. The two
groups combined had over 22% in 1851, roughly the same as
agriculture, forestry and fishing, as against the 43% for 'industry'.
In the next hundred years their proportion almost exactly doubled
while 'industry's' share rose more slowly, to nearly 50%. Agriculture and domestic service by then retained only about 5% each of
the occupied population. The outstanding characteristic of this scene
has been the decline in the gainfully-occupied rural population
and the steep rise in the proportion engaged in public and professional services, from 7% to 22%; and it is noteworthy that this
increase has occurred mainly in the twentieth century. In short,
the last hundred years has witnessed the rise of the 'white-collar'
worker to a position where he holds a position of decisive importance in society.

The interaction between population growth and economic

growth has already been touched on. The impact of each on the other must not be overstated. It is, however, self-evident that increased population would necessarily constitute a sharp spur to higher production, since it meant a greater potential home market for consumer goods. This was reflected, in turn, in the provision of better distribution, both of goods and people, through transport and other services. Apart from the effect this had on the expansion of foreign trade, for which a secure home market was a pre-requisite, there was the same direct association with overseas development, in that there was a large and continuing flow of people from Britain, especially to America and Australia, and with it a stream of investment. The *Report of the Royal Commission on Population, 1949*, sums it up thus: 'it would be entirely wrong to suppose that this alone [increased population] was the explanation of the fact that Great Britain also led the world in industrial development, in international trade, in foreign investment and in emigration to the new overseas countries. What can be said, however, is that if her population had not been growing, and growing rapidly, her leadership could not have endured more than a few years; that the economic development of the world would have been slower, so that the standard of living both in Britain and elsewhere would now be lower than it actually is; and that the influence of Britain and British ideas would be far less extensive than it is today. The growth of population in Great Britain was in fact the essential condition, not only of the development of Britain itself as a great and rich nation, but also of the growth of the new overseas countries inhabited mainly or largely by people of British descent, and of the spread of Britain's culture and influence all over the world through emigration, commerce and capital invest-ment.'

3   The Beginnings of Reform

THE party system is accepted in Britain today as a natural and essential condition of democratic government. As with all other British institutions, however, the party system and democracy itself have evolved slowly, fitfully, painfully, through the centuries. An effective party system can exist and work only within a highly sophisticated political framework. It assumes that the party in power has been returned by the vote of a free electorate, and that it will be confronted in Parliament by one or more parties forming a coherent official Opposition. It further assumes that the Opposition will seek through constitutional means to take over the government in due course — in short, that there will be switches of government reflecting changes in the opinion of the electorate. All this in turn presupposes that the views of the greater part of the electorate on the *raison d'être* of government are only marginally right and left of a given point of equilibrium; in other words, if the party system is to be effective, there must be a broad measure of agreement in the electorate — and in Parliament — on the fundamental principles of government. That is not to say that political thinking in Britain has not changed enormously over the centuries, but it has changed gradually, and any party which has sought to challenge the basic structure has made no headway. The party system, in fact, is a prerequisite of vigorous parliamentary institutions in a very advanced society.

Until the seventeenth century the nature of government in Britain did not encourage or even permit a party system of however primitive a kind. Government was vested in the monarchy, which might or might not call on Parliament as it thought it desirable or expedient in particular circumstances; but it ruled through its own agents, particularly the Privy Council. This was true of both England and Scotland before their Parliaments merged in 1707. The fact that there was a parliament meant that, however carefully it was controlled, there might be outbreaks of opposition, but it was not until the seventeenth century that the challenge to the power of the monarchy became critical. The Civil Wars were essentially a struggle between parties — those upholding the prerogative of the Crown and those who were determined to curb or destroy it — but they were not parties as we know them today; they were irreconcilable, for they represented an unbridgeable cleavage over religion and, much more, over what kind of government the country should have. In the outcome the Crown was overthrown completely and was succeeded by a Republican Constitution, still using Parliament, although sparingly. In 1660 the monarchy was restored, but the struggle continued, until the issue of principle was determined by the almost bloodless Revolution of 1688. The result was not a triumph for democracy, as was often asserted, but a compromise 'mixed constitution', with a hereditary monarchy, forming a part of, and retaining considerable authority in government, but working through a Parliament, meeting regularly, on whose goodwill it depended for its survival. By now a very loose grouping of parties was discernible: on the one hand the Tories, who laid much emphasis on the rights of the Crown, of the State Church and other established institutions; on the other the Whigs, who were the protagonists of parliamentary privilege.

The most that can be said is that at this stage the way was open for a parliamentary party system, but this proved to be a plant of very slow growth and the eighteenth century witnessed little real change in the forms of government, national or local. The first reason was that the Whigs and Tories had too much in common: in essence, they were both drawn from an oligarchy of land-owners. There were, of course, as always, the new rich — and their number multiplied in the eighteenth century — deriving their wealth from trade and manufactures, but they were not of the *élite* until they had acquired estates. Both categories were thus united in their support of the rights and privileges of property and in their resistance to any changes which might affect those rights. There was in fact no conflict of interest or policy so fundamental as to demand mutually exclusive parties.

The monarchy was not detached from politics in the way it is today; on the contrary, it was deeply involved, and in it was vested the power, which it exercised to the full, to choose its ministers from those acceptable to it who could command a large enough following in both Houses and thus ensure parliamentary support. Control of members there certainly existed although there was also a substantial independent element at all times; but it was exerted not through party machinery, but through patronage, including gifts of office, money and honours.

Towards the end of the eighteenth century there could be detected the growth of an Opposition. One finds the word actually used by commentators on the political scene. It was, however, like the Government party itself somewhat amorphous and fluid, depending a good deal on personality and lacking consistency even in its opposition. It was not so much the embodiment of a different set of policies as the expression of the right to criticise on the part of those excluded from the Government.

It was almost impossible for parties to grow in the hothouse atmosphere of a Parliament dominated by an aristocracy which, by its very nature, was largely impervious to public opinion as it then existed, and repudiated any obligation to defer to it. It should also be borne in mind that there was no Civil Service to maintain continuity of government and that this alone would have prevented the luxury of party warfare on a large scale.

Edmund Burke is much associated with the gradual emergence of the theory of a party system, since he was its most brilliant apologist at the end of the eighteenth century. 'Party' he defined as 'a body of men united for promoting by their joint endeavours the national interest, upon some particular principle in which they are all agreed'. The advocacy of parties by Burke or anyone else by no means implied support of democracy, that is, government by the people. He and others of a like mind insisted that 'the People' could have their interests looked after without their being directly represented, or even consulted. He argued, however, that it was right and salutary that Members of Parliament should on occasion withhold support of the king's Government without opposing the king as such. This became only too apparent in the reign of George III and, above all, with the American War of Independence (1776–81). The Government was assailed for its failures and the king condemned for his excessive and deleterious influence on State policies, and it was inevitable that the fierce debates should raise constitutional issues of crucial significance. George III's mental deterioration and his enforced withdrawal from politics made things easier for the opponents of undue royal power, and, without any pronouncements being made, the part of the monarchy in the 'mixed constitution' was much reduced.

The French Revolution and the long war-time period of domestic repression went some way to crystallise attitudes — 'policies' would be too strong a word — of the two parties. In so far as it is possible to generalise, it could be said that the Tories became more than ever confirmed defenders of the Constitution as it stood, in Church and State, and that they commanded the loyalty of all institutions concerned in its maintenance — the Anglican clergy, the municipal corporations, the Services and the great bulk of landowners. There were Tories who were conscious of the need for a carefully controlled degree of change: the younger Pitt, sometimes called the founder of the modern Tory Party, before the French Revolution would have carried through some much-needed improvements had he not been thwarted by his own followers and his sovereign. Such Tories were ready to exercise a benevolent paternalism in social affairs and there were some who subscribed to the need for more economic freedom; but on the whole they were adherents of the *status quo*. As late as the 1830s Tories could talk about 'the Demon Liberalism who is now stalking through the land, assuming first one name and then another, March of Intellect, Political Economy, Free Trade, Liberal Principles but always destroying the peace of the cottage and the happiness of the palace'.

The Whig leadership was also reluctant to change but more ready to admit that it might be necessary. At the same time, the Whig Party was associated with elements which had a vested interest in change. There were the Dissenters, a large, powerful and articulate body, and there were the commercial interests, with which Dissenters were often linked, who were in any case not averse to breaking a lance with the landowning fraternity. There were the Radicals, seeking reform for its own sake, and using both parliamentary and extra-parliamentary methods to secure it.

Even allowing for the presence in Parliament of individuals and groups of a progressive turn of mind and the existence outside it of a clamorous and ever-growing body of Radicals, the omens for making any drastic alteration in the composition or policies of Parliament itself were not hopeful in the early nineteenth century. Its membership was tightly restricted to an aristocracy based on land-ownership, although, as in the case of the Peel family, re-sources to acquire the land might have come in the first or second generation from manufactures or trade. The right to vote was confined to a few, whose qualifications were often at best dubious and at worst non-existent, and who, by reason of their very fewness and their vulnerability to pressure from landowners, lent themselves as a matter of course to electoral jobbery. The electorate was mostly in the wrong places, for the distribution of the franchise was still based on a distribution of industry and population which had been altered out of all recognition. Many seats had no justification in terms of people — not that people had ever been the criterion — while places like Manchester, Birmingham and Sheffield, to name but a few outstanding examples, lacked any representation what-soever. The total electorate in England and Wales before 1832 was well under half a million, out of a population of about 16 million. The position in Scotland was even more lamentable; out of over 2 million people, the right to vote was vested in less than 5,000, electing forty-five members; but in practice thirty-one of the forty-five seats were said to be in the gift of twenty-one peers. The control of the burghs was in the grasping hands of self-perpetuating cliques, without even a pretence of popular representation. In Ireland the incongruities and absurdities were even more flagrant, for political power in a predominantly Catholic country was in the hands of Protestant landlords. Of the total of 658 seats in Parliament, 273 were at the disposal of landed proprietors, and over 200 of them were Tory-controlled.

There was little apparent difference between the membership of the House of Commons and the House of Lords, except that in the former it was more youthful. The same ruling families were to be found in both Chambers, with the elder scions in the Upper House. It contained 360 members and in 1815 was predominantly Tory. It was arch-conservative in outlook and, what was worse from the point of view of representation, it provided the majority of ministers. Even when a comparatively progressive Whig Government came to power in 1830, nine out of the thirteen ministers were from the Lords. Yet there were forces of change building up which were irresistible. The French Wars had been a reason and an excuse for clamping down on agitation, however justified, although there was one remarkable stroke of reforming legislation in 1807, namely the abolition of the slave trade. This was a great credit to Parliament, but it was also a most impressive illustration of what could be achieved by 'public opinion', properly marshalled.

There was no lack of targets for the reformers. The structure, not only of government, but of society simply was not capable of accommodating the pressures created by new circumstances. There had been great changes both in agriculture and industry which, however desirable in terms of pure economics, had brought dislocation and hardship to a great many people. There was widespread and bitter poverty, yet the only official means of relief was through an archaic Poor Law. Population was increasing rapidly and its concentration in towns created the most serious problems of public health. These and other urgent matters could not be tackled under a hierarchical system concerned primarily with conservation. The hall-mark of the political and social order was property, since the property-owners were the law-makers and the governors. Interference with property was regarded by the law as the cardinal offence. There were well over 200 crimes, including petty theft, for which capital punishment was invoked, while transportation to the colonies was freely used for poaching and many other offences. Yet the gap between the ruling class and the 'People' was widening, with the increase of capitalist farming and

capitalist industry, which created a landless proletariat of large
and increasing dimensions. The post-war depression hit not only
much of industry, but agriculture, and Britain was still predominantly an agricultural country. Prices had roughly doubled
between 1790 and 1814, with wages lagging behind, but afterwards fell away sharply until, by 1830, they were back at slightly
below pre-war level. This was partly due to the policy of financial
deflation followed by the Government, through restriction of the
supply of money. There followed a period of comparative stagna-
tion with consequent unemployment. The succession of bad harvests helped to worsen the plight of agriculture, which felt the
situation the more keenly because it had done very well out of the
war and had invested much capital in the expansion of output.
The area of land under wheat had increased by one-third. The
slump meant that the landlords' pockets suffered — tenant farmers
and agricultural workers of course were also affected — and the
landlords dominated Parliament. So in 1815 there was passed a
Corn Law, which gave agriculture protection by prohibiting the
import of corn until the home market price had reached 80s. a
quarter.

There was nothing new in the idea of protection for agriculture,
and grain exports had been subsidised ever since the seventeenth
century by a Corn Bounty Act. But times had changed. As early
as 1791 a revision of the existing Corn Law had sparked off sharp
parliamentary controversy. There was a great increase in the
number to be fed and, although Government had not acknowledged
this yet in its fiscal policies, Britain now needed all the food it
produced and more. There was no danger of a flood of cheap
imports, since the Continent was the only source. The Corn Law
was therefore an anachronism. It was much more: politically
speaking, it was dynamite. It was denounced by liberal political
economists as an artificial impediment to free trade, by employers
and workers in industry as an encouragement to dear food, and
by radicals as the symbol of class selfishness inherent in a form of
government dedicated to the interests of the landowners. It
created ill-will abroad. It was not even efficient, for it failed to serve
its purpose of stabilising agricultural prices and ensuring agricul-

tural prosperity. It was, in fact, disliked by many landlords, although this was not the popular belief. Prices still fell when harvests were good and rose when they were bad so that both producer and consumer had to face sharp fluctuations.

The Corn Law taken by itself, however, was not so much a cause as a popular slogan. The great mass of the people was, literally, an unknown quantity to the rulers. It had to be kept in subjection, but there were bound to be eruptions and fear of the mob was an ever-present consideration in the minds of the Government, especially after the French Revolution. The mob was capricious, ignorant and easily roused in favour of reaction, as well as of progress. As the Gordon Riots of 1780 had shown, it could be directed against Roman Catholicism or dissent of any sort and could be most dangerous when it was aroused. There was no police force adequate to cope with riots until Sir Robert Peel introduced the concept of a civil arm of the law, and they had to be repressed by use of the military. The mob took its lead from above and the propaganda of the late eighteenth and early nineteenth centuries for reform had its effect on the masses in inciting them to resent oppression rather than, as previously, unorthodoxy.

More important was the middle class. Its ranks were being steadily swollen from beneath; it was prosperous and playing a vital part in the nation's economy. Yet, as a class, it remained formally shut-off from political privileges and, so far as that large part which was not of the Anglican persuasion was concerned, from the elementary rights of citizenship, such as entry to the Universities or admission to public office. Its challenge might be resisted, for a time, but it could not be ignored. It provided the sinews of the movement for change and, where any popular campaign such as Chartism was without its support, that campaign inevitably failed. It could afford to kick against the pricks and to organise accordingly. Its aspirations for reform might be selfish, although they often had a tincture of genuine liberalism — still in the early nineteenth century an ugly word to most people — and even, in nonconformist quarters, of religious fervour, as might be expected from people who clung to their own creeds in the face of political disadvantages. They did not preach revolution, rather the logical extension of the doctrine on which society was already based, that property and rights went together.

There were others who sought to assert principles of government such as the establishment of annual Parliaments and universal suffrage; they were actuated sometimes by abstract motives, but more frequently by a revulsion against social injustice. Sometimes the resentment took an extreme form, but most radicals, led by people such as Hunt and Cobbett, believed in constitutional change, not revolution. From this it followed that the first aim was to reform Parliament, from which the repressive laws emanated. To this end they set out to create and regiment and occasionally to inflame public opinion. This was done through mass meetings, monster petitions to Parliament and the founding of societies such as the Union Societies and the Hampden Clubs.

Then there was the growing power of the Press. In 1815 there were some 250 journals in circulation, and the introduction of steam-printing in the previous year greatly facilitated production on a larger scale. In 1817 the London *Times* had a public of between six and seven thousand and it was not for nothing that it was known as 'The Thunderer', even if Cobbett was constrained to find a less complimentary description for it. There were other influential periodicals — and again it should be noted that they were not owned or run on party lines and were often vitriolic in their criticism of the Government — such as the Whig *Edinburgh Review*, which sold 10,000 copies, and the Tory *Quarterly Review*. Finally there was a flood of pamphlets of all sorts. Illiteracy was widespread, but news and views percolated down to an ever-larger public.

Whether Parliament recognised it or not, the fact was that these forces simply could not be indefinitely contained. They were fairly easily dealt with when they took crude forms, as in the recrudescence of Luddism in 1816 and the riots in Spa Fields in the same year, both explosions of economic misery. The Government was not to be stampeded by such excesses, but responded with the suspension of the Habeas Corpus Act. A lightening of the economic depression brought temporary relief; then came a further recession and renewed agitation in 1819, when the credit of both monarchy and Government was at a low ebb. There was the 'Peterloo

Massacre', when a mass meeting of between 50,000 and 60,000 people in St. Peter's Field in Manchester was broken up by a cavalry charge which killed eleven and wounded hundreds more. The reaction of the Government was to pass the notorious Six Acts, the most important of which laid down that meetings should be confined to people of one parish, thereby hitting at mass meetings. There was an extension of the stamp duty, which was a tax on publications. In 1820 occurred the Cato Street Conspiracy, directed against the Government. There broke out in Scotland the so-called 'Radical War', with strikes and rioting, which ended with the hanging of three of the ringleaders.

The reputation of the monarchy was even further lowered by the squalid dispute between the new King George IV and his Queen Caroline. Nevertheless there was no real menace to the Government, for the Whigs kept aloof from popular agitation. The advent of Canning as Foreign Secretary and leader of the House of Commons in Lord Liverpool's Administration (1822) held out promise of better things. Canning was not in favour of constitutional reform, but he was progressive enough to appreciate that the old regimen must be softened unless worse were to befall. It was in this spirit that he advocated Catholic Emancipation, and the same attitude could be discerned in the willingness of his colleague Huskisson to relax the Navigation Laws and to modify the Corn Law. Peel was not of the same mind, but he, too, was possessed of a sense of realism, as might be expected of a man who was only one remove from the manufacturers' ranks. He was Home Secretary from 1822 to 1827 and initiated the relaxation of the penal laws, including the abolition of the death penalty for about 100 felonies. He also made some improvements in prison administration and in 1829 established the Metropolitan Police Force, with its headquarters at Scotland Yard; this was soon copied in the rest of the country. In 1824 the Combination Laws were repealed.

Canning had a short time as Prime Minister in 1827 with an Administration containing a small Whig element, and the period of enlightenment which had helped to abate popular unrest, seemed to end with his death in the same year. In 1828 an

ultra-Tory Administration was set up, with the Duke of Wellington
as Prime Minister. The Tories had been in office since the war,
but it seemed questionable that they could survive in power much
longer. The burning question was that of Catholic Emancipation
and, although the Whigs might be half-hearted about constitutional reform, they were solidly in support of removing Catholic
disabilities. The Toleration Act of 1689 had been a misnomer, and
the Test and Corporation Acts of Charles II still debarred all
Dissenters from holding public office and from admission to the
Universities, although in practice annual acts of indemnity had
been passed to condone breaches of the law. There were probably
2 million Dissenters in England and Wales out of a population of
13 million and, although Catholics only numbered 60,000, they
formed the great bulk of the Irish population and any relief to
them might have unknown consequences. Peel and the Duke of
Wellington were opposed to any concession of the sort, but
Wellington had the gift of summing up a strategic situation in all
its aspects. While he believed and had believed for years that the
country was on the verge of revolution, he was wise enough to
recognise that, with the election of O'Connell to Parliament, he
must make a tactical retreat. The movement for Catholic Emancipation was strong not only in Ireland but in England and even in
Scotland, because Protestant Dissenters appreciated that, for
obvious reasons, the cause was also in a measure their own. In
1828 the Test and Corporation Acts were repealed and in 1829
Wellington and Peel reluctantly forced through Parliament the
Roman Catholic Relief Act. They did it grudgingly and, as far as
Ireland was concerned, ungenerously — a section of the Irish
electorate was deprived of the franchise — but nevertheless they
split the Tory Party.

This surrender was important, both in itself and as an indication
that Parliament was not wholly impervious to outside pressures. It
was, however, Parliament itself that was the target of most of the
agitation outside, social, economic, religious and constitutional.
The year Eighteen-thirty was one of revolution, affecting all Western Europe, including France where the revolt against arbitrary
government was essentially *bourgeois* in character, as were most

revolutions. In Britain the time seemed ripe for a change. George IV had died, unlamented, and a General Election was therefore necessary. The Tories had had a long run, but, like the Bourbons, they seemed to have learned nothing and forgotten nothing. The industrial and agricultural depressions had deepened. Political unions such as the London Radical Reform Association and the Birmingham Political Unions whipped up a fresh bout of agitation, and when Wellington in the new Parliament made it clear that he and his followers were not interested, his party, already weakened by the election, lost office. The Whigs formed the next Administration.

The new Government was far from sympathetic to popular movements. Agricultural labourers rioted in southern England, and nine of their leaders were hanged and 450 transported. The Government was, however, fully convinced of the need for a moderate measure of reform and showed surprising determination to achieve it. Its first Bill in 1831 was defeated, and it insisted on an appeal to the country, which gave it a large majority in the House of Commons. The second Bill, in the same year, passed the Commons and was inevitably defeated in the Lords. The nation was in a fury. There were riots in town and country, and when the third Bill was again held up by the Lords, the Ministry resigned. After an abortive attempt by Wellington to form a government — Peel refused to be associated with him in any proposal for reform — the Whigs were returned, with a promise wrung from King William IV to create enough new peers to get the measure through the Lords. This threat proved sufficient and in 1832 the Reform Act was passed, with similar Acts in the same year for Scotland and Ireland.

There is no doubt that historians of the period for a long time tended to exaggerate the importance of the first Reform Act. On the other hand, it is equally easy to become so obsessed with its details as to depreciate its historical significance out of all proportion. In its actual provisions it was modest, and a bitter disappointment to the Radicals. It made no change in the principles of the franchise, which continued to rest on property and not, as the Radicals had hoped, on people. The vote was given to £10 householders — that is, those who were rented at that figure in boroughs

— and to £10 copyholders and £50 leaseholders in the counties, in addition to the 40s. freeholders, to whom the vote had previously been restricted. This did at least prescribe some rough standards to replace the chaotic and illogical procedures which had prevailed. A few working-class people were added to the register, where rents were high, as in London, and with the rising prices and standards their number would steadily be added to. The total electorate in England and Wales was increased by roughly one-half, from 435,000 to 652,000. In Scotland it rose more dramatically from the derisory figure of under 5,000 — from a population of close on 2½ million — to 65,000. Scotland's representation was raised from forty-five to fifty-three Members of Parliament and Ireland's from 100 to 105. Incidentally, the erstwhile Tory dominance of Scotland was destroyed from this juncture.

More important, in its recognition of new conditions, was the considerable redistribution of seats. Fifty-seven 'rotten boroughs' were eliminated and thirty cut down from two to one seats apiece, making a total of 143 seats available for redistribution. The redistribution was nothing like as comprehensive as it might have been, but twenty-two of the new industrial towns, such as Birmingham, Manchester, Leeds and Sheffield, were made constituencies for the first time, with two members each, and twenty other towns were also brought into the lists. Sixty-five additional seats were given to the counties.

There was, indeed, much left undone. There still remained 'pocket-boroughs', subject wholly to the influence of the landlords; but there could already be detected in the larger constituencies the beginnings of the system under which constituents made demands on their Members before and after elections, even if the Members were reluctant to accept such pressure. Not only in the small boroughs but also in some of the larger, with rural areas attached, the influence of the landlords remained decisive and the same was true of the counties. This was deliberate policy, as had been made evident during the passage of the Bill. Thus the Government was compelled to accept the so-called Chandos Clause which added to the electorate tenants-at-will, who were of course peculiarly subject to the dictates of the landlords. Even the Duke of

Wellington, who had been so apprehensive of the effects of the Reform Act, admitted that 'the gentry have as many followers and influence as many voters at elections as ever they did'. This influence was traditionally a part not merely of the political organisation of the country but of the whole social fabric, and would not easily be eradicated. The fact that some classes of voters were particularly vulnerable to the power of the landlords — and Britain was still a mainly rural nation, while in the towns, too, industrial magnates could be oppressive — helped to maintain the influence. It was bound to continue in such a society, especially while the system of voting did not provide for secrecy.

Parliament therefore continued to be the landlords' preserve. In the House of Commons of the year following reform, 500 members were representative of that class and 217 were the sons of peers or baronets. Corruption was if anything made easier, as inclusion on electoral registers was a condition of voting; the Parliament of 1841 was known as the 'Bribery Parliament'. Election expenses were still unlimited. There was no payment of Members, which meant that only the well-to-do could stand or serve. The redistribution of seats was not extensive enough, but at least it did make a belated recognition of some of the changes wrought by the Industrial Revolution.

Perhaps most important of all was that this was the first step, the first small indentation in the wall of privilege, which would inevitably be enlarged by the besiegers. Whig and Tory leaders alike believed that this was once-for-all: Peel in 1834 declared it to be 'a final and irrevocable settlement of a great constitutional question'; but it was impossible that the process should stop at that point. A great importance was attached to an increasing electorate. There had been, and would continue to be, a decaying of the power of the Crown, although this was retarded by the fact that the next sovereign, Queen Victoria, was, partly through personality and partly through the sheer length of her reign, to perpetuate for a time certain traditional attitudes, including the belief that ministers were responsible directly to the sovereign.

It could be held that the circumstances of the age required a fair measure of power to be vested in the sovereign. On the other hand, the prestige of the monarchy, already low, could be further impaired if it ostentatiously supported a party which the electorate then repudiated, as happened in 1835 and 1841. The Constitution as we know it was still in an early stage of evolution. The Reform Act, however, gave a decided fillip to change in this direction. Party loyalties had become better defined as a result of the pre-1832 struggle, and with it the conception of party programmes and policies. The House of Lords had had a rude shock, but it was well-entrenched and recovered quickly. It continued to be a centre of reaction and a barrier which, Bastille-like, would have to be stormed sooner or later. In this connection, it is of interest that the idea of life peerages was put forward in 1858, only to be summarily rejected.

Certain of those trends can be traced from the eighteenth century, and would have been pursued whether or not there were a Reform Act; but the Act could reasonably be regarded as a sort of watershed in the evolution of the modern party system. More voters had to be wooed and the compulsory registration of voters was an invitation and a challenge to organise the electorate in the constituencies. In this matter there was a lesson to be learned from the Radical 'political unions', which had directed and rallied opinion before 1832. In 1831 the Tories founded the Carlton Club, and in 1835 a Committee was established there to supervise the registration of voters. The fact that registration cost one shilling offered a mutually advantageous way of getting on terms with the voter. In 1835 the Radicals also set up London headquarters with provincial branches for the same purpose, and the Reform Club was the natural sequel.

The building-up of the Conservative Party — a title first used in 1831 — was much more than a matter of office organisation. Peel was the architect, and the definition of the Party's interest, 'to resist Radicalism, to prevent those further encroachments of democratic influence which will be attempted' (after 1832), was a restatement, not a departure. He was also the first, in his Tamworth manifesto (1834), to send a message from a parliamentary party to a national electorate; but this was a *ballon d'essai*, and not regarded as a precedent for party manœuvring of this sort.

Perhaps the chief import of the Act was that it demonstrated that the British Constitution, rigid as it appeared, did not need, like those of the continental pattern, to be destroyed if anything better were to emerge. As it proved, the Reform Act of 1832 was the first of a series which ran on well into the twentieth century. The title of the Act might be misleading in that it read an Act 'to amend the representation of the people'. In fact, in spite of the critics, the people were brought more fully into the scheme of things. What was more, it was the people who had provided the driving force behind the reform, through extra-parliamentary agencies. The lesson of this was not lost, and bodies outside Parliament such as the Anti-Corn-Law League and The Chartists were to follow as pressure groups.

The reforming movement under Whig auspices was not limited to national government. In 1833 the Burgh Act for Scotland extended reform to municipal government, by giving the local franchise to £10 householders. England and Wales got a similar, though better, Act in 1835, the Municipal Corporations Act, which also attacked the oligarchy in local government and introduced some uniformity into the electoral system by giving the franchise to all rate-paying occupiers.

The period of Whig rule was marked by a whole sweep of reforms. While in a coalition ministry, they had been mainly responsible for the abolition of the slave trade in 1807, meaning that British subjects and ships were forbidden to take part in the traffic. In the post-war period the task was carried on, with Britain converting France, Spain and Portugal to formal abolition, although, unfortunately, the trade continued, with even greater horrors, because of its clandestine nature. Wilberforce kept up the campaign and an Anti-Slavery Association was formed in 1823 to take up the work of the previous Abolition Society. There was very strong opposition from the West Indian planters, whose economy was rooted in the system, but public opinion, irrespective of party, had been educated by all the propaganda, and finally there was passed, in 1833, an Act abolishing slavery in the British colonies. The West Indian planters were given £20 million compensation, which worked out at a price of £37 10*s*. per slave.

The year 1833 also saw the first effective Factory Act. The Tories had made the first moves in this sphere, and members of both parties helped to pass the measure. It was pioneered in the House of Commons by a Tory, Michael Sadler, and, on his failure in the 1832 election, by another Tory, Lord Ashley, later the Earl of Shaftesbury. The conflicts inherent in the party system and within the one Party were reflected in Lord Ashley, for, arduously as he worked for factory reform, he had entered the House as an opponent of parliamentary reform. The Act fixed maximum hours for children and young persons up to eighteen in almost all factories and, what was most important, created the nucleus of an effective factory inspectorate, which not only 'inspected' but revealed in its reports the conditions of work, and thus gave the material for further reform. Working-class agitation for the restriction of working-men's hours was ignored by Parliament; a distinction was made between those who were deemed to be helpless and those who were not.

In 1834 there was passed the Poor Law Amendment Act. It was in many ways a very harsh measure, which showed little or no understanding of the problems of poverty; but at least it marked a departure from the old and now completely inadequate system dating back to Elizabethan times. This had been made even more arbitrary in its operation by the expedient popularised by the parish of Speenhamland, in Berkshire (1795), under which wages were supplemented from charitable funds. The old system was local, being based on the parish, so the Commission of Inquiry which reported in 1832 recommended a greater degree of central administration. It is interesting to note that Royal Commissions, which could enlist the services of experts outside Parliament, were becoming a stock device of Government and not always as a delaying device. The system had provided for outdoor relief; now that was abolished and the rule — fortunately not always observed in practice — was that the destitute could get relief only by entering a workhouse, and under the most appalling conditions. Parishes were for administrative purposes grouped into 'unions', and a central Poor Relief Commission was established, later the Poor Law Board. The combination of local administration with central control set a pattern which was to be widely copied as government became more pervasive. The new system was felt most harshly in the industrial North and resentment of it was one of the grievances behind Chartism.

Chartism was another manifestation of the pressure for reform, deriving from economic servitude. The basic sources of the unrest which engendered it were untouched by the reform of Parliament in 1832. The new Parliament was nowhere near democratic and gave no assurance that it would be sympathetic to the needs of the masses. The new Poor Law confirmed that, whatever its intentions, it was not in touch with the harsh realities of the new society.

A growing body of wage-earners was seeking protection against economic exploitation and vicissitude, but in a variety of ways, which sometimes crossed. It is difficult, therefore, to distinguish between the several reform movements of this period and to tag them 'political' or 'social' or 'economic'. The trade-union movement was regarded by many of its champions as very much more than a movement to improve the wages and hours of the working class; it was thought of by some, like Robert Owen, as an instrument to transform the whole of society. All the movements had an element in common, the belief that *government* must be changed, and this found a platform for a time in Chartism.

In 1836 William Lovett and others founded the London Working Men's Association, and in 1838, in association with Francis Place, the Radical tailor who had already engineered a successful campaign against the Combination Law, brought out the 'People's Charter' as a statement of their programme. It included manhood suffrage, vote by ballot, equal electoral districts, abolition of the property qualifications for Members of Parliament, payment of Members and annual Parliaments. The Charter asked for too much too quickly; nearly a century elapsed before some of the points were conceded, and one of them (annual Parliaments) has always been dismissed as undesirable. It had inherent weaknesses. Its genuine radicalism was tinctured with a false nostalgia for a 'golden time' which in fact had never existed, and which encouraged the belief that turning the clock back would re-create a 'merrie England'. It inevitably attracted many extremists, foremost of whom was an Irish demagogue, Feargus O'Connor, who, by his very intemperateness, made tremendous appeal to the depressed hand-loom weavers, and others steeped in misery; they were not concerned with logic; they wanted, and needed, miracles. The movement also had solid artisan support in both England and Scotland. It was backed by the resuscitated Birmingham Political Union, using the now well-proved methods of mass agitation. Much in its doctrine, however, was alarming to the moderate reformers and to most members of the middle class.

Under the sponsorship of the movement, a National Convention met in Westminster in 1839. A petition bearing 1¼ million signatures was presented to the House of Commons in the same year, but Parliament refused even to discuss it. There was a great deal of loose revolutionary talk in England at this juncture by a section of the Chartists and there were riots, including a serious outbreak in Newport (Mon.) which had to be quelled by the military. The Government, however, kept its head and refrained from panic measures.

Scotland took the initial defeat in a different spirit. There Chartism continued to cherish its ideals, but it widened its appeal by adding to the programme such aims as temperance — always and with reason a plank of social reformers during the nineteenth century — and the abolition of capital punishment. It abjured violence in principle and endeavoured instead to educate, through Chartist churches, Chartist schools and Chartist newspapers such as *The Scottish Patriot*.

Then came the 'Hungry Forties' and in 1843 another and even bigger petition, ostensibly carrying over 3 million signatures, was presented to the House, which discussed and rejected it. There were more riots and strikes. In 1848, under the stimulus of the revolution in France in the same year, there was another Convention and petition, the signatures on the latter clearly in part forged, and the Government refused to allow the great procession which was to bring the petition to the House of Commons. As a result it was taken in cabs. The movement then collapsed and died, except in Scotland, where it survived, in a quiet way, into the sixties.

It failed partly because its inspiration was poverty and the resentment it bred, for which quick wholesale remedies could not be found, even if they had been sought — and certainly not the remedy which the Chartists wanted. It suffered from the outset from disunity, for O'Connor and his followers represented one sector, and Lovett another, although they might have a common ultimate aim. The superior artisans had little sympathy with the grievances of the landless and chronic poor, and the trade unions did not ally themselves with Chartism. The middle class, although attracted by much in the political programme, was alienated by the revolutionary methods and pronouncements of the more extreme leaders and by the excesses which they fomented. The public as a whole, too, was torn between different allegiances at this time. In the lull following the first Reform Act there were competing claims from the Anti-Corn-Law League, the Factory Reform movements, Chartism and the trade-union movement.

Although the movement was a failure, it served some purpose in fanning the embers of revolt and keeping Parliament aware of social discontent. It thus helped to keep under way such developments as factory legislation. When Chartism collapsed — and it was significant that its collapse synchronised with an improvement in the economic situation — there were other agencies to carry on the work.

4 The Triumph of Free Trade

THE Whig régime gradually lost its impetus. It had never been consumed with zeal for change and various things combined to slow it down. Viscount Melbourne, who succeeded Grey as Prime Minister in 1834, was no reformer. Peel was busy refurbishing the Conservative Party image and for a brief interlude in 1834–5 headed a Government. Even more deadly were the implacably obstructive tactics of the House of Lords, which, as usual, had an ally in the monarch, William IV. The balance of power in the Commons was at best precarious, for the Whig majority rested on the support of the Radicals, and that of Daniel O'Connell's Irish adherents.[1] Nevertheless, valuable legislation on a variety of matters continued to be enacted, and some of it could be regarded as part of the long-term erosion of oligarchical government. There was the commutation of tithes in England in 1838, and the lowering of the stamp-duty on newspapers from 4d. to 1d. The Whig Government had survived the death of King William in 1837 and the accession of Queen Victoria, but it was running out of steam. In the dying years of the Administration, perhaps the most notable measure was the introduction by Rowland Hill of the 'penny post' in 1840. Cheap newspapers and cheap post were notable advances in the communication of ideas, at the same time as the railways were introducing a new era of physical communications. They were powerful agencies in the process of educating the public and crystallising political differences.

Finally in 1841 Peel became Prime Minister, with a clear majority. He was fundamentally *bourgeois*, the son of a great manufacturer (himself a practical reformer) and in outlook he was

[1] See Chap. 10.

dispassionate and critical, to the point where he could be accused of cold-bloodedness. In the day-to-day prosecution of government, while mistrustful of theories, and especially of radicalism, he was prepared to accept the logic of circumstances, which was more than could be said of many of his party colleagues or opponents.

He quickly showed his disposition for sober, empirical reform. The Whigs had not distinguished themselves in the realm of finance, and the State revenue was inadequate. Most of it came from indirect taxation — it was estimated that four-fifths of the national income was from this source — and any departure from that basis, involving the adoption of direct imposts on wealth, was bound to incur the hostility of landowners and manufacturers alike. The business of replenishing the Exchequer was therefore much more than a fiscal question. Peel found this a task to his taste, and faced the problems involved with intelligence and resolution. He revived the income tax in 1842. It had been brought in first by Pitt in 1798 as a war-time money-maker, and was duly abolished in 1816, against the wishes of the Tory Government, which was defeated on this issue by its own followers. Peel himself and his successors right through the century regarded it as a temporary expedient, but in fact it never disappeared and with it the principle of a direct levy on wealth could be said to have been firmly established.

At the same time he resumed the policy, on which William Huskisson, when President of the Board of Trade (1823-7) had set his seal, of relaxing the framework of high protection within which British trade operated. This system had been accepted as sacred for the last two centuries. The first great challenge to the doctrine came from Adam Smith, Professor of Political Economy in Glasgow University, with the publication in 1776 of his *Inquiry into the Nature and Causes of the Wealth of Nations*. This was an attack on what was called 'mercantilism', which, broadly speaking, meant that the terms of trade were to be artificially manipulated and controlled in favour of the mother country; that accordingly, under 'navigation laws' harking back to the seventeenth century, traffic with the colonies was to be as far as possible an exclusive business, conducted through her merchant navy; and that there should be a premium on exports and a deterrent on imports other than useful raw materials. This was part of the national economic philosophy in Britain and on the Continent. Adam Smith in general condemned restrictions on commerce, including those inherent in the colonial system as it stood. His work was a classic exposition of the advantages of free enterprise and free trade, of the benefits accruing to the community as a whole from economic individualism, tempered only — and this was an important qualification, for he had no love for 'merchants and merchant-manufacturers' as a class — by the forces of competition.

It made an immediate and powerful impact. Pitt the Younger was much impressed by it. When he became Prime Minister in 1783 he tried, and failed, to lower the tariffs against Ireland, which were one of the most repugnant features of the navigation system. His motives were not simply political, although the policy would have eased Anglo-Irish relations. He did achieve a major reduction of tariffs with France in 1786. He was, however, up against the traditions and prejudices of centuries, and he was soon after faced with the preoccupations of war. The delay was temporary. It was not only Adam Smith's theories at work. The breakaway of the American colonies had been a damning judgment on the old restrictions against which the colonists' revolt had been officially directed; Adam Smith had powerfully endorsed their attitude, in the interests not only of the colonies but of Britain. In any case, the economic climate was changing. With the Industrial Revolution British manufacturers and merchants not only had no need of protection; nor did exporters need the incentive of bounties; the more far-seeing and energetic were impatient of restriction, including the special trade privileges reserved for the old chartered companies. Britain had carved out a new Empire, which was waiting to be exploited both as a source of raw material and as a market; for, despite the glamour and wealth of the East India Company, much the greater part of British trade in the eighteenth century had been with Europe. As the century advanced Europe became, comparatively speaking, less important, but only because Britain was now bidding for the trade of the world. How could this be achieved within the trammels of a policy of exclusiveness?

The props of the old régime were already one by one being knocked away. The monopoly of the East India Company in trade with India and China went in 1813 and 1833, and the monopoly of the Levant Company disappeared in 1825. In 1820 the London merchants presented to Parliament a 'petition for free trade', although the trading community as a whole was far from being converted to the proposition at this juncture. Merchants in Glasgow and Manchester followed suit. The logic of free trade was compelling. Britain was far ahead of Europe and the rest of the world. In 1830 'Britain was producing three-quarters of Europe's mined coal, half of Europe's cotton goods and iron, and most of Europe's steam engines'.[1] Exports were necessary but so were imports, both of raw materials such as cotton, and of such things as tea, sugar and tobacco, fast ceasing to be luxuries. There was not yet a party of protection and a party of free trade. Indeed it was the Tories, such as Huskisson, who in the earlier part of the nineteenth century had made the first inroads into mercantilism, for they had no objection to the removal of tariffs as such, so long as agriculture retained protection.

This was the background of Peel's fiscal policy. During his Ministry he reduced the import duty on a range of food supplies — sugar, butter, cheese, etc. — and a host of other commodities, especially raw materials, were freed from duty altogether. By the end of his Ministry he had removed duties on some 600 out of about 1,000 commodities. In 1843 he completely freed the export of machinery, as well he might. He made many other reforms, notably in the administration of the excise system, as part of a reconstruction of national finance. He reduced the National Debt and in 1844 passed the famous Bank Charter Act.

Perhaps the keystone of the mercantile system was, however, the Corn Laws. The Anti-Corn-Law League had been founded in 1839, and the advent of the penny post and cheaper periodicals in the last years of the Whig Government, already noted, facilitated nationwide propaganda methods to supplement those previously used in the form of monster meetings and petitions. Peel had

[1] R. M. Hartwell, *The Industrial Revolution in England* (Historical Association, 1965), p. 17.

tentatively approached the problem in 1842, when he improved the
sliding scale by lowering the duties, and this, with better harvests,
dulled the agitations. There were competing schemes at this time.
Some reformers, notably the Chartists, distrusted the League
because it diverted attention from their political programme, and
because (they said) it would mean reduced cost of living, reduced
wages and agricultural unemployment. Similarly the Leaguers disliked the Chartists. In Parliament the League had what the
Chartists had not, able protagonists, Richard Cobden and John
Bright, who stumped the country on the issue, arousing a remarkable moral fervour, not least among Dissenters, who saw the Corn
Laws as the symbol of monopoly and reaction in Church as well as
in State. It also enlisted competent lieutenants outside Parliament,
like Duncan McLaren in Scotland, whom Bright complimented on
the fact that 'the later meetings and all your printing must have
saturated the Scotch mind with Free Trade Doctrines'.

A decision was precipitated in 1845-6 by the disastrous Irish
potato famine, together with a bad harvest in England. The Whigs
plumped for repeal. Peel himself was convinced of the need for it,
but failed to carry his Cabinet with him and resigned. The Whigs
could not or would not form a Ministry; here was a dangerous
situation bristling with risks for any party that took a positive line
either way. Peel returned, and in the face of formidable opposition,
including that of many of his own party, notably Disraeli, carried
repeal in 1846. His Government was immediately thereafter defeated by a vindictive combination of Tories, Whigs and — less
ironically than might appear, for relief came to their country too
little and too late — Irish M.P.s. The Conservative Party was
broken for two decades until the man who had helped to break
it, Disraeli, in turn revived it. It never lost its partiality for
protection, which fitted in very well with its political philosophy,
although for the greater part of the century it remained reconciled
to its impracticability.

The end of protection did not prove calamitous for British
agriculture, as the pessimists had prophesied. As the total of
population swelled and the standard of living advanced, so did
the home demand for foodstuffs become more buoyant. Railway

transport brought the market closer to the producer, and in particular the carriage of vegetables, meat and fish to the large towns was speeded up to an extent undreamed of by the early railway pioneers. As the economy changed from being predominantly rural to being predominantly urban, so it became incumbent on the agricultural industry to become more intensive and more efficient if it were to meet the demands on it and take full advantage of the sellers' market. Agriculture, taking it as a whole, responded to the challenge. An era of 'high farming' began in the 1840s, which was characterised by a variety of improvements. These included the use of artificial manures and synthetic feeding stuffs, the introduction of deep drainage, and some attempts at mechanisation, although a revolution in this last department had to await the coming of the internal-combustion engine; steam-engines could be and were used but there was an obvious limit to their scope. There was a spirit of research reminiscent of what had appeared in the late eighteenth century. Inevitably there was a trend towards the creation of bigger, more commercial units, which, as in manufacturing industry, could afford to sink capital in the pursuit of greater production and reap the full benefits. More land was brought under the plough, until by 1872 the arable acreage reached an extent never before attained. Along with this went greater production of livestock and wool.

The period of prosperity, which has been called the 'golden age' of British agriculture, lasted until the seventies. In that decade a rapid decline set in. British agriculture had become more efficient, but so had agriculture on the Continent, notably in Holland and Denmark, which had an exportable surplus. As the development of transport had brought the home producer closer to his market, so it helped the overseas producer to tap the enormous, almost insatiable demand in Britain for more and cheaper food. The overseas producer might and often did have advantages which were lacking to the British farmer. In the United States and Canada, in South America, in Australia and New Zealand, there were vast new lands opening up for growing wheat and rearing sheep and cattle on a scale which made British farming appear nothing short of puny. It was cheap farming in those territories, in that it was extensive rather than intensive and needed less effort and less capital; but capital was available and Britain had been largely instrumental in providing it, purely as a good commercial proposition.

The centre of influence in Britain was moving from the country to the town, and the towns wanted cheap food and cheap raw materials in exchange for manufactures. Steamships could carry grain — indeed, the sailing clippers had carried it in fantastically speedy voyages from America and Australia even before the steamships asserted their dominance. The fate of the British farmer was bound to become precarious once mutton and beef could be transported in good condition for long distances — and this was achieved with the use of refrigeration and of canning. As in other fields, mass-production was putting the small man out of business and the only hope for the farmer was in specialisation and large-scale production. The choice appeared to many to lie between the almost hopeless task of attempting to compete with bulk imports and a return to protection. Most European countries chose the latter course, although some of them also made sure that their farming was brought to a high standard which enabled domestic agriculture not only to survive, but even to export. British Governments, however, whether Conservative or Liberal, were not disposed to espouse the unpopular doctrine of protection, with its corollary of dear food for the masses. There were some palliatives, such as rating relief for agriculturalists, but these did little to relieve the depression. Britain's prosperity was based on industry, and so long as industry accepted free trade, there was little hope of a change in fiscal policy; nor did it come until the twentieth century was well advanced.

In the twenty years following the repeal of the Corn Laws, much of the fire seemed to have gone out of domestic politics. The Conservative Party was in ruins, and the Liberal Party, as it became known after 1847, representing a coalition of Peelites, Whigs and Radicals, was still far from being a close-welded entity, nor would it ever be. Whig industrialists and Radical politicians made uneasy bedfellows. There was a great deal of party flux in the House of Commons, partly because discipline was lax, and partly, perhaps, because the issues dividing them seemed to be smaller after the titanic struggles of the thirties and forties. This was a reversion to earlier habits, but there was a serious danger that the House would solidify into fragmentary groups, as happened on the Continent.

There was, nevertheless, a continuity expressed not in principles but in persons. Palmerston was the supreme example of how apparent paradoxes could be reconciled in politics. He had begun, like Gladstone, as a Tory. He became a Whig who wanted no more constitutional reform after 1832 and who in home and foreign policy was liberal-minded without ever being Radical. From 1830 to 1841, with one brief interval, and again from 1846 until his death in 1865 he held high office continuously and was Prime Minister twice. He might connive at constitutional revolts abroad but he would not countenance 'agitation' at home. There was little chance of Parliamentary upheavals while he could control the temper of the legislature. Asked in 1864 what proposals for domestic legislature should be made at the opening of the new Parliament, he said: 'There is really nothing to be done ... we cannot go on legislating for ever.'

That is not to say that there was not a vast amount of constructive legislation in this period. Gladstone, who had been President of the Board of Trade under Peel, completed the destruction of the old fiscal system during his tenure of the Chancellorship of the Exchequer from 1852 to 1855 and again from 1859 to 1866. His Budgets of 1853 and 1860 were landmarks in the transition to free trade, which included the jettisoning of colonial tariff preferences (1853). Colonies at this juncture were out of favour, in a political sense; but if there were ever to be a return to protection it would be through the imperial connection. Gladstone was a convinced exponent of liberalism in many forms and his party became definitely identified with the policy of free trade during his long association with it. He had lengthy spells in office over a period of some forty years (1852–93) and in this period the change-over was made complete. Duties and taxes ceased to be a means of protection, and were looked on as primarily a source of revenue. This meant that, if the now accepted policy of liberating raw materials and food supplies were to be fulfilled, the only things left would be such consumer luxuries as tobacco and alcohol; this conception fitted very well with Gladstone's austere personal views. There was no real difficulty in carrying through the programme, since protection was no longer practical politics.

Britain naturally did her best to promote free trade all over the world, for protection anywhere was against her commercial interests. The year 1860 saw a famous treaty, often called the Cobden Treaty, between Britain and France, by which wines and silk from France were to enter duty-free, in return for the free export of cotton and iron manufactures. This was an extremely important departure, since it had repercussions on the rest of Europe; there was a general and progressive lowering of tariff walls there, operated through the reciprocal principle of 'most favoured nation' treatment. In 1865 and 1867 Britain herself made treaties with Belgium and the German Zollverein, in which she agreed not to give or accept colonial preferences.

It is worth noting that, as late as 1870, perhaps two-thirds of the State revenue still came from indirect taxation, despite the abolition of so many duties in the previous thirty years. The reason is that there was a high return from a comparatively few items, especially alcohol and tobacco, together with tea and sugar. The rest of the revenue came from direct taxation, including income tax.

As with protection, so with free trade, it was easy to find a political philosophy. Mercantilism had been an expression of national rivalry and exclusiveness. In the same way, Cobden and the others saw in the abolition of tariff walls a valuable contribution towards international goodwill, as well as a potent factor in domestic politics. To many Liberals its corollary, direct taxation, was a way of redistributing wealth, a deterrent to monopolies, and a socially acceptable way of financing State activities.

Although no major changes in the franchise took place in this period there were some well-intentioned, if not very effectual, improvements. The Corruption Act of 1854 provided for an audit of candidates' expenses and made an attempt to define corrupt practices. The death of Palmerston in 1865 put an end to the uneasy balance of forces which had prevailed in Parliament. Not only had Russell, who headed the next Administration, for long nursed proposals for further electoral reform, but he took over a team in which the Leader of the House of Commons was Gladstone, who in the previous year had made a declaration in support of household suffrage and was chided for it by Palmerston. Gladstone had begun as a Conservative, a defender of the Constitution in Church and State to the point of denying university entrance to Dissenters. He was, however, in the tradition of Peel, a descendant of a commercial magnate, who, having served a long apprenticeship in politics, had become persuaded that domestic reform was necessary and desirable, and that he himself was equipped physically, intellectually and morally to carry through the great causes which were beckoning. It was typical of his detached, 'professional' approach that the Government of which he was Prime Minister in 1871 opened the English Universities to men regardless of their creed. 'Whenever he gets my place, we shall have strange doings,' prophesied Palmerston. He had comparatively little interest in foreign affairs, and had fallen foul of his chief because his reductions in taxation had left too little money for defence. The reform of the franchise was an issue which might not split the House of Commons, but it was likely to start electoral battles and compel the 'marginal' voters and members to state their party allegiances. Disraeli, scenting the challenge and the opportunity, said, 'The truce of parties is over.'

Public opinion, whipped up by bodies such as the Reform League and orators like John Bright, once again was vociferous. The electoral position was not only unsatisfactory in itself, but the anomalies left by the first Reform Act had become much more flagrant in the interval. Of the adult male population of England and Wales one-fifth was enfranchised and even fewer, one eighth, in Scotland, and one-twentieth in Ireland. There had been further growth and concentration of population in industrial centres, yet half of the borough population of England and Wales had thirty-four seats, the other half 310; while the southern counties, with a quarter of England's population, had one-third of the representation.

The Russell Government was divided on the precise measures

to be taken, and a small but powerful group of Whigs was opposed
in principle to concessions on any large scale. The modest Bills
brought forward by Russell and Gladstone met with such obstruc-
tion that the Ministry resigned and the Conservatives, under
Derby, formed a minority Government. The situation was ready-
made for party manœuvre, and Disraeli, now Chancellor of the
Exchequer and Leader of the House of Commons, had come to the
conclusion that here was a golden opportunity to dispose of the
question and at the same time 'dish the Whigs'. A sharp economic
recession, coupled with a bad harvest, had heightened the temper
of the people and made further procrastination dangerous. So in
1867 the second Reform Act was passed — corresponding Acts for
Scotland and Ireland were passed in 1868 — with Liberal approval.
It was a compromise, but, as amended in the Commons, went a
good deal further than its designers had intended. In the boroughs
the franchise was extended to all householders and £10 lodgers,
which in effect enfranchised the artisan class. In the counties
property remained the qualification, although the limit for copyholders was now reduced from £10 to £5. There was partial or
complete disfranchisement of a number of the smaller boroughs,
producing fifty-two seats, of which nineteen went to towns in
England and five to Scotland, with twenty-five to the counties,
two to the four Scottish Universities and one to London University. It was estimated that the borough electorate went up by 134%
and the county electorate by 45%. This reflected the lop-sidedness
of the Act, since it denied the countryman rights accorded to the
town dweller. It could be only a temporary measure.

The increase in the electorate meant that the parties had to
improve their own organisation and finance in order to keep in
touch with it. In 1867 there was formed the National Union of
Conservative and Constitutional Associations, and then the Conservative Central Office, to co-ordinate local activity and make
available lists of suitable parliamentary candidates. In 1877 the
Liberal Party followed suit with the National Liberal Federation,
of which Joseph Chamberlain was first President. The Cabinet
system was taking shape and the status of the Prime Minister as its
leader was being enhanced. Gladstone, who became Prime Minister

in 1868 (as did Disraeli in a Conservative Government), did much both to woo the electorate and to promote Cabinet solidarity. Leaving out Peel's Tamworth Manifesto, it was Gladstone who started the business of literally going to the country, to make direct appeal to the voters. In order to appeal, a Party must have a policy in advance, as well as personalities. Here the Liberals led the way; in 1891 the National Liberal Federation set forth the 'Newcastle Programme' which every Liberal condidate was expected to adopt, which in turn meant toeing the Party line on his return as a Member.

Meanwhile there had been further electoral reforms. In 1872 the most effective way possible to eliminate intimidation and undue influence was taken with the passing, in Gladstone's first term as Prime Minister, of the Ballot Act. In 1883, during his second Government, there was passed the Corrupt and Illegal Practices Act, which placed a limit on election expenses according to the size of the constituency and required a return of expenditure from election agencies. This was a shrewd blow at bribery, and indirectly strengthened the control of the central Party organisation, whose expenditure was not affected. This the same Government followed with a Franchise Act in 1884 and a Redistribution Act in 1885; they made fundamental changes and laid down the principles on which the further reform of the franchise in the twentieth century was to be based.

The former extended household franchise to the counties and the second for the first time attempted to find a logical ratio between population and seats. It worked out at about 50,000 electors to each Member, although in practice allowance was made for medium-sized boroughs of 15,000 to 50,000 and for sparsely-populated counties. Boroughs with less than 15,000, were to be disfranchised and merged in their counties. Twenty-two towns with 50,000 to 150,000 population remained undivided, returning two Members. The effect was to give London forty-two seats and north-west England forty, while Scotland now had seventy-two; and the total rose to 670, with an electorate of $5\frac{3}{4}$ million.

In the General Election of 1868, the Liberals swept the board, much to the chagrin of Disraeli, who had calculated that the enfranchised artisans would give his Party credit for the Reform Act. Liberal programmes, however, were to work on his Party's behalf. In 1865 Gladstone, in pursuit of a solution to the Irish Question, had declared for the disestablishment of the Anglican Church (of which he was an ardent member) in Ireland, and this was done as soon as he returned to office. Even more serious was the Licensing Act of 1872, for it was not only intensely unpopular with publicans and their patrons — and the public-house was a common meeting-place for groups of all sorts, including trade-unionists — it alienated the brewers, who tended thereafter to help finance the Conservative Party. On the other hand, nonconformists had been disappointed by the Education Act of 1870, which empowered local school boards to use the rates to provide schools, but excluded denominational establishments from their scope. The fact that nonconformists no longer found such cause for partisanship in the Liberal Party as they once had may have contributed in some measure to the Liberal defeat in 1874. The Conservatives, on the other hand, tended to garner support from the old Whig landowners as well as from the middle class, including merchants and industrialists who were having second thoughts about the advantages of free trade. Its attractions were being dimmed for them, as for farmers and landowners, by the late seventies, with the onset of an economic depression with disturbing implications.

The Conservative Party also offered a foreign and imperial policy which was much more positive and glamorous than that of the Liberals, although imperialism was not the prerogative of any one party, and, in this as in other things, there were Liberals who were not of Gladstone's mind. It was the tragedy of Gordon's death at Khartoum which finally brought down his second Government, in 1885. Before then the canker of the Irish Question had begun to eat into the Liberal Party's vitals, sapping what energy it had left for domestic reform. There seemed, for one reason or another, to be a waning of radicalism in its leadership and one able individual in particular was prepared to put new fire (with himself carrying the torch) into Liberalism even if it meant a certain amount of incendiarism. This was Joseph Chamberlain; and when the Liberals returned to power in 1886 he led a breakaway movement, ostensibly over the Irish Question, which he saw as part of an imperial pattern. The loss of Chamberlain and his followers greatly enfeebled the Liberals and conversely strengthened the Conservatives, with whom they made an alliance as Liberal-Unionists. The net result was that the Liberals went out of office for almost twenty years. They were to have a partial revenge when Chamberlain, by his insistence on a return to protection in the guise of imperial preference, helped in turn to split the Conservative Party in 1904. Before this a third political party had emerged, which lacked the long traditions of the Conservatives and Liberals and could present itself to the electorate as the embodiment and voice of new influences and aspirations.

5   The Financial Structure

IT has been said that, in the growth of an industrial economy, the decisive factor is the availability of capital. Labour and a modicum of raw materials are, of course, also essential, but their presence is a minimal requirement and can be taken for granted. Capital, on the other hand, is not a natural resource and has to be created or procured elsewhere and brought to bear on the natural resources if these are to be exploited. Britain was fortunate and exceptional in that, at the critical stages of her development, she had a sufficiency of all three at her disposal.

Capitalism has never, in the modern age, been wholly 'private' in the sense of being concentrated in the individual. The finance necessary for industrial and commercial enterprise was often beyond the capacity of one man, and, even where it was not, there was likely to be an element of risk which made it highly desirable to spread the responsibility. This could be effected through a partnership of a few intimates, with, in theory, ownership and management going together. This kind of association, however, would clearly not be appropriate to the financing, and still less to the management, of large-scale undertakings, and so there evolved the joint-stock company structure. In this, shares might be bought and sold by people concerned only with the return on their investment, and as early as the seventeenth century one finds mention of 'that new mistery we call stock-jobbing'. Joint-stock companies were becoming an accepted feature of industrial and commercial organisation, notably in the extractive industries — iron, coal and copper — and in overseas trade, where both the outlay and the hazards were high, as were the returns. Of this distinguished assembly were the great trading associations such as the

Russia Company, the East India Company and the Hudson's Bay Company, which were accorded a quasi-governmental status as the pioneers and upholders of English mercantile prestige and influence against foreign rivalry. By the eighteenth century the joint-stock system was popular also in banking and insurance, but not, as a general rule, in manufactures, although here, too, there were examples, not least in Scotland, where capital was much scarcer than in England, and where there was a burst of joint-stock activity in a variety of trades at the close of the seventeenth century.

Such companies might be incorporated by royal charter or special Act of Parliament, which conferred valuable privileges. These could include monopolistic rights, and afforded the protection of the law of corporations, which gave a legal identity — necessary if the company were to be able to sue or be sued in the courts — together with the precious limitation of its liabilities to the extent of its corporate assets. Unincorporated companies, on the other hand, were subject to the law of partnership, which meant that a shareholder — like a partner — was liable for the whole of the company's debts 'to his last shilling and acre', and not simply for his own share-portion. This was a frightening prospect, which repelled many would-be investors, as well it might. There were great profits to be earned, but even a well-founded concern could go bankrupt, saddling the participants with unforeseen debts — as Sir Walter Scott, partner in Ballantyne's, a publishing firm, found to his cost. An entrepreneur often had a stake in several promising businesses, and might lose his all if one of the more expensive ones failed.

The development of joint-stock companies was administered a severe set-back in 1720, at which stage their total capital was about £50 million. In that year the Government, alarmed by a frenzy of ruinous speculation involving the South Sea Company, in which the Government had a direct interest, passed the so-called Bubble Act, aimed at wild-cat flotations. There had been an earlier and relatively more catastrophic débâcle in Scotland when the joint-stock Darien Company, which the Scottish Government and nation had hoped would establish Scotland in the colonial field, completely collapsed (1700); but since the English Government had done its best to bring this about, it had no legislative aftermath. The Act of 1720 in passing incorporated two insurance companies and then went on, in effect although in imprecise language, to declare that unincorporated companies, with public share issues, were henceforth proscribed, leaving only incorporated concerns and partnerships within the law. The Act was practically a dead letter from the start, but it did set a stigma on the usual run of joint stock. Yet incorporated companies continued and flourished; in 1820-5 they were believed to represent not less than £160 millions' worth of capital.

The huge capital requirements of canals and railways alone were enough to demonstrate that the law was out of keeping with the times. Railway projects were carried out under authority from private Acts of Parliament, but these were difficult and extremely costly to secure. Railway companies, although sometimes shady in their promotions, were conceded limited liability as a matter of course, partly because they were so new in conception as to fall outside the traditional restrictions, partly because of their size and public usefulness, and partly because there was a powerful railway 'lobby' in Parliament. They showed, however, that there were a host of schemes, some of undoubted public benefit — docks, municipal improvements, etc. — which could be fulfilled only through public investment, government finance being out of the question. They further revealed that there was a public willing and able to provide the funds, but that the channels through which this could be done were artificially narrow and tortuous. Yet change came slowly. 'The strong conservatism of the legal profession [which found the existing procedures very lucrative], the example of a great Lord Chancellor (Lord Eldon), the lingering influence of the moribund Bubble Act and its suggestion of common law prohibition, the indifference of the legislature, the relative novelty of the economic changes, the conservatism of many business men, the relatively small number of companies in existence — all combined to check the correction of an unsuitable body of law.'[1] There

[1] H. A. Shannon, 'The Coming of General Limited Liability', reprinted in E. M. Carus Wilson (ed.), *Essays in Economic History* (1964).

was, too, the genuine fear that unlimited liability would encourage mismanagement, fraud and uninhibited speculation. It was argued that, as things were, there was no serious shortage of investment capital for sufficiently attractive, if not necessarily sound, ventures. Finally, in face of the new pressures, Government did not quite know what to do: where, if anywhere, lay the *via media* between public and private interest?

As with other reforming movements, the argument in favour was given a moral tone. It was urged by Christian Socialists, co-operators and other champions of the working class, that the small saver could not possibly risk his meagre capital without the safeguard of limited liability. That there were many such the growth of trade unions and friendly societies testified, although it by no means followed that they would sink their money in chancy industrial equities. This argument found a response in the upper echelons of society, for already it was being preached that wider share-ownership was a barrier to social unrest and political instability. Canals and railways were all very fine, but they could not absorb investment funds for ever. The situation was full of anomalies. The law on the Continent was more enlightened in this regard and this, it was contended, was a positive inducement to capital to go abroad. Perhaps the most damning indictment of all was that the prohibitions on the many and the exclusive privileges for the few could be construed as a kind of protection, a denial of commercial freedom and a relic of plutocracy.

There were no criteria by which Parliament could decide applications for incorporation, and this remained true even after the Bubble Act was repealed in 1825 and the procedure for incorporation further relaxed in 1834 and 1837. Slowly the breach was widened and in 1844 the Registration Act, applying to England and Wales only — in Scotland there was no need of it — allowed the incorporation of companies, not including banks, for which different regulations were prescribed, with more than twenty-five partners; but unlimited liability still applied. In spite of the 'railway mania' in the forties and other speculative excesses, in 1855 came an Act sanctioning the granting of limited liability to companies coming under the Registration Act, and this was quickly replaced in the following year by the Joint-Stock Companies Act. Its sponsor was Robert Lowe, then at the Board of Trade, who saw this reform in its true historical perspective as a natural progression 'from prohibition to privilege, from privilege to right'. The Act offered limited liability to all companies complying with certain fairly simple stipulations, including the signature of seven or more on the memorandum of association, specifying the names and objects of the company, the presentation to shareholders of an annual balance sheet, and provision, if required by one-fifth of the shareholders, for inspection of accounts by the Board of Trade. Banks were again excluded, until 1858, when the privilege was extended to them, except as regards their note issue. In 1862 a Consolidating Act included insurance companies.

It looked at first as if the opponents of freedom had been justified in their attitude. There was a flush of conversions to public companies in the fifties and sixties, especially in coal, iron and engineering; between 1856 and 1862 nearly 2,500 companies, with a total paid-up capital of over £31 million, were registered. Over one-third of the companies formed were defunct within five years and this proportion tended to increase rather than diminish. After 1862 there was a rush of new issues, averaging £120 million a year over the next three years. In 1866 came the crash of Overend, Gurney & Co., a great discount concern with limited liability, and the figure fell to under £29 million in 1867. It recovered slowly, until by 1872 it again exceeded £100 million, and thereafter the movement tended to speed up, with periodic crises having a decelerating effect. In the seventies and eighties there was a tendency for firms to go public in the Lancashire cotton industry, and many operatives there became small investors; but on the whole manufacturers were slow to adopt the device.

The private business not merely survived but flourished. In 1907 it also was given the right to limited liability by the Companies Act. It was, of course, usually a much smaller unit than the public company, and while in number it easily outstripped the latter, its share in the national economy greatly declined. By 1938 there were ten private for every one public company, but the capital investment in the latter category was more than twice as large.

No doubt the spirit of speculation was encouraged by the relaxation of the law, and limited liability certainly had its unsavoury side, but the development was necessary and justifiable. Joint-stock companies played an ever more important role in the economy: between 1885 and 1925 the capital invested in them increased ninefold (from £482 million to £4,470 million), which roughly corresponded to the increase in their number.

Joint stock was a prime factor in expansion. It implied, among other things, a growing gulf between ownership and management, and between employer and worker. These were not necessarily evils. The thrusting employer, forcing his way up from the ranks, was often, by the nature of his experience, and because of his lean resources, a parsimonious employer. Family businesses could mean ownership and management in the hands of incompetent heirs. On the other hand, they also symbolised a personal relationship between employers and employed, which might or might not apply in practice. Joint stock was the inevitable preliminary to large-scale management through boards of directors, acting on behalf of a body of shareholders whose interest was confined to their dividends. Management of this sort was strictly functional, while the larger scale offered opportunities for the 'economies of size'.

The other great institutional development in the field of finance was in the machinery for making credit available to industry and commerce. In the sixteenth century, the depositing of money with, and the loan of it by goldsmiths, at interest, was well known; there was even a rudimentary mechanism of credit, in the form of written promises to pay. This came to involve payment of interest on deposits and loans, which was contrary to the old medieval hostility to usury, but in the seventeenth century it made considerable headway, without guidance or restraint, and banking became a lucrative profession. The restraint was not likely to come from Government, since the sovereign was himself so often a debtor.

The expansion of industry and commerce made nonsense of an insistence on cash transactions only. The bigger the business, the more it was necessary to have advances made for the installation of machinery, for the promotion of a trading venture, and so on; to cover the gap, the widening gap, between the initial expenditure and the final payment by the customer. Credit was a local growth: a bill of exchange, or promise of deferred payment, would pass between supplier and customer, and such a bill might pass through several hands and in different places as the equivalent of money and might be accepted by a local bank, on discount, in recognition of the trouble and risk involved in collecting cash payment. Paper money in the form of notes, redeemable in cash, was also issued.

The beginning of some kind of central regulation, although it was not recognised or intended at the time as such, came in 1694 when the Bank of England was founded, largely at the instigation of George Patterson, a Scot. The Bank of Scotland was founded in the following year, the prime mover being John Holland, a London merchant. Both were joint-stock banks, incorporated by charter, and enjoying limited liability. There were, however, substantial differences between the banking systems as they evolved in the two countries. The Bank of England was created largely to be the instrument of government borrowing — England was at war at the time of its inception — and it started off by lending the whole of its capital (£1·2 million) to the Government at interest, partly in the form of notes. These in the early days also bore interest. There was always a very close relationship between the Bank of England and the Government, despite the fact that the Bank was not re-garded as a State bank. In return for its support, the Government extended certain privileges to the Bank, notably that of being in-corporated and joint-stock, with limited liability. It was supposed to possess a monopoly of joint-stock banking in England, and did in fact enjoy it throughout the eighteenth century; other banks existed, but they were private or partnerships. No bank of more than six partners was allowed to issue notes. There were other banks in London, such as Child's and Hoare's, which, until 1770, issued notes, mainly, like the Bank of England, for large amounts —that is, for merchants' purposes. There were many private banks in the provinces, some originating from the goldsmiths, some from rich industrialists such as Boulton and Watt, who needed such facilities for the prosecution of their own affairs. Lloyds had its origin in a bank started in Birmingham by the ironmasters Sampson Lloyd and Partner, and Barclays in one started by the Gurney family at Norwich in 1775. By 1815 there were perhaps 900 provincial banks in England and Wales, unincorporated and mostly short-lived.

The Bank of Scotland, on the other hand, was established to further commerce and industry, not to finance government spending. Scotland was much less rich in natural resources, so abundant credit facilities were imperative, hence the greater laxity conceded in regard to the right of note issue. The Bank was given a monopoly, but only for twenty-one years. Other banks were soon established, on a similar joint-stock basis, and also enjoying the right of note issue. There was the Royal Bank (1727), which had its origin in the Equivalent Company set up as a result of the Union of Parliaments to administer funds accruing from the financial settlement. There were the British Linen Bank (1746), which started as a finance house for the promotion of the linen industry in Scotland, the Commercial Bank (1810), and others. These were all joint-stock, and, to meet local needs in the light of communication difficulties, they developed branch systems, unlike the Bank of England, which regarded itself as primarily a London bank. The reputation of Scottish banking stood high, partly because it rested on a joint-stock basis, partly because of its extensive coverage, and partly because, as a rule, it was cautious — some would have said over-cautious — in its use of resources. Scotland's system was called the 'classic banking system' and was widely copied in other countries.

Partnerships were also fairly numerous in Scotland, but they gradually disappeared or were absorbed by the joint-stock banks. John Coutts started a modest kind of establishment in connection with his corn-merchanting in Edinburgh, early in the eighteenth century. His sons went to London and founded the banking-house of Coutts & Co., leaving the Edinburgh institution to flourish for about a century before it finally joined the Glasgow Union Bank in 1838, which in turn became the Union Bank of Scotland.

A severe financial depression followed the end of the Napoleonic Wars and a crisis in 1825, was, perhaps unfairly, blamed to some extent on the Bank of England. In fact it was mainly due to the over-stretching of resources, attributable to the boom in investment in South and Central America. Seventy-two country banks failed in England and one in Scotland. There had been half a dozen similar crises in the last fifty years, and this and the arguments of the reformers convinced the Government that the English system was dangerously rigid, and particularly that the Bank of England was too circumscribed in its dealing with crises. In 1826 Parliament sanctioned the establishment in England of joint-stock banks with any number of partners with a right of note issue outside a sixty-five-mile radius of London. The Act prohibited the issue of £1 notes in England and Scotland. This provoked an agitation in Scotland, led by Sir Walter Scott and others, which was successful in securing Scotland's exemption. The Bank of England at the same time was expected to open provincial branches and did so to a limited extent. In 1833 joint-stock banking was permitted within the sixty-five-mile limit, but without note issue. This greatly encouraged joint-stock banking: in 1823 there were 32 in England and Wales, in 1836 98, in 1841 115, while during the same period the number of private banks fell away sharply. A small straw in the wind was an Act of 1833 repealing the old Usury Act of 1713, which forbade interest at a higher rate than 5%, a relic of the distrust of usury as such.

There was still no limitation on the right of note issue, and over-issue had been blamed for the 1825 crisis. There was another in 1837–40 for which over-issue of paper money was again said to be responsible. This resulted in the famous Bank Charter Act of 1844. Briefly, the Bank of England's right to issue notes was limited to a certain aggregate value (maximum £14 million), against which first-class securities were to be held; this was the fiduciary issue. Beyond that amount gold and silver coin or bullion cover was required, and not more than one-fifth of this was to be in silver. No new bank of issue could be set up, and the note issue of those already so privileged was strictly limited. If a bank of issue ceased to operate, two-thirds of its lapsed issue could be added to the fiduciary issue of the Bank of England. Note-issuing banks other than the Bank of England dwindled in number, and the last went in 1921.

The special position of Scottish banking was recognised by the Scottish Bank Act of 1845, which still governs Scottish banks' note issue, and gave much more latitude than was enjoyed by their English counterparts. Issue rights were confined to the banks already having them; each bank could have in circulation an amount of notes (minimum denomination £1) equal to its average circulation during the seven years ended 1 May 1845, plus the average amount held at its head office from time to time. Amalgamating banks could issue notes to the amount of the aggregate enjoyed before amalgamation.

The idea of the 1844 Act was to impose a limit on credit, by restriction of note issue, and so prevent crises. It did not succeed, partly because notes were not the only media of credit. There was another crisis in 1847, precipitated by a trade recession the previous year, and a disastrous harvest, leading to abnormally heavy imports, which made for uncertainty and the export of gold. The Bank of England was slow to appreciate the position, its freedom of action was limited, and the gold reserve fell. Eleven banks and many firms went bankrupt. The Government eventually publicly authorised the suspension of the Bank Act; that is, it allowed an increase in the fiduciary issue by promising an Act of Indemnity if the statutory limit were exceeded; intimation of this alone relieved the panic and the money flowed in again. There was another crisis in 1857 — in fact, down to 1870 there was at least one crisis per decade – this time started by a collapse in the United States, in which Britain had heavy commitments, and by undue speculation at home. Two large Glasgow banks, the Western Bank of Scotland and the City of Glasgow Bank failed, and Liverpool also was hard hit. Again the Government suspended the Act, and this time the Bank had to take advantage of it briefly. In 1866 there was another crisis, partly due to the operations of finance houses which, like Overend Gurney, took advantage of limited liability to a dangerous extent in their discounting and other operations. The collapse of Overend Gurney, for over £5 million, shook the financial fabric, and in a few months 180 joint-stock companies had joined it in the bankruptcy courts. The Bank of England had held aloof from the finance houses' troubles, but the crisis

demanded action; the Bank Act was suspended, and the bank rate
was raised to 10%, the highest until 1914, on the outbreak of the
First World War. Variation of the bank rate became a stock device for
control of the credit temperature, in the last quarter of the nineteenth
century. There was another famous crisis in 1890, when over-exten-
sive speculation in foreign securities, particularly in South America,
resulted in the near-failure of the famous house of Baring Brothers.
This time the Bank checked the panic before it reached disaster
proportions by guaranteeing a fund to meet Baring's liabilities.

But the foundation of credit and money is confidence, and confidence in the stability of the system was growing steadily. Banking
experience was lengthening, and was becoming a steadying factor.
More settled political conditions in the world helped. There was
less wildcat investment, and fewer booms followed by bursts.
There was, too, not only the gradual acceptance by the Bank of
England of its obligations as a central bank (a part which it had
come to play by force of circumstances rather than as a voluntary
policy) but the tightening up of the whole financial structure,
resulting from numerous amalgamations. Between 1877 and 1907
over 200 banks were absorbed in larger concerns, and this process
reached a crescendo in 1918, with a record number of fusions,
resulting in the 'Big Five', which became responsible for some
five-sixths of banking transactions.

Gold had been tacitly acknowledged to be the currency standard
in the eighteenth century. It was abandoned in 1797, because of
the run on the banks induced by war-time fears, and the gold
currency was replaced by note issue. In other words, the Bank of
England was released from its obligation to redeem notes in gold
on demand; it was a suspension of cash payments. The free issue
of paper money helped to create inflation. In 1821 the gold
standard returned and Britain remained on it until 1914. Officially
it was not abandoned until 1919, but gold coinage had simply
vanished. In 1925 there was a return to the gold standard, but not
to gold coinage — that is, a return to gold bullion, with the Bank of
England being required to buy and sell gold bars at fixed prices.
The gold standard was again abandoned in 1931 as a result of the
depression and the adverse balance of payments.

In 1914 there was a brief run on the Bank of England, and measures on what were by now accepted lines were taken. The Currency and Banknotes Act of that year empowered the Government to increase the fiduciary issue as necessary, without a statutory limit, and the Treasury was also authorised to issue notes for £1 and 10s. In 1928 the Currency and Banknotes Act restored the right of note issue in England to the Bank of England; Scotland was not affected. The Treasury could now raise or lower the fiduciary issue at the request of the Bank for six months at a time, but not beyond a total period of two years without Parliament's consent. This gave a good deal of elasticity, and the latitude was used in 1931, and again in 1939. After 1932 the Bank and the Treasury worked very closely together, through the Exchange Equalisation Account, which was controlled by the Treasury, and operated by the Bank of England. In short, Britain was moving rapidly towards a managed currency. Finally the Bank of England was nationalised after the Second World War.

The Bank of England has played a greater part than the legislation might suggest, since from an early age it became the bankers' bank, with provincial and Scottish banks holding their reserves in the Bank of England. Another development making for centralisation has been the amalgamation of Scottish banks in the big English banks.

Of course the banks lent money at interest to sound or likely creditors, and this was an orthodox way of financing enterprise. There were, however, many other sources, and it is important to remember here that Britain was a pioneer. It borrowed little or nothing in the capitalisation of its industry from abroad, although it was to lend and invest a great deal in other countries when the time came. The capital for British industry came from domestic sources. It was essentially private investment, and in this it differed from much of the investment in the expanding economies of Europe, where the State might direct or encourage investment in one way or another; but then there was an acceptance of Governmental control in, say, Germany or Russia, whereas in Britain there was a deep-rooted distrust of it. Even public spending of any sort was looked at askance, except in the realm of military and naval affairs, and even here, for most of the nineteenth century, it was looked on as a necessary nuisance, necessitating taxation. In industry, education, etc., the Government made little financial contribution for a long time, even in what came to be known as the public sector of enterprise.

Land had always been a field of investment, for profit, for security, for prestige, for political power. The 'nabob' returning from India, the merchant prince, the industrial magnate, invested in land, and the Agricultural Revolution made possible very good returns. Landowners in turn sank money in the exploitation of the mineral resources of their own estates. 'In the early nineteenth century agricultural rents had long ceased to be the sole source of income for an enterprising landowner, especially if his estate had industrial or mineral potentialities. Landowners dominated many turnpike trusts, and inland waterway proprietories; their urban ground rents multiplied as towns and industries developed; in many cases they engaged in entrepreneurial industrial activities.'[1] Coal and iron were obvious cases. The Duke of Norfolk owned coal-mines and ironworks around Sheffield; the Duke of Leeds had mines at Barnsley; the Duke of Atholl in Scotland operated mines on his estates; local landowners were associated with iron and coal development in the Midlands, Yorkshire, the North of England, South Wales and Scotland. The Duke of Bedford promoted urban development in Bloomsbury. The great trading companies were another safe and lucrative field for investment. Wedgwood invested in canals, with an eye on his own particular kind of manufacture. Merchants, too, invested in industry. There was ample capital in Liverpool from the overseas trade in cotton and slaves. The tobacco barons of Glasgow had money to spare for shipbuilding and engineering. The merchant adventurers of Bristol sank money in the industries of South Wales at the end of the eighteenth century. The Darby ironworks at Coalbrookdale was partly financed by a Bristol merchant banker.

Most of the investment in the first half of the nineteenth century

[1] J. T. Ward, 'The Earls Fitzwilliam and the Wentworth Woodhouse Estate in the Nineteenth Century', *Yorkshire Bulletin of Economic and Social Research*, xii. 1 (1960).

was local. The London Stock Exchange dealt in a very restricted range of Government securities, and the shares of some of the large trading undertakings. There was 'a great deal of money about', at least in a fairly limited circle. Taxation was light, again reflecting Government attitude and the role of the State. On the other hand, the opportunities for investment were limited. Industry did not attract or seek as much capital as might have been expected. Much of what was required was secured through the ploughing back of profits, as in the South Wales iron industry, or through the private efforts of directors and their friends. The canals in the last twenty years of the eighteenth century needed great infusions of capital, which was usually raised locally by interested parties. The railways, however, demanded much more, and it was this 'railway mania', which reached its peak in the 1840s, that, more than any other single agency, was responsible for the wider spread of the invest-ment habit. It was said that £300 million was invested in railways before 1855, of which one-half came in the frantic rush of 1846–50. Relatively small investors put their savings in those presumably ultra-safe securities, and most of the railway capital came in lumps of from £200 to £2,000, raised through public sub-scriptions.

The relaxation of the law concerning joint-stock companies made public issues of shares simpler, and a much greater variety came on the market. The London stock-market widened its scope, and provincial stock exchanges developed, as did merchant bankers such as Rothschild, and Baring, which previously had concen-trated mainly on foreign loans. When Guinness became a public company in 1886 Barings handled the issue.

The investment trust began in the last quarter of the nineteenth century, and its home was in Dundee. This was a method of finding an outlet for capital diversified to the point where the overall risk was reduced to a minimum. Robert Fleming, the founder of the first, the Scottish American Trust (1873), returned from a visit to the United States full of the potentialities of that country. The funds of the Trust were usually put into railway mortgage bonds, but they were spread over various undertakings. The massive Alliance Trust, whose origins can be dated to the same year, concentrated at first on land mortgages in the same country.

Even with all this extension of facilities, however, the investing public in the nineteenth century remained comparatively small, being drawn mainly from middle-class and upper-class people. The working class had not got the habit, and such savings as they were able to put by were mostly invested in Friendly Societies and savings banks. The majority of enterprises still got their capital from private sources, without reference to the public, right up to the First World War.

Investment abroad was not merely a profitable utilisation of financial resources surplus to domestic needs; unco-ordinated as it was, it was still vital to Britain's role as an economic power. It was essential to other countries well endowed in other respects in enabling them to exploit their potential in the production of manufactured and primary commodities, and, while it could be argued that in the long run their development of manufactures might work against Britain's interest, it brought in its train great and immediate benefits. It gave rich dividends to the shrewd investor, and these, together with the very substantial 'invisible returns' from shipping, insurance and other services, helped to pay for the imports of raw materials and foodstuffs on which the country increasingly relied, as well as the 'extras' which were part of a higher standard of living. Here, and especially in the period between the mid-nineteenth century and the early seventies, was free trade at its best, with Britain accepting without let or hindrance the products of the rest of the world, secure in the knowledge that her own surpluses in capital and goods, and her own expertise, would command a ready market.

Surplus capital had been building up in England during the seventeenth and eighteenth centuries, but there is no evidence of an outflow to other countries before the peace of 1815. Until the Napoleonic Wars, Holland had been the world's investment centre. Before this time, surplus income found its way to Bank of England stock, the stock of the great chartered companies, such as the East India Company, home Government securities and the comparatively few home commercial ventures which had a public appeal, notably canal construction. Various factors tended to encourage the movement of capital abroad after the end of the Napoleonic Wars. It was true that the investment habit was still in its infancy; the man with money to spare was still constrained by suspicions of 'bubble' schemes, but this inbred caution was being dissipated by the growth in the nineteenth century, not only of exciting new opportunities but of creditable media of investment, in the form of joint-stock companies, and the orthodox credit agencies. The coming of limited liability helped greatly to promote the investment habit. At the end of the Napoleonic War, there was a slump in returns at home, so that investment abroad looked more attractive. At this juncture, too, foreigners turned naturally to Britain as a source, since she had emerged from the struggle with her sinews stronger and more supple than ever. It was a striking commentary on this that the French Government should borrow from her conqueror (through Baring Brothers, a merchant bank which had started off as a woollen-merchants' business in Exeter) the wherewithal to pay off the indemnity imposed on her by the Allies. And the habit grew more and more widespread throughout the nineteenth century, although there were set-backs from time to time; one can almost detect a cyclical movement, due to the fairly regular recurrence of various circumstances, such as defaulting on the part of borrower-states, especially in America, or the failure of large-scale enterprises, often caused by periodical 'overheating' of the economy.

With Britain becoming the workshop of the world, there was a natural temptation on the part of private firms doing a large exporting business to leave some at least of the balance accruing to them in less-developed countries, since enterprises there might offer a remunerative field for this surplus capital. British capitalists were developing industries on the Continent in the early nineteenth century, and not infrequently used their own men as well as their own money. Ingenuity and skill had been the chief contributions to continental growth, despite the prohibitions of English law, but capital also had found its way into canal projects, and Boulton and Watt sold steam-engines in Europe. In 1798 a German manufacturer was given exclusive rights in Crompton's mule and

another in Arkwright's water-frame in the following year. In both
cases British engineers were employed to fit the machinery and
supervise its running. Later British contractors, like Brassey, with
British labour and British capital, played a very large part in the
finance and building of railways in France and Belgium. The same
story was repeated in the coal-mines of the Ruhr and the ironworks at Le Creusot. Continental tariff restrictions helped to promote investment, since it was easier to invest capital on the other
side of the wall than to try to send native manufacturers over it.
But the movement was in any case inevitable, in view of the relatively advanced economy of Great Britain, and the high returns
that capital and skill could command abroad. The City of London
in the first half of the nineteenth century was more favourably
disposed to foreign than to home investment, especially the
merchant banks, such as Baring Brothers, and Rothschild, which
specialised in State loans. It is, however, impossible to assess the
gross amount of British foreign investment for the period before
1870.

Capital was not only invested by capitalists in this manner;
a considerable amount was taken overseas by emigrants — considerable, that is, when taken *in toto*; many of them, especially
Irish and Highlanders, took little or nothing — and a rough estimate suggests that between 1830 and 1845 there was from £20
million to £30 million of 'unrecorded capital', in addition to
private investment, which went abroad from Britain.

Those early investments might look lucrative, but they did not
always prove so; English investors lost £10 million in South
America in the 1820s. Yet the movement went on steadily; native
industry in Britain at this stage was largely financed out of profits,
so the income from agriculture, trade and Government securities
flowed readily into colonial and foreign channels. There were also
official British loans to foreign governments, sometimes with
political motives, as in the attempt to keep alive the 'sick man of
Europe', Turkey; but this factor was fairly uncommon in British
circles, whereas in France it was an accepted feature of diplomacy.

Investment in the early part of the century was mainly in
Europe and America; it was estimated that in 1827 £93 million of

British capital was already invested in Russia, Germany and America, both in Government securities there and in bank and canal enterprises. By the 1830s the European capital market had begun to fall off, but the demand from elsewhere more than compensated for this. The development of the United States from now on continued to attract an increasing amount, especially to railway development, through the purchase of State bonds or shares. Central and South America, too, offered glittering prizes, particularly in mining, and many investors lost money there. Railways never failed to attract capital, and towards the mid-nineteenth century the shares of Canadian and Indian railways also began to appear on the stock-market; although about this time (1847-8) the flow abroad was severely checked by commercial and on the Continent political crises; in fact, there was some flow back from Europe, and around £6 million worth of stock was realised, but this was only a temporary check.

There could be, and often was in Britain's case, a strong connection between the export of capital and the export of capital goods; India was a very good example of this. One-third of the capital invested in Indian railways down to the 1880s was spent on taking British rails there. But this was by no means an invariable rule and it was not the practice to 'attach strings'; nor indeed would it have been practicable, short of a degree of state direction which would not have been tolerated. By the mid-nineteenth century, the total of British investment abroad, in Government securities and private enterprises, totalled probably £300 million.

With the recovery of the United States after the Civil War, the flow of British capital there went on apace, but the period up to 1873 was marked by intense activity in investment in many quarters. Governments generally were borrowing, including British colonies. Canada was an outstanding case, for, like India, there was a vast amount of opening-up and development to be undertaken, while Australia and New Zealand were similarly preoccupied. Railways were still perhaps the main draw, and Britain still had plenty of money to lend. By 1870 the total of British investment abroad was probably about £800 million. France, too, had been lending a great deal, but the Franco-Prussian war, and the necessity for France to pay her indemnity, compelled her to sell her foreign investments, and Britain bought up a considerable amount of them. The export of capital reached a very high level in 1872. There was another check in 1876–8 deriving from an adverse trade balance, due to bad harvests, the unsettled political situation on the Continent, and the development of continental industries, accompanied by high protection. Between the early 1850s and the middle eighties, the amount of British capital invested abroad increased by about £1,000 million, and, by the latter date, the total British capital thus invested was estimated at £1,302 million. A substantial amount of this, probably over half, was in Government securities.

In the eighties the balance of trade was steadily becoming more adverse. On the one hand, Britain was importing an increasing proportion of her needs; on the other, her suppliers were becoming more self-sufficient. They sheltered behind tariff walls, while Britain remained an open market for the world, and the metropolis of a huge area whose monetary standard was sterling. In the years before the First World War, the unfavourable balance was running at £150 million per annum, but this was comfortably cushioned by the income from investment services. The export of capital did not cease, but conditions were less favourable to it. America had by the end of the century amassed capital of her own — she was indeed exporting capital — and was recovering the dominant control of her own business by buying back securities from European investors. The South African War (1899–1902) still further reduced the export of British capital, which the British Government needed for its own purposes. But there was a recovery after the South African War; in fact, there was a revival of the movement on an intense scale, from about 1905 onwards. It rose between then and 1912 from £50 million to around £200 million. 'It was estimated', says Clapham, 'that during 1911–12 about 30 per cent more capital was exported than during the whole decade between 1890 and 1901, and in each of the two years vastly more than in any peak year of capital export during the eighties or seventies.'[1] The years 1912–13 saw the biggest recorded exports of

[1] *Economic History of Britain* (1938), bk. iv, pp. 61, 475.

British capital. By 1914 £4,000 million was invested abroad. Of this figure, nearly one-half was in the Empire, or over £800 million in the United States, and over £300 million in Latin America.

It was believed by some that the movement of capital abroad before the war, while it greatly contributed to the country's commercial and political power, went too far; that Britain was investing capital and reinvesting the proceeds of established investments abroad, and was concentrating her resources, too, on exporting capital goods, to too great an extent, since this might mean that the opportunities and positive needs of British industry were being neglected. It was argued that if there had been less concentration on other countries, conditions at home, including living conditions, could have been greatly improved.

It is hardly necessary to add that foreign investment and the new imperialism were closely linked. The direction of the flow changed in the late nineteenth and early twentieth centuries, partly because of the diminishing pull of America, partly because of the opportunities elsewhere. The expansion of the British Empire was bound up with the need for new markets and raw materials, and also with the need for new fields of investment. Patriotism and self-interest frequently went hand in hand for the British investor — not that he would invest in the colonies because they were colonies, but simply because the return might be high. Investment and State policy were also linked; the defence and protection of British capital interests in the Far East largely prompted the 'Opium War' against China in 1842. One can note certain broad tendencies in the nineteenth century. The chief incentive for capital investment abroad, was, of course, profit, so the bulk of investment was in fairly speculative enterprises, promising high returns. But in the 1890s the small investor was coming to the fore, and safety was becoming more important, and by 1914 about 30% of British foreign investment was in Government and municipal securities. The fixed-interest issues of British colonies and dominions had become popular. The Colonial Stocks Act elevated issues of Colonial and Dominion Governments, which complied with certain conditions, to the rank of 'trustee' securities. It was significant that, in this period, the flow of emigrants from Britain to the Empire trebled.

Politics had comparatively little effect on British investment, except in so far as the Government's policy in the third quarter of the nineteenth century of guaranteeing interest on the securities of railways and certain other public utilities in British colonies was a special (and effective) inducement to home capital. This contrasted very much with the policy followed in France, Germany and the United States, which aimed to channel lending to those quarters where the home governments thought it would do most good politically.

The First World War made severe inroads into Britain's overseas holdings. She had to make heavy purchases abroad, while she also made very large loans to her allies. She was still well able to shoulder those financial commitments out of her own resources, and the position had been restored, on paper, by the twenties. The strain was, however, much more exhausting than before, for the balance of trade had deteriorated further. The situation was worsened by the Depression, since earnings fell away, particularly those from the primary-producing countries, while invisible earnings, especially from shipping, contracted with the shrinkage of international trade.

The Second World War was a repetition of this experience, but in a sharply exacerbated form. This time well over £1,000 million worth of holdings, representing above one-quarter of overseas investments, were sold, often at disastrous prices, while the total of merchant shipping had fallen by close on the same proportion. An external debt of some £3,000 million had been contracted, so that over all Britain was 'in the red'. Normal exports had been cut by nearly two-thirds. How to rectify this state of affairs has remained Britain's most intractable and most vital post-war problem.

6 The Development of Transport

INDUSTRY could not quicken and expand without improved transport, for, however much production might associate itself geographically with the native resources of raw materials and power — and there were obvious and increasing limitations to this process — the enlargement of the market could not be achieved without mobility of materials and finished products.

In the sphere of internal transport, roads came first, and, while their early development has been overshadowed by that of canals and railways, it is significant that there was a 'road era' roughly contemporary with the period of the Industrial Revolution. In the early eighteenth century, most roads in Britain were not worthy of the name; they were merely tracks, maintained by compulsory service — at the order of the State, but on a purely local, parish basis — exacted under a statute of the mid-sixteenth century. This prescribed six days' direct labour in a year, or, if one's income were over £50 per annum, the use of a man, horse and cart for the same period. The State, in fact, enforced self-help; in the eighteenth century it increasingly left the initiative to private enterprise, in the form of turnpike trusts. These were formed by landlords primarily for their own convenience, and tolls were charged for the improvement and maintenance of the more important stretches. Each trust had to be authorised by a private Act of Parliament. The first recorded Act of this kind was in 1663, but such Acts were uncommon until the eighteenth century, when there was enough demand to warrant a General Turnpike Act (1773) to facilitate such private legislation.

The Government had a direct interest in good communications.

Troops might have to be moved, while the post had always been a royal monopoly. It did not entirely deny its responsibility, and built military roads and bridges in Scotland after the Rebellions of 1715 and 1745. Even so, by far the greater part of the roads when the Industrial Revolution began were maintained by compulsory service either directly, or indirectly, through the rates, pauper labour being commonly used. In 1820 perhaps one-sixth of the highways — apart from private roads — were under trusts. After 1815 those trusts were beginning to combine for compelling reasons, especially the need to pool capital resources, to cover greater stretches and to eliminate wasteful competition. It was the trusts, unpopular as they were with toll-payers, which enlisted the help of such engineers as Thomas Telford (1757–1834) and John McAdam (1756–1836) and thus fostered the science of roadmaking. Government again was interested, and McAdam, who was a Road Commissioner in Scotland from 1783, became surveyor to the Bristol Turnpike Trust in 1816 — in that year he also published his book *The Present System of Roadmaking*, which made him famous — and became Surveyor-General of Metropolitan Roads in 1827.

There was much to be done and much to be learned: the techniques of surveying and engineering and actually constructing roads were still in their infancy. Telford in particular showed how to design roads, and McAdam how to give them a durable surface. In 1835 the Government passed the Highways Act, which did away with compulsory service, and empowered the parish to levy a road rate and appoint paid surveyors. The tendency towards centralisation and uniformity in the highways' system, which the Government professed to encourage, languished, partly because Government had not yet really accepted the idea of roads as traffic arteries, and partly because long-distance traffic was now finding another and better medium in canals and railways. Railways in particular began to force the trusts out of business, leaving the onus to local authorities. But even by 1874 there were still 854 trusts, of which the last gave up the ghost in 1895.

In 1888 the county authorities, which had always had the responsibility for bridges, with a county rate, were given the task of

looking after the highways in their area, while the rest were entrusted to the urban and rural district councils. This attitude of
leaving development to local initiative contrasted unfavourably
with that applying in, for instance, France. There, before and after
the French Revolution, the central government built, improved
and maintained main roads. 'In Great Britain', says Professor
Knowles, 'transport improvements were regarded as the business
of individuals ... transport was a business like anything else, and
a government had no concern with business undertakings except
to prevent abuses ... in France the transport developments came
from above, and were planned on a uniform system; in England
they came from below, and grew up in a patchy, haphazard, piecemeal fashion.'[1] This was true of all forms of transport; and the
contrast between unco-ordinated private effort and State supervision applied equally between Britain and other European
States.

With the advent of the motor-car, there was a new urgency and
a new potential source of funds for road-making. In 1909 the
Budget for the first time introduced taxation of motorists, and of
the fuel they used, from which was to be financed, through the
Road Fund, the activities of a Central Road Improvement Board,
which gave grants to local authorities. As with other types of
machine, so with the means of road locomotion, there was an intermediate stage of evolution, when manpower was used. In 1868
the Coventry Machinists Company began to make bicycles. The
location was not by chance, for Coventry had already become a
centre of precision engineering, for turning out watches, then
sewing-machines and finally bicycles. First there were the 'bone-
shakers', then the penny-farthings, then, after 1885, the 'safety
bicycle', that is, the modern type with, after 1889, pneumatic
tyres. Bicycling became the rage, for pleasure and business, around
the end of the nineteenth century.

Public transport in the towns was mainly a matter of horse-
buses until the 1870s. In 1871 London began to build its under-
ground (steam) railway; the Inner Circle was finished in 1884.

---

[1] L. C. A. Knowles, *Industrial and Commercial Revolutions*, p. 240.

Horse-drawn or steam-trams became common around the same time. These were gradually replaced towards the end of the century by electric trams, which confirmed the social habit of using public-service vehicles for travel within town areas, and they maintained their popularity until midway between the two World Wars.

But motor transport was nothing short of a revolution. Steam-coaches had been tried, with a good deal of success, but the competition of the railways, the bad surfaces of the roads, the costliness of turnpikes, and governmental unfriendliness, symbolised in the Locomotive or 'Red Flag' Act of 1865 — which insisted that road users must be preceded by a man with a flag, and restricted speeds to four m.p.h. in the country, and two m.p.h. in the towns — finally killed this experiment. (The first car rally in 1894 was won by a steam-engine.)

There had been various developments of the internal-combustion engine — such engines were in use as early as 1832 — using gas, oil, and finally petrol. The credit for pioneering in this field goes to a German, Daimler, although Benz had made a motor-tricycle earlier. In 1886 Daimler produced a motor-bicycle, and in the following year a motor-car, to be produced in Coventry. In 1895 Lanchester and Austin designed their first cars, and the latter's enterprise helped to make Birmingham a centre of the automobile industry. France and Germany, not Britain, were the leaders; by 1893 France was producing 500 cars per year. Britain by contrast moved forward slowly, but in 1896 the 'Red Flag' law was repealed. The motor-bus quickly followed, and gradually drove horse-buses off the streets. The First World War forced the Government to a realisation of the potentialities of the internal-combustion engine, and after it motor transport became firmly established. For the first time it became a serious rival to rail transport. There were 389,000 motor vehicles registered in 1914, 2,200,000 by 1929, and by 1939 over 3 million, of which 2 million were private cars.

The Government reluctantly had to play a more direct part. The modernisation of trunk roads could be said to have begun in 1924. Slowly, too, the Government accepted responsibility for some degree of regulation of the traffic. In 1930 there was passed the Road Traffic Act, which established thirteen road districts, reduced in 1934 to twelve, each under three traffic commissioners. The purpose was to regulate the expansion of motor transport through the issue of licences. At first control was exercised over private and passenger service vehicles; then in 1933 there came the Road and Rail Traffic Act, which did the same thing for goods transport by bringing under the licensing powers of the traffic commissioners road haulage vehicles, with a special kind of licence for different methods of operation. In both cases the commissioners were desired to have due regard to the other facilities, including rail facilities, already available, but there was no systematic policy of transport integration. London presented a special problem, and in 1933 the London Passenger Transport Board was given responsibility for passenger transport in all its forms, within the London area, except for what went by the main railway system.

Yet another medium of transport was launched by the beginning of the twentieth century. In 1903 Wilbur and Orville Wright made a half-hour flight in a plane, and in 1909 Blériot crossed the Channel. The First World War decisively proved the value of aircraft as it proved the value of the motor-vehicle, and the first commercial line began in 1919. Here, again, the British Government went no further at first than providing landing and navigational facilities for privately-operated concerns, in line with the official view that competition and not control was to be aimed at. Private enterprise, however, could not compete with foreign State-aided undertakings, and the inevitable introduction of subsidies in Britain quickly led to the amalgamation of the companies concerned, to form Imperial Airways (1924), with a proportion of the directorate nominated by the State. The exploitation of internal and continental routes by private enterprise compelled a further amalgamation between Imperial Airways and British Airways, in the shape of a public corporation, British Overseas Airways Corporation (1939). Immediately after the Second World War British European Airways took over the domestic and European operations, while a separate corporation was set up for air transport to South America.

The latter was soon afterwards merged in the British Overseas Airways Corporation.

The demands of commerce also were responsible for the development of canals. Water transport had always been the chief agency, whether by river or by coast, for the transport of heavy goods, and the improvement of river channels — inland navigations — and the construction of canals were a logical extension of it. At the beginning of the nineteenth century canals seemed to offer a much better prospect than road transport, partly because water transport would be about half the cost of road transport, and partly because the roads were so intolerably bad. The 'canal era' was also roughly that of the Industrial Revolution, and was associated particularly with the name of James Brindley (1716–72). Telford was also a canal builder, of, among others, the Caledonian Canal (1823). Brindley was a wheelwright by trade, and in 1759–61 he engineered the first canal for the Duke of Bridgewater, from the duke's Worsley Colliery to Manchester. Then he made a second canal for him, linking Manchester with Runcorn on the Mersey. These were expensive propositions: the duke's canals cost him £200,000, but his collieries prospered, for their transport costs were greatly reduced. It was a matter of self-interest, and others were not slow to follow the example; indeed, a 'canal mania' set in. Not all the projects were well-founded, but there were outstanding achievements, such as the Grand Junction Canal between London and the Midlands, authorised in 1793, and the Forth and Clyde Canal, engineered by Brindley, and constructed between 1767 and 1790.

Canals were also built by private enterprise, either by individuals or by companies. They involved a limited amount of government regulation, in so far as each project required an Act of Parliament. By 1830 there were almost 2,000 miles of canals, and 1,312 miles of inland navigations. Government interference or help was confined to fixing maximum rates, except in the case of the Caledonian and Crinan canals in Scotland, which were financed and owned from the start by the Government. So, as with roads, there was no uniformity of design or overall plan; there were variations in depths, widths and rates. They were often too small to accommodate worthwhile ships. Yet, with all their deficiencies, the canals were of vital importance at a crucial stage in the expansion of British industry. They helped to open up inland areas such as the Potteries. They gave experience in civil engineering, and incidentally produced a nucleus of navvies for other and perhaps greater projects, in both Britain and Europe.

The canals were merely water roads. The undertakers were not carriers themselves, until 1845, when an Act permitted this — too late — and a good many were neither prosperous at the best of times, nor very efficient. Their tolls were often exorbitant, and, above all, they suffered from the lack of a common design, which prevented through traffic. After 1830 there was a relative decline, relative in the sense that even as late as 1909 canals carried more goods absolutely than they ever had before, but by then the total tonnages of United Kingdom traffic had increased enormously. After this date, canals played a lesser part in the expansion of transport because of the deliberate policy of the railways in buying them up to eliminate their competition. By 1875 the railways had possession of half the canals of the country.

Government might have helped them at this difficult period in their history, but its policy was one of non-interference. In 1873 it went so far as to set up the Railway and Canal Commission to check the absorption of canals by railways, and so help to maintain competition between the two agencies. But nothing could save the canals. The fact was that the railways suited industry far better: they were much faster, which was a most important aspect for, say, farm produce, and especially dairy produce, to which British agriculture was changing in the later nineteenth century. They were handier, even for coal, which had inspired the earliest canals, and also for small consignments. The only exception to this story of decline came from the Manchester Ship Canal Company. This daring and imaginative piece of private enterprise, to give Manchester direct access to the sea, was authorised by Parliament in 1885, begun in 1887, and opened in 1894. It was thirty-six miles long, and in due time made Manchester one of Britain's major ports.

The railways followed a similar pattern of development, the responsibility being left to private enterprise. Again, in this respect,

Britain stood in marked contrast to continental powers, such as France and Germany, where railways were subject to overall governmental planning and control. One could say that in Britain railways, so far from being in any way helped, had to fight against Governmental interference, which could at times reach the point of being a threat to their very existence.

The transport of coal was again the main original incentive. In 1804 Trevithick built a locomotive to haul coal at Merthyr Tydfil, and George Stephenson's first locomotive was used between 1814 and 1825 for the same purpose. The Stockton and Darlington Railway, opened in 1825, was the first railway intended for public traffic. Like roads and canals, it started as a means for the transport of a client's goods by his own vehicles, including horse-drawn wagons. The Newcastle–Carlisle Railway was opened in 1829, and used horse-traction until 1834, after which the locomotive was accepted as the method of traction. But the railway epoch may be said to have begun with the Liverpool–Manchester Railway, opened in 1830, which was started largely as a kind of revolt against the inadequacy of canals. It had a length of twenty-nine miles and cost no less than £820,000, of which £70,000 was spent on getting the Bill through Parliament. George Stephenson (1781–1848) and his *Rocket* were associated with the Stockton–Darlington and the Liverpool–Manchester Railways — the *Rocket* was used on the first, but operated with complete success on the second — as well as with other railway developments in the North of England. His son Robert (1803–59) was also a notable railway engineer, and built not only the Menai Strait tubular bridge, 1850, but also the Newcastle High Level Bridge, and other great engineering projects.

Among many famous names connected with development of railways, one of the most illustrious was Brunel. The name became well known when Brunel *père* (Marc) undertook to build the world's first tunnel under a navigable river, and, after eighteen years' frustration, completed the Rotherhithe–Wapping Scheme (1843). Again both father and son (Isambard Kingdom) won scintillating reputations; but the latter was probably the better known, as engineer to the Great Western Railway, and thus responsible for the early stages of one of the greatest and best-run railways in Britain. He built railways, bridges, a lighthouse and ships, of which the *Great Eastern* was the most famous; incidentally, he hoped to make Milford Haven a port, an idea which has only recently been brought to fruition.

In 1835–7 there was the first railway boom, but there was a much greater one in 1844–8 and the years immediately following. This was the era of George Hudson, the 'railway king', who became a byword for his insatiable appetite for promoting new constructions and for consolidating existing undertakings, during the 1840s. Consolidation was in fact badly needed, for most schemes were completely independent of each other. In 1846 alone there were no less than 272 Acts of Parliament for the promotion of separate railway undertakings. In 1844–6 around £180 million of capital expenditure was undertaken. A good many of the embryo schemes, perhaps 40% of the total, disappeared in the collapse of 1847, but even so there was a vast amount of new construction.

The early railways were short and expensive for various reasons. There was the cost of securing parliamentary sanction, and then the preliminary expense of surveying and planning, which was estimated at £4,000 per mile, not including compensation to land-owners, which was often exorbitant. The capital cost of British railways has been estimated at not less than £54,000 per route mile, compared with a cost in Prussia of £21,000, and in the United States of £13,000. Other factors making for expense were the difficulties of terrain, and, of course, the inevitable frustrations and set-backs associated with pioneering. By 1838, 490 miles of railway had been constructed in England and Wales, and 50 miles in Scotland, at a total expenditure of over £13 million. Despite the vast outlay, the development went on apace: in 1843 the railway mileage in the United Kingdom had risen to 2,036, in 1848 to 4,600, in 1855 to 8,280, in 1870 to over 15,000, in 1880 to 18,000 and in 1900 to nearly 22,000 miles.

Railways were usually profitable: a return of 10% was common. One of the major defects resulting from the total absence of national planning was, as with canals, the impediments to through routes. Two gauges were used, Stephenson's narrow gauge (4 ft.

$8\frac{1}{2}$ in.), and Brunel's wide gauge (7 ft.). Not until 1846 did Parliament pronounce in favour of the former — even then it may have chosen unwisely — and it was not until 1892 that the Great Western Railway finally abandoned the broad gauge.

Those were some of the factors responsible for what was generally regarded as the over-capitalisation of British railways, at least in the period before 1850. But they were not the sole, or even perhaps the main, factors in the extravagant capital costs. A huge amount of money was sunk in railways in the last quarter of the nineteenth century, before there was any worth-while degree of rationalisation through amalgamations or mutual understandings. The delay in achieving a working relationship was partly attributable to the active government discouragement of such a trend. In this later period, there was the need to modernise the railways, in order to keep pace with the growing demand, to face up to and if possible beat competition from other lines, and all this under the dead hand of government restriction. Trains became bigger, and more powerful locomotives had to be designed, which in turn necessitated stronger tracks and bridges. A more sophisticated age demanded improved amenities in railway stations, in restaurant cars, in lavatories; and there was the progressive demand for more safety, with better signalling systems, more adequate sidings and so forth. All this, of course, meant that more money had to be pumped in.

Parliament not only allowed competition; it insisted on it, for, apart from not wishing to be involved in enterprise, except to make use of it, as for the carriage of mails, it was worried about the possible implications of this great new sprawling force in the country. In particular it was apprehensive about possible monopolistic tendencies, since the idea of monopoly was abhorrent. In 1842 the Board of Trade was given an oversight over new railways, although this meant in practice little more than an assurance of certain safety regulations, about which the Government had always been concerned. In 1844 Parliament made appropriate noises; it reserved to itself the right to revise railway charges if the dividend were over 10% (an early attempt to insist on some relationship between charges and profits), together with the right to compulsory purchase by the State of railways built in and after

1844; while it insisted on one daily passenger train on passenger lines, at one penny per mile third class.

In 1842 the railways themselves established the Railway Clearing House, merely to make arrangements, including rates, for through traffic; this was incorporated by Act of Parliament in 1850, and it became a common meeting-ground for all the companies. The units tended to become bigger, both by a process of amalgamation and by reason of the bigger lines sending out branches, and by 1850 there were strong individual systems like the London and North Western, the Midland and the Great Northern, and, further, there was a good deal of collusion of a somewhat clandestine nature between the different systems to offset the rigours of competition. In 1846 Parliament set up Commissioners to keep a critical eye on proposed amalgamations, but these had little or no effect, and they were disbanded in 1851. In 1854 there was passed what was known as 'Cardwell's Railway Act', which prescribed certain safeguards for railway users, facilities for through traffic, no undue preferences, etc.

Parliament continued to be torn between its policy of free enterprise, and the need to safeguard the public welfare. In the 1860s amalgamations went on apace, and in 1871 there were such far-reaching proposals for further amalgamations that Parliament established the Railway and Canal Commission of 1873, whose function was mainly to keep an eye on railway rates, and to exercise a general vigilance about proposed amalgamations, and the take-over activities of the railways as regards canals — a follow-up of Cardwell's Act. In the last quarter of the nineteenth century there was a great expansion of the railway system, but mainly in the elaboration of existing routes — that is, connecting lines, together with the building of suburban lines — as well as a good deal of improvements, such as the Severn tunnel, which was opened in 1886, the Tay Bridge — or rather Bridges — of 1878–87 (the first collapsed), the Forth Bridge of 1890 and the Mallaig line of 1901. This kind of expansion was essential, but of course it greatly increased the high capitalisation of the network.

The railways not unnaturally wanted some relaxation of their original Acts of Incorporation, in particular to enable them to charge higher rates to cover the kind of expenditure described. On the other hand, there was a depression in trade, accompanied by a demand from traders for more protection from higher railway charges. The result was the Railway and Canal Traffic Act of 1888, which sought to introduce some measure of standardisation into schedules of maximum charges. These were to be determined by the Board of Trade, and were to come into force in or by 1893. The Railway and Canal Commission was to be the authority responsible, and was to become a permanency. The railways retaliated by raising all their rates to the maximum permitted, and the result was the Railway and Canal Act of 1894, which insisted that rates must not exceed the 1892 level, unless the railways made a case for an increase to the Commission's satisfaction. This system continued until relaxed in 1903, and it meant that, since competition in rates was difficult and dangerous, it must be restricted to the provision of better facilities, or avoided through amalgamation or some working arrangement. A Parliamentary Inquiry in 1911 said, 'the era of competition between the railway companies is passing away'.

The restrictive system imposed so far could not be indefinitely maintained alongside rising costs, not least those of labour, which had been organised in trade unions since the early seventies. Even in matters of railway employment, the State had insisted on a right of intervention. In 1846 a Committee of Inquiry into the conditions of navvies had, with reason (the casualty rates were very high), recommended compensation for injured workers, and statutory control over the standard of accommodation for them. Neither recommendation, of course, was accepted. In 1893, following a railway strike in Scotland for the reduction of hours, the Board of Trade was given authority to investigate and fix maximum hours if necessary.

In 1909 a Royal Commission recommended that the State should acquire the railways for a total compensation of around £6 million. No action was taken in this direction, but during the First World War the railways were temporarily taken over, and a kind of unified control was imposed through the Railway Executive Committee of General Managers. Then came the Railways Act of

1921. There were 214 railways in Great Britain, and 121 were now formed into four groups; the L.N.E.R., the L.M.S., the G.W.R. and the S.R. A Railway Rates Tribunal, which took the place of the Railway and Canal Commission, included three Crown-appointed members, its duties to fix standard rates, and approve variations of them as required, and also to determine such things as conditions of carriage. The Ministry of Transport was to be the final arbiter in such matters. The intention was that the rates should return a 'standard revenue', which, in fact, was never achieved by any of the Companies. Finally, there was to be a Central Wages Board, with appeal to a National Wages Board, which included a Ministry of Labour chairman, and representatives of the users. This last device was modified in 1935, with the establishment of the Railway Staff National Council, and the Railway Staff National Tribunal. In 1947 the railways and railway ports were nationalised, along with canal and road transport, by the Labour Government. A large proportion of road transport was in 1953 restored to private ownership.

In common with much of industry, the railways attained a peak for traffic immediately before the First World War. The loss of coal markets hit them hard, including the railway ports in South Wales and elsewhere. In the 1930s railway traffic had fallen by one-eighth, and the fall would have been greater but for the diversion to railways of traffic from coastal shipping, which lost over 15% of its traffic between 1913 and 1924. In the case of coastal shipping much of the loss was also in coal traffic. Both railways and coastal shipping were losing traffic, including coal, to the roads.

Even the briefest survey of the development of British transport is not complete without some reference to shipping. Britain is, after all, an island nation, and shipping is still overwhelmingly the chief vehicle for her overseas trade. Steam was first used with sails; the first steamship to cross the Atlantic also used sail-power (1819), and it was not until 1839 that the first cross-Atlantic voyage was made by a vessel relying on steam-power alone. Britain had lagged behind the United States during the era of the fast wooden 'clipper' ships, but led the way in the exploitation of the steamship, and encountered the usual pioneering difficulties. Coal at first did not appear to be the answer, since a great deal had to be carried to serve the clumsy engines, which meant that the ship had to carry a proportionately smaller amount of cargo. To some extent this impediment was met by the creation of coaling stations at suitable places along the coasts, but the real remedy was found in economy through the evolution of the engine, and especially the arrival of the Elder compound engine and the Parsons steam turbine. The use of steel, instead of iron, made for increased cargo space. Finally there came the oil-driven engine. Curiously enough, what marked the doom of the sailing ship was the opening of the Suez Canal (1869), which the sailing ship could not navigate. From then on, steam took over, aided in Britain by the availability of coal and the growth of marine engineering and shipbuilding.

Up to the First World War, Britain was supreme in shipbuilding and in the sea-carrying trade. Until then, British ships carried over one-half of the world's sea-borne trade (52%). The Government, faithful to its doctrine of refusing responsibility for transport as for other forms of enterprise, was reluctant to give any direct help. It gave subventions for the carrying of mails to the Cunard Company, the Peninsular and Oriental Steam Navigation Company, the Royal Mail Steam Packet Company and the Pacific Steam Navigation Company, but there was no help to cargo shipping, and aid was only given for 'services rendered'. Britain indirectly benefited from the American Civil War, which had disastrous effects on the United States, rapidly becoming before then a rival. After the war, the United States shipping industry stagnated, and American capital was diverted into railways. In the 1880s European nations began to subsidise their shipping in various ways; Germany especially advanced rapidly, the State giving special low rates on State railways for shipbuilding material, and for exports going by German ships, while it also gave direct subventions to the shipping industry. Much of the increasing emigrant traffic across the Atlantic was diverted to German ships. Other factors helped Germany, including the development of the German iron and steel industries and the compact organisation of German shipping; 60% of it was in the hands of ten lines working together, and the rest had links with the ten.

This kind of thing hit the British shipping industry, which in any case was suffering after 1873 from a trade depression and a surplus of world tonnage, intensified by the advent of the steamship. This, and the growth of economic nationalism, encouraged the formation of shipping rings, making agreements as regards rates, etc., sometimes even between different nations. The British Government was moved in 1903 by the intensity of German transatlantic competition to give a substantial loan to the Cunard Company to help build two fast ships, the *Mauretania* and the ill-fated *Lusitania*. It also gave a subsidy to the Elder Dempster line to foster trade with the West Indies. These were quite exceptional expedients.

The First World War dealt a grievous blow to British shipping, from the sheer destruction of ships, the loss of trade to other countries, especially the United States and Japan, and the building of rival fleets. As a temporary relief, a British Shipping (Assistance) Act, 1935, gave a subsidy to tramp shipping until 1937. The Government made a loan to the Cunard Company to help finish the *Queen Mary* and to build the *Queen Elizabeth*, again as quite special cases. Britain held firmly, and has continued to do so, to the policy of free trade in shipping, with no discrimination on the basis of the national flag such as has marked some other countries, including the United States.

With the growth of shipping went the development of the ports. The London Docks were built in the early nineteenth century by joint-stock companies incorporated by Acts of Parliament. Even here the Government was apprehensive of monopoly and each undertaking was given exclusive rights in particular trades; but the force of competition led to amalgamations and finally, in 1908, the Port of London Authority, a public body including nominees of the Government, was set up. In other cases, such as Bristol, the municipal authority was in control; the Port of Liverpool was governed by a Board representative mainly of dock users; the railway companies took command of Southampton and some other ports; and the Manchester Ship Canal Company was the outstanding example of private enterprise, operating under statute.

The results of the revolution in transport were momentous.

Within Britain, the coming of canals, and, above all, the building-up of a railway system, meant the opening-up of the country to an extent undreamt of previously. With the advent of railways, people could and did move from one district to another with ease, whether in search of work or for pleasure. The popularity of railways for passenger transport took their promoters by surprise, and until well into the twentieth century this remained the favourite means of travel outside the towns. Seaside towns began to be holiday resorts. Labour became more mobile.

More important, from the economists' point of view, was the comparative simplicity of marketing and the greater accessibility of supplies. Dairy produce, for instance, could be dispatched quickly and with a fair assurance of safe delivery, to London from the north of England, fish and meat from Aberdeen, and so on. The marketing of perishable produce gave a new lease of life to farming at a time when it was sorely needed, and helped to improve the lot of town-dwellers. Goods could be sent regardless of weather conditions, no small consideration in so variable a climate. Equally, the retailer or wholesaler need no longer rely on building up his own large stocks, since replacements could easily be sent to him. The inland builder could get his timber and bricks with little difficulty. Communication was greatly simplified; no longer did the mails or newspapers take days to arrive by stage-coach, and this speeded up the creation of a public opinion and a national consciousness. Parliament was no longer remote, and politics became everyone's business.

Canals, and more especially railways, as has been observed elsewhere, were the chief influence in creating the investment habit, and this not only in Britain but also overseas. They stimulated other industries, particularly iron and steel manufacture and engineering, to the point where the construction of locomotives, of rails and the other paraphernalia of railway operation, became nothing short of an industry in its own right, in its own centres.

Railways served the ports, and the ports responded with improved and often specialised facilities. Bigger and better-equipped vessels docked there, unloading their raw materials and foodstuffs, taking abroad coal or manufactured goods to pay for them. The steamship recked not of wind or weather. The railway could push into the depths of an African jungle or connect the prairies with the Atlantic seaboard. Neither Britain herself nor her Empire could have developed as they did in the nineteenth century, lacking the railway and the steamship. The world as a whole was contracting, and nations were brought closer to each other, with all the possibilities for greater co-operation and greater competition which this carried in its train, not least for the nation which had started it.

7 The Growth of Socialism

PROTECTION versus free trade has long been and remains a matter for debate; but, while the working of the Industrial Revolution had as a natural concomitant *laissez-faire* in the commercial field, it provoked quite the opposite reaction in the field of social relationships. The impact of industrialisation had repercussions throughout the structure of society which made it inevitable, quite early on, that there should be a degree of protection for those sections of the community most vulnerable to its asperities. True, there were restrictions here dating from earlier times, which had been designed for the good regulation of society, but while they became anachronistic, there was never any real question but that they would be replaced by other restrictions and safeguards more in keeping with the new ethos. The Industrial Revolution accelerated the transition in that the brash, rough, new organisation intensified the old social problems and created new ones. The economy was becoming more complex and interdependent. In such an environment, *laissez-faire* on the social side simply could not be tolerated.

There was no real contradiction between the belief that the individual should have the maximum possible freedom to work out his destiny and the acceptance of a modicum of artificial control on behalf of the common good. Even Adam Smith conceded that there were departments, such as education, where the Government should exercise direction. Samuel Smiles, the supreme apostle of self-help, condemned *laissez-faire* as 'a dreadful theory' in so far as it encouraged inertia in regard to social needs. The man whose preaching is most often cited as the quintessence of individualism is Jeremy Bentham (1748–1832). He initiated a school of thought which profoundly influenced the nineteenth century. Certainly he believed strongly in individualism, but, unlike Adam Smith and his followers, he never argued that uninhibited self-interest was bound, by some law of nature — the 'invisible hand' — to make for the collective good. On the contrary, he held that a degree of restraint was imperative if 'the greatest happiness of the greatest number' were to be achieved, and that this must be exerted through an improved Constitution and improved laws. From this it followed that there should be State intervention in certain sectors of human activity. His disciples, like the Radical Edwin Chadwick, found little if any difficulty in applying and adapting his principles to such diverse social problems as poor relief, factory reform and public health. Yet, potent as was this philosophy, it drew its inner strength, as did the doctrine of free trade, from the circumstances of the age. State intervention was increasingly accepted by leaders of both political parties, and by different schools of reformers, though for different reasons besides the common acknowledgment of the need to mitigate injustice. On the one hand, it might be seen as an essential part of the evolution of democracy and an attack on the power of the landed oligarchy, on the other as a form of paternalism, which might also have the effect of slowing down or preventing the growth of democracy, while at the same time dealing a shrewd knock to industrial plutocracy.

Laissez-faire then, in this context, never properly took root; the significance often attached to it, as a determinant in nineteenth-century social affairs, is little more than 'a political and economic myth'.[1] Nevertheless, there was much resistance to change, and there were many dogmas advanced in support of a more rapid adaptation or reconstruction of society than was sought by the orthodox reformers. One of these was Socialism.

It would be difficult and perhaps unwise to define Socialism, for it has taken many forms, each claimed by its protagonists to be the only true gospel. Professor Gray, in *The Socialist Tradition*, having described different variants and exponents, concludes that it 'demands the abolition of the private ownership of much (if not

---

[1] G. Bartlett Brebner, 'Laissez-faire and State Intervention in Nine-teenth Century Britain', *Journal of Economic History*, viii (1948).

all) wealth and requires that the wealth so transferred should in some way be vested in and operated by the community as a whole'. This will not satisfy the purists, but the qualifications made are certainly appropriate to the British species.

Socialism emerged in its modern form as a natural and logical offshoot of capitalism, with the growth of a wage-earning proletariat. It was in its genesis a revolt against the inequalities of the capitalist system and in this country Robert Owen (1771–1858) has been dubbed 'the father of socialism', not so much because of his ideas, which he preached and published freely, but because he embodied the revolt, and in a limited sphere, translated his philosophy into practice.

He was a capitalist and a very successful one, rising quickly as a manager until, in association with others, he took over his father-in-law, David Dale's, New Lanark mills in 1799 and quickly began to apply his theories to their operation. The mills became a platform for the exposition of all sorts of ideas of reform, bearing not only on the running of industry but also on education and living conditions in general, since he was convinced that environment was all-important. Labour, he held, was the true begetter of value, so the essence of his scheme lay in production through workers' co-operation. This, of course, was nothing new; in Britain one could find earlier examples of the creed in Sir Thomas More's *Utopia* (1516), in the views of the Levellers of the seventeenth century, and in Thomas Paine's *Rights of Man* (1790). With the great expansion of production the idea that the workers should share the wealth which (it was said) they alone created gained force, and found expression in a variety of manifestations, including the co-operative movement for making and retailing goods — the outstanding example being the Rochdale Equitable Pioneers' Society, started in 1844 — the giant trade unions and Christian Socialism. Chartism contained an element of Socialism among its mixed components, but with its practical extinction in 1848 the doctrine languished, except in intellectual circles, for a generation.

Owen's experiments owed such success as they had mainly to his own personality, and they soon collapsed. Generally speaking, it could be said that Socialism as such, certainly for the first three-quarters of the nineteenth century, made little headway, although the preaching of Owen and others like him helped towards certain practical reforms such as the Factory Acts.

Karl Marx (1818–83) lived and worked in London from 1849 to 1883. He and his collaborator, Engels, preached what they called 'scientific socialism' because it was said to represent the logical and inevitable outcome of historical processes, as distinct from the 'Utopian socialism' of such as Owen, resting on human aspirations. Marxism made little or no impression on the working class. This was partly because, while industrialisation and capitalism brought much that was evil in their train, conditions in Britain were improving and were seen to be improving. It could not be argued, as it could in some other countries, that the Government was implacably rigid in its form or in its social policies, and reform of all sorts came slowly but fairly steadily. In short, the atmosphere was never one of complete frustration and despair. The other reason, associated with this, was that after the middle of the century, the trade-union movement was gaining ground. It was based on the 'aristocracy of labour', that is, on the craft industries, who could by no stretch of the imagination be called socialist. The trade unions were denounced by socialists, fretting at the failure to rouse the working class, as bastions of capitalism; and certainly many of their leaders had no mind to challenge the system, which, in a sense, was their natural habitat. Marx himself, who hoped to find in them an instrument for his International, finally abandoned them — and Britain — to their capitalistic errors, and concentrated on the Continent, where, because of political and social reaction, the soil was much more promising.

It was not, of course, that there was any lack of ammunition for socialist artillery; but mass misery does not make for articulateness, and it was difficult for the intellectual reformers' ideas to permeate the mass, which was too obsessed with its immediate needs and too ignorant and illiterate to formulate or even endorse social policies. Extension of the franchise in 1867 and 1884 helped to leaven the whole; but its main effect was to give more 'body' to a political labour movement, meaning nothing more than working-class representation. The enfranchisement of the miners in particular was a powerful factor, but miner politicians, like mining trade unions, were first and foremost sectional in outlook. Labour, however, was becoming more aware of its 'class' grievances, and the falling away of trade in the seventies made the artisan sector a little more receptive of suggestions for changes in society.

There was a clear distinction between socialist movements and the demand for labour representation in politics, although they might merge on occasion. Even after the enfranchisement of the working class, the Liberal Party usually commanded their political support and there was little thought at this stage of a separate party. The London Working Men's Association, formed in 1866, and echoing the views of its predecessor, demanded working-class representation in Parliament and set afoot a national campaign in support. In the following year one of its founders, George Potter, in his paper *The Beehive*, suggested a trade-union political levy for the purpose. Potter and his L.W.M.A. had for long been at variance with the powerful 'Junta', as the Webbs called it, an informal association of secretaries of national unions with London head-quarters, which dominated the London Trades' Council. Like the craft unions of which it was a nucleus, it was much more conservative in its policies than the L.W.M.A. In 1869, however, there was a reconciliation, promoted by the need to ensure a common policy towards the trade-union legislation which was then impending. In that year the Trades Union Congress passed a resolution in favour of labour representation in Parliament, but this was little more than a paper decision, and the T.U.C. did nothing then or for some years to come to follow it up.

In the same year the Labour Representation League was set up. Its aim was to fight by-elections, but on behalf of candidates who would take the Liberal 'ticket', and the real purpose was to compel the Liberal Party to take full account of working-class demands. In 1874 twelve working-class candidates were put forward and two of them, both miners, Thomas Burt and Alex. Macdonald, were returned, with Liberal support, and both were deemed to be Liberal M.P.s. The Miners' Union began paying the election expenses of their candidates in the same year, and more trade unions began to follow the same policy. In 1880 the Secretary of the

Labour Representation League, Henry Broadhurst, was elected, as a Liberal.

There was a great deal of activity in the way of propagandist work. Henry George's *Progress and Poverty* was published in America in 1879 and the author in the eighties made lecture tours in this country. He was not a socialist but a land reformer, but the socialist movement found in his teachings support for such things as land nationalisation. In 1881 Henry Hyndman, a wealthy student of Marx, founded the Democratic Federation which later became the Social Democratic Federation. This body made no bones about being socialist and 'anti-establishment'. It had a planning programme somewhat on Chartist lines, with a variety of panaceas for the ills of the age, including State socialism and self-government for Ireland. It seems to have made comparatively few converts, although its dissemination of ideas, through literature and mass meetings, must have had an important educative effect. The same thing could be said of the Fabian Society, which was formed in 1884. It included such notable individuals as Sidney Webb and Bernard Shaw; but its approach was essentially academic and it was not a political group as such.

The fact was that the organised workers — i.e. the trade unions — and the Radical Clubs were still at best lukewarm and often positively hostile to the idea of separate party representation for Labour in Parliament. The Labour Representation League decayed and finally expired by 1881. It seemed possible that the Liberal Party and, to a much lesser extent, the Conservative Party — which commanded considerable support in the textile trade unions of north-west England — would continue to be the channels of labour's special wants, since both were ready to recognise the existence of social problems and the need in principle to take practical steps to deal with them. Lord Acton described Gladstone's land legislation as socialist. A Liberal, Sir William Harcourt, could claim that 'we are all Socialist now', meaning that progressive politicians accepted the need for State intervention for the promotion and protection of working-class interests and a certain modest redistribution of wealth to that end. This might not be socialism, but it was well on the way towards it.

There were new impulses at work in the eighties, which provoked discontent with society as it existed and therefore with the
political and constitutional organisation. The 'brashness' referred
to earlier was wearing off and there was more time, as well as more
experience, for criticism of society's shortcomings. Bouts of economic recession heightened the feeling of disillusionment among the
newly-enfranchised workers. In agriculture the long depression
never lifted, and this tended to diminish the income and the power
of the landed class and to tilt the balance further towards the
industrial proletariat. Britain had one of the highest standards of
living in the world, but there was little room for self-congratula-
tion, as Charles Booth revealed in his *Life and Labour of the People
of London*, published in 1889. He estimated that nearly 31 % of the
city's inhabitants, or roughly one million people, were living in a
state of chronic destitution. Similar investigations followed, in
England and Scotland, all equally dismal in their evidence. They
cast grave doubts on some of the assumptions which had previously
dictated social policies.

In the General Elections of 1885 and 1886 respectively eleven and
ten working-class candidates were returned, who aligned themselves with the Liberal Party and were called Lib-Labs for short.
The Labour Electoral Association, which was established in 1886,
was in a sense an offshoot of the Trades Union Congress but
resolutely refused to support anti-Liberal candidates. It was
another phoenix, rising from the ashes of the Labour Representation League, and, like it, was neither effective nor long-lived. It
lasted until 1895. In 1888 Keir Hardie stood as an Independent
Labour candidate for mid-Lanark and failed abjectly, but in the
next year he helped to organise the Scottish Labour Party, with the
support of a wealthy Radical landowner, Cunninghame Graham,
and became its secretary. Other regions followed suit, with the
establishment of the London Labour Representation Committee,
the Bradford Labour Union, etc. Here was a more modest approach, and all the more promising for that reason.

In 1892 Keir Hardie was returned to Parliament for West Ham
(South) and John Burns for Battersea — both without Liberal
opposition but not on the Liberal 'ticket' — while Havelock Wilson

was also returned for Middlesbrough. There were in addition twelve Lib-Labs, mostly miners. The untiring Keir Hardie thought this might be the moment to achieve that fusion or at least alliance of labour which he had dreamed of. In 1893 he and others called a conference at Bradford, of various interests, including the T.U.C., the Social Democratic Federation and the Fabian Society, and the political labour organisations. As it turned out, this proved a turning-point, even if it did not justify Philip Snowden's description of it as 'the most important political movement of the nineteenth century'. It led to the formation of the national Independent Labour Party; it is noteworthy that the conference rejected the title of 'Socialist'. It was joined by the Scottish Labour Party and other similar bodies. This was far from being a united labour movement and it was on the cards that it might even have a fissionary effect. John Burns and Havelock Wilson, for instance, refused to join the new party and became openly antagonistic towards it.

There was little electoral gain from all this activity. The Party, although pledged to a fairly general sort of socialism, 'played it down', and concentrated on medium and sometimes rather pedestrian reforms of a severely practical nature, such as the statutory abolition of overtime and piecework, and the establishment of a minimum eight-hour day, which it was hoped would make an appeal to moderate working-class voters. Keir Hardie was well aware of the need for more strength and cohesion in the movement and strove continuously for a 'labour alliance' with the trade unions. But the T.U.C. still refused to commit itself to the idea of an independent Party in Parliament. Support for this was coming from the 'new' trade unions who were trying to organise the more depressed sections of the workers, including the general labourers, and who had more reason than most to believe that society itself had to be recast as a pre-condition of the betterment of their members. This was useful, and infused a left-wing element into the T.U.C., but it was not enough; nor was the enthusiasm of the intelligentsia, led by people like Robert Blatchford, who did very useful work through his paper *The Clarion*. The propaganda work undoubtedly helped to indoctrinate public opinion and so paved the way to eventual success.

In 1895 membership of the Party was estimated at a meagre 6,000. In the General Election of that year there were twenty-eight Independent Labour Party candidates, but the Party's only Member, Keir Hardie, lost his seat, and it was left with no representation at all. In spite of the setbacks and hope deferred, the core of the Party refused to become heart-sick. One of the circumstances working in its favour was the refusal of local Liberal Associations to sponsor working-class candidates except when, as with miners, they were backed by trade-union funds. This attitude was not surprising, especially having regard to the fact that Members of Parliament were still unpaid and elections cost much money. The Liberal Party had by its policies alienated many of its wealthiest supporters among landowners and industrial magnates. Some of those policies, like the lines taken on imperialism, militarism, temperance and the Irish Question, appealed to many — though by no means all — supporters of political labour; but this did nothing to fill the Party's coffers. At the same time, the failure to take over Labour aspirants helped to create a political vacuum and drove some politicians to seek another fold. Keir Hardie himself started off as a Liberal, as did Ramsay MacDonald, whose rejection as a candidate turned his mind to the possibility of an alternative political vehicle.

The prospect of a bridge between socialism and trade unionism appeared to receive a damaging blow in 1895, when the T.U.C. expelled the 'politicians', including Keir Hardie and John Burns, as not being 'bona fide' trade unionists. In spite of this reaction on the part of the union hierarchy, there persisted an inter-play between the two movements, fostered by individuals with a foot in each camp. Thus in 1898 a member of the Party, G. N. Barnes, was elected Secretary of the powerful and sober-minded Amalgamated Society of Engineers. At last, the pressure from the militant section in the T.U.C. broke the barrier, and in 1899 the Congress instructed its Parliamentary Committee to summon a conference of trade unions, co-operative societies, socialist organisations and other bodies concerned with the promotion of labour interests, in order to concert methods for increasing the number of 'Labour' M.P.s — a declaration of intentions which was sufficiently

vague not to alarm those in the ranks — and they were numerous —
who did not want a separate party. In 1900, accordingly, delegates
of the I.L.P., the Social Democratic Federation and the rest, met
in London. It was significant that the Co-operative movement
found itself unable to be represented.

The Conference was a success and decided to set up the Labour
Representation Committee, with Ramsay MacDonald as its
Secretary. It was agreed that candidates for Parliament need not
necessarily be working men, so long as they were in sympathy with
'Labour Movements', which, in effect, was a rejection of the
division affirmed by the T.U.C. in 1895, and let in the socialists;
that there should be a trade-union political levy, as had been
advocated for years past; and that there should be in Parliament
a distinct Labour Group — not Party — which, therefore, did not
constitute a separate political entity, was not committed to socialism, and could support either of the existing Parties. It was a
compromise, certainly the best that could have been achieved in
the circumstances of the time, but it was regarded by Keir Hardie,
Ramsay MacDonald, and other socialists as a foundation on which
to build. This, they well appreciated, they would have to do very
carefully, for there were still eminent trade-union leaders who were
positively and categorically opposed, as they made clear to Ramsay
MacDonald, to the conception of a separate party. They were
apprehensive of socialist ambitions, and indeed of socialist policies,
and were determined that the Labour Group should be subservient
to the trade-union movement and be in effect its mouthpiece in
Parliament.

In 1900 there was a General Election and fifteen candidates
were put up by the L.R.C. There was little money available; the
L.R.C. income for 1900–1 was £243. The Miners' Federation
refused to join, as did local miners' associations, which were Liberal
in complexion, while the Co-operative Societies also held aloof.
Not surprisingly the L.R.C. had little success. Keir Hardie was
returned, as was Richard Bell, who was Secretary of the Amalgamated Society of Railway Servants, and had figured prominently
in the Taff Vale case; but he vividly illustrated the dichotomy in
the Group, for he had been highly critical of his own members on

that issue, was elected an M.P. with Liberal support, and soon joined the Liberal Party. There were also a number of Lib-Labs, mostly miners.

It was clear that the 'breakthough' had not yet been achieved. One thing lacking was finance, so that more candidates could be promoted, and in 1903 the L.R.C. started its own political fund. This was on a voluntary basis at first and was not made compulsory until the following year. In 1901 the Social Democratic Federation had withdrawn its support, because the L.R.C., it claimed, was not nearly socialist enough. Ramsay MacDonald and his colleagues had good cause to be gloomy, but the Labour Alliance was now a fact, and, even allowing for abstentions, it held out exciting possibilities. It needed above all else a *casus belli*, a grievance which would transcend internal differences and convince the unions finally that they had in the Labour Group the perfect political instrument for the furtherance of their causes. The Taff Vale case provided it.[1] The trade unions, for their part, saw their interests threatened and naturally rallied to the support of their Labour spokesmen in Parliament. In 1902–3 the membership of the L.R.C. almost doubled, to 861,000, and its income rose to £800. In 1903 Arthur Henderson, fighting in its name, won a by-election against Liberals and Conservatives. This was a famous victory. Funds continued to pour in and in 1905–6 the income reached the handsome total of £12,000.

As a result of all this, the L.R.C. was able, in the General Election of 1906, to put forward fifty-one candidates, of whom twenty-nine were elected — thirty if one includes a trade-union candidate who joined it after the Election — while there were also fourteen miners' M.P.s, in addition to some Lib-Labs. This represented a very great advance; but it was in no small measure due to an electoral arrangement, the result of delicate negotiations between Herbert Gladstone for the Liberals and Ramsay MacDonald, by which it was agreed that twenty-four of the L.R.C. candidates should have a straight run against the Conservatives. The advantage of this arrangement went almost wholly to the L.R.C. Certainly there were Liberal candidates who must have gained Labour support by promising to amend the trade-union law, but this was a

[1] See Chap. 9, pp. 148–9.

minor element in the Party programme and the Liberals won their victory over the Conservatives on issues which had nothing to do with the Labour movement as such. At the same time, it was significant that in Scotland, which since 1832 had been traditionally a Liberal stronghold, the L.R.C. won two seats, although there the Liberals with some prescience had ended their alliance with Labour.

Charles Booth's survey had raised a challenge to the comfortable belief that poverty was necessarily a token of individual irresponsibility, especially among the able-bodied. A Royal Commission on the Poor Law had been set up in 1905 and took five years to finish its deliberations. It was not unanimous in its conclusions, but some reform of the system would have resulted but for the immovability of the President of the Local Government Board, John Burns — who, ironically enough, had been a fierce socialist but had become enmeshed in bureaucracy. Fortunately, the problem of want was approached from another direction.

In 1908 there was passed an Act to give non-contributory pensions to those over the age of seventy with less than a certain income. Labour Exchanges on a national scale were established in 1909, as recommended by the Poor Law Commission, and this was followed in 1911 by the National Insurance Act, the central idea of which was borrowed from Germany, where a scheme had been in operation for over twenty years. It was to be financed by contributions levied on employers, workers, and the Exchequer, and, in its sick-pay provisions, applied to all workers. As regards unemployment benefit, it was restricted to seven industries peculiarly susceptible to fluctuations, but even so it covered 2¼ million workers. Friendly societies and trade unions ranked as 'approved societies' for purposes of administration. The measure was furiously contested by the Conservative Party, and, in its sick-pay features, by the British Medical Association.

This revolution marked a new awareness of the State's social obligations and of the responsibility of the prosperous to the less fortunate. The reform of taxation was a part of it. Harcourt, as Chancellor of the Exchequer in Lord Rosebery's Liberal Administration, had made a resounding break with tradition when in 1894 he revised death-duties so that they were graduated in scale to the size of the estate. Income-tax had varied only infinitesimally throughout the nineteenth century, because it was regarded as an unfortunate and temporary expedient; but in 1909 a graduated scale was introduced here, too, with super-tax for all incomes over £5,000, following the distinction created in 1907 between earned and unearned income. Before the First World War, those taxes were bringing in close on £75 million annually, which was as well, since in the first decade of the twentieth century expenditure on the social services increased fourfold. It was small wonder that the House of Lords threw out the Budget of 1909, or that the Liberals, who had long chafed under the obscurantism of the Upper House, dissolved Parliament on this issue, and ultimately in 1911 forced through the Parliament Act, which limited the Lords' right to reject a measure to a suspensory veto for two years.[1]

The Election of 1906 gave the L.R.C. a new confidence and in the same year it became officially the Labour Party. By the following year its membership was over one million and it had an income of about £15,000. In 1909 the Miners' Federation joined it, not without some misgivings; some of the miners' M.P.s, including the pioneer, Thomas Burt, refused to enlist. The going was still by no means smooth. As the breakaway of the S.D.F. had shown, the partnership between socialism and trade unionism was half-hearted and unsure. This manifested itself in 1911 when a rival body, the British Socialist Party — in effect a reincarnation of the S.D.F. — was founded. Yet things were still going the Labour Party's way. In 1909 there had been the Osborne decision, which laid it down that a trade union, as such, had no right to participate in politics by lending financial support to a Party; but this contributed to the institution, in 1911, of the payment of Members of Parliament, which relieved the Labour Party of a burden it could ill afford and left its funds free for other purposes. The law, as it was interpreted in the Osborne judgment, was soon amended (1913), and trade-union money, which was absolutely vital to the Labour Party organisation, could, under certain conditions, be allocated to its support, while trade unions could also, and did, supplement the salaries of their own successful candidates.

[1] The Parliament Act of 1949 reduced the delaying period to one year.

In spite of all this, the Party made little apparent headway. It continued to rely to a great extent on Liberal goodwill, and in the first General Election of 1910 Liberal support was available, as in 1906, in a large proportion (one-third) of the seats contested by the Party. Both Liberals and Labour lost ground. The Labour Party's representation fell by five, leaving it with a total of forty, including the newly-joined miners' M.P.s. This was raised slightly in the next General Election of the same year to forty-two. It did not seem after all that Labour would ever be anything more than a substantial minority Party, and there were many trade-union supporters who were happy that it should remain so. There were various factors operating against it. It was working in the shadow of the Liberal Party, which was travelling as fast as most reformers believed possible, and was breaking down opposition with unheard-of rudeness. At the outbreak of the First World War the status of the Labour Party was not high and its prospects were not thought by the political prophets to be very bright. It was accepted by its opponents and by many of its members as essentially a pressure group operating in a two-party system, holding the balance as necessary between the giants.

The Labour Party was given its due share in the war-time Coalition Governments, headed first by Asquith and then by Lloyd George. At the end of the war, to all outward appearances the political scene had not greatly changed; but appearances were in this case deceptive. The Liberals had had a brilliant spell between 1906 and 1910, and, in carrying out their far-reaching social reforms, had successfully challenged and chastened the House of Lords, and temporarily subdued the Conservative Party. Some commentators hold that by the end of this period the Liberal Party had spent itself — its Parliamentary strength was certainly already weakening — and that its power had in reality begun to wane towards the end of the nineteenth century when it had been damaged by internal disputes over various issues of principle, including even free trade. It has been argued that its eclipse was made inevitable by changing circumstances and particularly the fact that the bulk of the new electorate would want a different brand of political philosophy. This contention is a little difficult to reconcile with the fact that the

Party was so much in tune with its time as to lay the foundations of
the Welfare State. There were more obvious reasons for its attrition.
The Irish Question had been a harassment from the beginning and
was to remain so until its end, and even its end was to be disruptive.
It might have survived this, since defections to the Conservatives
might have been offset by accessions. What did not permit of any
such compensation was a civil war between people of the same
persuasions. Of such a nature was the rift which split it from top to
bottom in the shape of the bitter quarrel between Lloyd George
and Asquith, dating officially from Lloyd George's appointment
as Prime Minister in 1916.

In 1918 there was the 'coupon' Election — a term of ridicule
coined by Asquith. It meant that the candidates sponsored by
Lloyd George for a section of the Liberals and by Bonar Law for
the Conservatives, were officially endorsed by the respective official
leaderships; this left out over 100 Asquithian Liberals. The
Labour Party had wisely decided to withdraw from the Coalition.

In 1918 the Representation of the People Act extended the
suffrage to men over twenty-one and women over thirty, thus adding some six million women voters and two million men to the electorate. The Coalition was successful, but the balance of power had
changed greatly. The Conservatives were now predominant, while
the Liberals' previous strength was nearly halved. Labour's gains
were not spectacular, but it could summon a grand total of fifty-
nine, of whom almost all were trade unionists. The new Parliament
took office in 1919, with Lloyd George Prime Minister, and Bonar
Law Lord Privy Seal and Leader of the House of Commons.

8   Towards a Planned Economy

T HE political and economic climate had been greatly changed
     by the war. The emergency had compelled a degree of
government intervention which would have taken a generation or
more to evolve naturally. Regulation by the State, although still
disliked by many, had acquired a new respectability in the eyes of
most sections of the electorate and all Parties. Winston Churchill,
campaigning in Dundee — unsuccessfully — in 1918, as a Liberal,
advocated the nationalisation of railways. Not only had industry,
services and manpower been subject to controls; there was much
more government and, of course, Government machinery. The
Ministry of Health and the Ministry of Transport were both
established as permanencies in 1919, which was an indication of
changed outlook on the part of a Government representative of
Conservatives as well as Liberals, and there were war-time sur-
vivals, like the Ministry of Labour, which had been set up in 1916,
the Ministry of Pensions and the Air Ministry. It is true that the
Government quickly and deliberately proceeded to divest itself of
much of its special powers; but it was clear that further 'socialisation' was on the way and that the machinery to operate it was
already in existence. The Civil Service had been largely increased;
in 1914 it totalled just over 57,000, in 1923 over 116,000. In
1919 there was passed the Housing and Town Planning Act
and in 1920 the Unemployment Insurance Act. Both could be
regarded as nothing more than extensions of previous principles
and legislation and in fact they went through Parliament
without any serious opposition. The first entrusted the
housing programme to local authorities, with State subsidies,
and the second greatly enlarged unemployment insurance;

domestic servants, agricultural labourers and civil servants remained excluded.

The Labour Party had, even while the war was in progress, been
refurbishing its image. In 1918 it had promulgated a well-defined
Constitution, which was something no other Party possessed. It
included a specific set of objects, the acceptance of which was to
be binding on every Labour M.P. Official constituency organisations were created, to be representative of local membership.
Propaganda methods were improved. The *New Statesman* started
life in 1913. The *Daily Herald*, founded in 1912, had become a
weekly during the war but reverted to being a daily paper in 1919.
Militancy was in the air. There was no thought of depression
either in politics or in industry as yet, and it seemed that the war
might have opened up a new era for the more left-wing Parties.
The British Communist Party was founded in 1920, and, while the
Labour Party would have no official truck with it, the attitude of
many Labour politicians and trade-union leaders was much more
aggressive and even revolutionary than formerly. They had seen
capitalism toppled into ruins in Russia and liked what they saw —
or thought they saw. For the first time the militants in both camps
saw the opportunity to launch a powerful challenge to the capitalist
structure of society in Britain and they were ready to take advantage of it.

The immediate post-war period proved to be a time of boom
and burst. Prices rocketed, as did profits, and there was rampant
inflation, which was countered by severe Government deflation in
1920 and damped down by de-control of railways and mines, in
1921. 'Take-overs' were popular, affecting not only business enterprises but also trade unions. Industrial depression soon followed, and
with it came labour troubles. The Government had wisely anticipated the possible recrudescence of unrest by improving the
machinery of industrial relations, but this did not prevent, although it might alleviate, trouble in the mines and on the railways.
The Government passed the Emergency Powers Act in 1920,
authorising the State to safeguard essential supplies and services in
a crisis; this was a sort of insurance against large-scale stoppages
but was never directed against strikes as such.

Demobilisation, although it covered about 4 million men, went off surprisingly well, and there was comparatively little unemployment up to 1920. Then it rose sharply and by the middle of 1921 amounted to some $2\frac{1}{2}$ million. It remained serious, averaging $1\frac{1}{4}$ million until 1930, when the figure again rose to the 1921 total and to no less than 3 million by 1933. There was a great coal strike in 1921; the threat of the Triple Alliance was revived and the Emergency Powers Act was invoked, but the Alliance ended on 'Black Friday', when the N.U.R. and the Transport Workers withdrew their support for common strike action with the miners. There was a drastic falling off in British exports. Wage-rates were cut. There were 'hunger marches' in 1922 and afterwards. The 'dole' — that is, relief beyond what the person's insurance contributions warranted — was introduced. Then came the inevitable economy drive, following the Geddes Committee's recommendations in 1922. Free trade, dented by the McKenna duties (1915) received another knock from the tentative Safeguarding of Industries Act of 1921, which helped to reveal and widen the cracks in the coalition between Conservatives and Liberals.

The coalition was in any case highly unpopular with many Conservatives, and with a good many Liberals. Protection versus free trade was only one of the issues dividing the two main parties; there was also real trouble between them over Lloyd George's policy in Ireland and in India, as well as over his handling of foreign affairs. Charges were bandied about, including the well-founded accusation against Lloyd George about the sale of honours, although, since the Conservative Party shared equally in the spoil, the taunt came ill from that quarter. The Irish Question was got out of the way in 1921, but it left a great deal of bitterness behind. In the face of international failures and domestic crises, the only thing that helped to keep Liberals and Conservatives together was the common fear of a Socialist victory. Finally, however, the bulk of the Conservatives decided to abandon the Coalition and showed themselves unscrupulous in their manner of doing so. Some of the most eminent members of the Party, such as Austen Chamberlain, refused to be associated with what they considered a shabby party manœuvre. Lloyd George resigned

office, anticipating a defeat in Parliament, and Bonar Law formed
a new Government, with Baldwin Chancellor of the Exchequer and
Neville Chamberlain Postmaster-General — 'a government of the
second eleven', said Winston Churchill.

The General Election of 1922 justified in electoral terms the
Conservatives' break-up of the Coalition by sending back
almost the same number as last time, which gave them a clear
majority. The Liberals were shattered; both sections returned a
total of 117, and the fact that this represented over 4 million votes,
in comparison with over 5 million for the Conservatives, was little
comfort. The real shock, however, was the emergence of the
Labour Party with 142 seats and an electorate slightly larger than
that of the Liberals. The Labour Party had a strong and vociferous
left-wing in the I.L.P., but its chief spokesmen were careful to put
the emphasis on evolutionary Socialism. Sidney Webb, one of the
chief policy-makers, reminded the annual Conference in 1923 that
Owen, not Marx, was the founder of British Socialism, while the
Party leader, Ramsay MacDonald, had ever since 1900 been forced
to a strategy that was often ambiguous and devious in order to allay
apprehensions within as well as without his movement.

The Conservatives resumed office, and in 1923 Stanley Baldwin
succeeded as Prime Minister. Perhaps more portentous was the
fact that Joseph Chamberlain's son, Neville, who had followed in
his father's footsteps in Birmingham, now became Chancellor of
the Exchequer. With such a partnership in the administration, it
was no surprise that the Government formally declared for protection. Partly it was a political expedient, with which to restore
unity in the Conservative ranks; partly it was a reburgeoning of the
faith as preached by Joseph Chamberlain. The General Election
of 1923 was fought on this issue and the Conservatives lost heavily,
with their total membership in the Commons down to 258. The
Liberals, temporarily reconciled, rallied and aggregated 159 seats,
while Labour continued to forge ahead, gaining 191 seats. While, in
their share of the electorate, there was still little between the two
latter Parties, in parliamentary strength the Labour Party was now
second to the Conservatives. If Labour and Liberal made common
cause, the Conservatives would be defeated. This, in fact, was what

happened almost immediately, resulting in the formation for the first time, in 1924, of a Labour Government.

As a minority Government, it was bound to have a precarious existence and it ended in the same year. In the ensuing General Election the Conservatives exploited the misgivings that existed about Labour's sympathy with Russian Communism, although it was doubtful if this was the main reason for their success; rather it was the desire for a strong, stable administration. In any case the Conservatives were returned with an overwhelming majority, having 419 seats, representing an electorate of over 8 million. Labour's strength fell by over forty, but it increased its proportion of the electorate; and the Liberals suffered quite catastrophically, being reduced to a total of forty M.P.s, although they had the backing of some 3 million voters. It was perhaps a straw in the wind that Winston Churchill, after twenty years and two successive defeats as a Liberal, this time stood as a Conservative, successfully, and became Chancellor of the Exchequer in the new Government.

Britain, and not Britain alone, was floundering more deeply into an economic depression. The return to the Gold Standard in 1925 might have been a contributory factor, but there were deeper causes at work. The figures of the balance of trade were ominous. In 1929 British imports were 20% up on pre-war and exports 20% down. The position would have looked even more desperate but for the fact that the prices of primary products, on the import of which Britain depended for its food and raw materials, fell heavily in relation to the price of manufactured exports. This, however, meant that the primary-producing countries could afford to buy fewer manufactured goods, which was bound to affect Britain gravely in the short run, and which, too, in the long run would encourage those same nations to turn inwards, build tariff walls and develop their own industries behind them. British exports of manufactured goods fell by 45% between 1929 and 1931. Britain had lost and was losing markets, and she had also lost, as a direct result of the war, a great deal of her invisible exports, that is, overseas investment, insurance, shipping services, etc., which had been liquidated or destroyed. The Conservatives had their own nostrum for all this, namely protection, and although it had never been specifically endorsed by the electorate — quite the contrary, indeed — the Government proceeded to introduce it, in gradual doses, between 1925 and 1927.

There was ample justification for a reappraisal of economic policies. Gone were the days when Britain could rely on an assured world market for her goods. Other countries had become industrialised; Britain had helped them, for her own benefit, with machines, capital and skill. Those emergent nations had never subscribed to the doctrine of free trade. Even the British Dominions and colonies — some of whom, like the West Indies, had been hurt by the Mother Country's abandonment of economic imperialism — had not been slow to resort to international tariff bargaining in defence of their nascent industries. The British economy was still advancing, but that of other countries was advancing much faster; after 1880 the rate of growth was 2%, while that of Germany was 3.9% and of the United States 4.8%. Britain's export of manufactures rose by 121% between 1893 and 1913; Germany's increased by 239% and the United States' by 563%.

After 1870 British agriculture, exposed to the full blast of overseas competition, had shrunk deplorably. British industry had relied over-much on its old staple products — coal, iron and steel, and textiles, which in 1907 provided 46% of all manufactures and 70% of exports — and had comparatively neglected the new branches, such as the manufacture of chemicals and motor vehicles, because of conservatism on the part of management and labour, an undue diversion of capital investment overseas, and failure to rationalise production, as well as a lack of certain natural advantages possessed by competitors. The staple industries, too, were hard-pressed and the British economy with them. In 1907 nearly 90% of cotton goods went overseas, one-half to the Far East; but Indian and Japanese competition cut Far Eastern exports by 38% between 1913 and 1925, and there was no compensation elsewhere. Coal exports fell from 94 million tons in 1913 to 77 million in 1929, and iron and steel production in the same period dropped by one-quarter.[1]

[1] J. H. Dunning and C. J. Thomas, *British Industry: Change and Development in the Twentieth Century*, pp. 13–21.

Agriculturalists and industrialists were before 1914 drawing together in their common desire for protection. After 1905 the Association of British Chambers of Commerce regularly passed resolutions in favour, albeit grudgingly, since the fortunes of cotton and other industries had, after all, been built on free trade.

As the depression grew, so did the despondency among the workers. There was a recurrence of disillusionment with political action and a turning towards direct industrial action. The coal-miners were as usual in the forefront; the coal industry had been one of the worst hit by the slump in exports, so that the miners were faced with the threat of reductions in wages or longer hours or both. Many other workers saw in the miners' case the forerunner or reflection of their own. Militancy was encouraged by the example and inspiration of Russia, while the Government tended to be regarded as at best indifferent and at worst hostile to the workers' cause. Ernest Bevin tried to resuscitate the Triple Alliance. The net result of all this was the General Strike of 1926.

It should be recalled, however, that this was not simply a period of rebellion and reaction. 'Socialisation' continued to make progress. The Electricity (Supply) Act of 1926 removed the generation of electricity from private enterprise and vested it in the Central Electricity Board. In the same year there was established the British Broadcasting Corporation. In 1928 there was passed the Representation of the People (Equal Franchise) Act, which gave the vote to all women over twenty-one. State control was now recognised by all Parties to be necessary to the maintenance of a sound economy; or, to put it another way, it was accepted that the economy had to be, to a certain (unspecified) point 'managed' or directed from above. This view was quite consistent with the Conservative — and, of course, even more the Labour — creed, but it was most strongly brought out in the famous Liberal 'Yellow Book', properly called *Britain's Industrial Future* (1928). This even called for the establishment by the Government of an Economic General Staff.

All in all, the economic situation seemed ready-made to advance the cause of Labour, and when the General Election of 1929 came along, it was well ahead of the rest, winning 288 seats, with an electorate of over 8 million votes, as against the Conservatives with 260 seats, representing an electorate of much the same size. The Liberals bettered their position with 59 seats, which bore little relationship to their electorate of over 5 million. The Labour Party was once again entrusted with the formation of a government.

In spite of its posture of readiness, it was from the start in trouble. It was soon to be faced with a combination of circumstances which had not been anticipated in its socialist planning or dreamed of in the leaders' worst nightmares. The economic situation was deteriorating at a tremendous pace, whereas the doctrines of the Party had been formulated at a time when capitalism, with all its faults, was working reasonably well in a society which was securing an increasing share of the proceeds. Now it was not a matter of compelling capitalism to disgorge, or taking over its assets, for capitalism was seemingly bankrupt. What made matters worse was that the causes of the depression were to a considerable extent world-wide, but the fact remained that Britain as a trading nation was particularly vulnerable. The Government was, in a sense, there on sufferance, since it was dependent on the goodwill of the Liberals. It soon became apparent, too, that the Party was not united on any definite economic policy. There was an early split in the ranks, when Oswald Mosley broke away — on the grounds that the Party was not socialist enough — and there was constant wrangling with the I.L.P. for the same reason. There were various other factors which did not help, including suspicions that the pure socialism of Ramsay MacDonald and other Labour leaders had been corrupted by the atmosphere of 'upper-class' circles.

In the course of the year 1930, unemployment rose from $1\frac{1}{2}$ to $2\frac{1}{2}$ million and by mid-1931 it was even higher. The crisis had started with the Wall Street crash of 1929 and worsened steadily until 1931, when the Continent, too, was in a state of financial insolvency. There was clearly an imperative need for a resolute policy on the part of the British Government, but it became only too apparent that the crisis had accentuated the differences always existing between the trade unions and the Socialists until there was every danger of open rupture.

The drain on the unemployment insurance fund was bound to be severe and by 1931 the fund was bankrupt, to the tune of £115 million. The Report of the Committee presided over by Sir George May revealed the situation with fearful clarity and so increased the panic and the drain on the gold reserves. The obvious, although not necessarily the only or the right course, was to have a large-scale economy drive. The Cabinet set up a Committee to this end, and met representatives of the Labour Party and the T.U.C. General Council. The burning question was where the economies were to fall, and a plausible answer was to start off with a cut in unemployment pay, but this was anathema to trade unionists and to many Labour politicians. The Cabinet split over this issue and Ramsay MacDonald finally agreed, to the disgust of many of his Party, to head a National Government. He took with him a few of his supporters, including Philip Snowden. He himself became Prime Minister in a Coalition Government representative of Conservatives, Liberals and a section of Labour.

In October 1931 there was a General Election, which resulted in the return of the so-called National Government, which was over-whelmingly Conservative; the Party with its Liberal and Labour allies, had 521 seats, while the remaining Liberals numbered 33 and Labour 52.

It was a foregone conclusion that the Government, with Neville Chamberlain Chancellor of the Exchequer, would follow Conservative policies. Its parliamentary strength was such that it could reasonably claim to have been given a mandate by the electorate to use whatever prescriptions appealed to it. Besides, the economic situation appeared to justify all the claims ever made on behalf of protection. The Government duly proceeded with its programme of new or higher tariffs, import quotas, and marketing boards to control production and prices. In 1932 a fairly tentative beginning was made, in the Import Duties Act, and even so it met opposition from the Labour and Liberal elements in the administration. In the same year there was convened the Imperial Economic Conference in Ottawa, where the theories of Joseph Chamberlain at last materialised, with the creation of a form of imperial preferences embodied in the Ottawa Agreements. This precipitated the secession from the Government of the independent, as distinct from the

National or 'Simonite' Liberals, and of Philip Snowden. From 1933 onwards there was a slow economic recovery in Britain, as in the rest of the world, and by 1935 a favourable balance of trade had been restored. It was not that exports had improved very greatly, but that the prices of primary products continued to fall, so that imports were costing less and home and export prices could be kept reasonably low. This, of course, was reflected in the fairly stable cost of living.

It made little difference that in 1935 Ramsay MacDonald resigned and was replaced by Stanley Baldwin; or that, in the General Election of that year, the Conservatives lost some ground, for they still summoned the impressive total of 387 Members, without counting their allies. The Labour Party staged a good recovery, collecting 154 seats, while the Liberals fell to their lowest total so far, of twenty seats. In 1937 Neville Chamberlain became Prime Minister and remained so until displaced by Winston Churchill, as leader of a war-time Coalition, in 1940.

The National Government was much criticised for its alleged inertia in regard to the social misery engendered by the depression. It was, however, by no means idle. Cuts made in unemployment benefit were restored in 1934 and an Act of the same year created the Unemployment Assistance Board, which was financed by a new and separate fund; this effected a separation between unemployment insurance benefit and State assistance for the unemployed not eligible for relief under national insurance. It marked, in short, the end of the old Poor Law principles, as had been advocated in 1909, in its practical recognition of the fact that unemployment should not carry a stigma.

What was more remarkable, although it could be regarded as the other side of the coin, was that from the thirties onwards the State took it for granted that it should accept a measure of responsibility, not merely for the unemployed but also for unemployment as a national deficiency and, *ipso facto*, for national planning. This was partly a matter of natural evolution. State control had been firmly and permanently asserted before the war, in the manner and financing of social legislation. Then there was the spread of 'gas and water socialism' — that is, the operation of public utilities by municipalities — fostered by central legislation. It was but a short step from there to national control through public bodies, like the Central Electricity Board.

There were other reasons than simple evolution. In the second half of the nineteenth century there were not many to gainsay, publicly, the view that unfettered competition was the best way to safeguard the consumers' interest. In practice there had always been a measure of collusion or combination among producers, and in the latter part of this period this tendency was much intensified. Other States were giving their industries protection through tariffs and subsidies of one sort or another, as well as by condoning or encouraging cartels or other monopolistic forms. In Britain, in-dustrialists grouped themselves in units or rings, often aiming at creating quasi-monopolies; complete monopolies were impractic-able while imports remained free. Brunner Mond & Co. (1881) was a massive incorporation in the heavy chemical industry. The United Alkali Company ten years later brought together no less than forty-eight companies controlling 80% of soda production. The Fine Cotton Spinners' and Doublers' Association (1898) started off with thirty-one firms and soon absorbed more. The Imperial Tobacco Company (1901–2) consolidated thirteen companies to withstand the threat of American competition, and the Wallpaper Trust (1900) included thirty-eight firms. There were many more, equally distinguished: Lever Bros., the Distillers' Co., the Associated Portland Cement Co. and so on. Their purpose was not simply to corner a market: large enterprises were the media for large-scale investment and mass-production and marketing. The number of joint-stock banks fell, by amalgamation, by about two-thirds between 1880 and 1914. There were besides many associa-tions to regulate prices and output, in iron and steel, building materials, electrical equipment, shipping, etc. Individualism in industry, as in other fields, was being outmoded, and it was a serious question how long the State could continue to ignore these developments.

As things turned out, the State was compelled by the First World War to give added impetus to the trend, both directly and indirectly. It found the large, comprehensive type of organisation a near-necessity to control production; for instance, British Dyes Ltd., later the British Dyestuffs Corporation, set up with Government backing to fill the gap in supplies left by the cessation of imports from Germany; or as an intermediary, like the Federation of British Industries (1916). After the war, the clock could not be turned back without damage to the mechanism. Amalgamation went on apace: in 1926 Imperial Chemical Industries fused together British Dyestuffs, the Nobel Co., Brunner Mond and United Alkali. In 1929 Unilever was formed from a combination of Lever Bros. and its chief Dutch and Central European rivals. Like Courtaulds, J. & P. Coats and others, it had an international scope.

In 1921 the State, having given up control of the railways, disengaged itself from its traditional policies by helping to promote the great amalgamation which left only four large groups outside London. The 'Big Five' established their dominion in the banking world. Price-fixing was rampant: retail price maintenance covered perhaps 3% of consumer expenditure at the beginning of the century; by 1938 the proportion was close to one-third.

The Depression finally swept away the façade of free competition within the country, as well as free trade outside it. The two went together, and, conversely, protection meant not only tariffs but state subventions to and regulation of industry. 'Rationalisation' was the word. The Coal Mines Act (1930) set up a Reorganisation Commission to co-ordinate output. Marketing Boards appeared in agriculture. In cotton-spinning, shipbuilding, iron and steel manufacture and a host of others, agencies were set up, with Government endorsement or participation, to control production and prices. The Government lent money to the Cunard Line to complete the *Queen Mary* and to Richard Thomas Ltd. for a new steel works at Ebbw Vale.

As already noted, the Depression affected certain areas, particularly those relying on heavy industries, with exceptional severity, and there was a great exodus of people from there to the Midlands and South-East England. One of the disturbing features of this was the heavy concentration in and around London, which, on strategic grounds alone, was thought undesirable.

In 1934 the Special Areas (Development and Improvement)

Act designated four depressed regions (North-East England, West Cumberland, South Wales and Monmouthshire, and Central Scotland), and appointed two Commissioners, one for England and Wales and one for Scotland, to stimulate industrial development; special powers were given to build factories to let, and grants or loans were available for incoming firms. As a result, by 1938 there were ten Trading Estates employing 12,000 workers — a pitiful total, since there were 300,000 unemployed in those areas alone. In 1937 the Government appointed a Royal Commission on the Distribution of the Industrial Population (the Barlow Commission), which reported in 1940, after the outbreak of war. During the war, labour was directed to essential work as thought necessary and there was, of course, no problem of unemployment. In 1945 there was passed the Distribution of Industry Act, by which the 'special areas', the original four, were added to as the years went on, financial provisions were widened, and the duties of the Commissioners were taken over by the Distribution of Industry Division of the Board of Trade. In 1946 there was the New Towns Act, followed next year by the Town and Country Planning Act, through which could be exercised a measure of control over the location of industry. All this legislation laid down certain lines which successive Governments have followed.

Having regard to the pattern of pre-war developments, it was in no way remarkable that, when the Labour Government came to power in 1946, it strengthened State control of certain industries and services through nationalisation. A Ministry of Economic Affairs was set up in 1947. The coal industry, electricity, gas, a large sector of transport, including civil aviation, iron and steel, and the Bank of England were covered. Alongside this went the creation or continuation of various quasi-governmental bodies of an advisory nature, such as the National Joint Advisory Council and the National Production Advisory Council, with Regional Boards. The fact that the Conservative Party returned to power in 1951 and remained there for the next thirteen years did not fundamentally change the progression. Certainly the bulk of the steel and transport industries was denationalised; on the other hand, the State asserted its interest in the most debatable sphere of all, when the National

Council on Prices, Productivity and Incomes, and then a National Incomes Commission, were established.

At the same time there was some appreciation of the danger of monopolistic structures in industries other than those under State supervision, and in 1948 there was passed the Monopolies Act, which set up a Commission with powers to investigate monopolies which appeared to threaten public interest. This was followed in 1956 by the Restrictive Trade Practices Act, which appointed a Registrar to take action as necessary against employers working together to regulate prices or output.

9 Industrial Relations

THE spread of industrialism brought a widening cleavage between 'masters' and 'workers' — in other words, between capitalist employers on the one hand and an increasingly numerous wage-earning class on the other. This, with the social tensions which it generated, was causing concern even in the sixteenth century, for it was a symptom of the gradual disintegration of the old order in industry regulated through the guilds. Because of this disharmony, the State was much disturbed and sought to reinforce the system by legislation. The most notable example was the Statute of Labour (1563), which, among other things, provided for an annual review of wage-rates by justices of the peace, who were required in this task to take account of the prevailing cost of necessities.

The whole structure of industry, however, was changing under the impact of market forces. The 'domestic system', under which work was farmed out by entrepreneurs, who furnished the raw material and paid for the finished product, marked a transitional phase. With the development of more elaborate and more expensive machinery, with its corollary of concentrations of full-time labour, came the factory system. Not until its advent did associations of workers become a natural and permanent feature of the industrial scene. Apart from anything else, it was extremely difficult, if not impossible, for workers to combine for common purposes when they worked in their own homes for a variety of employers. In factories, however, they were forced together both at work and in such leisure as was left to them, and so discovered their mutual grievances.

True, long before the nineteenth century there had been frequent combinations among particular sets of craftsmen, usually for very temporary ends, and such associations were therefore ephemeral in character. In the eighteenth century there were scores of them. They might be mutual benefit societies and therefore respectable; the State officially recognised such bodies in the Friendly Societies Act of 1793, and it was estimated that by 1815 nearly a million people were covered by them. The real prototype of the trade unions, in their modern connotation, however, was the genus of bodies whose primary aim was to maintain or promote the workers' interests against the exploitation of employers. This kind of association survived only with difficulty and in a somewhat unreal fashion; they were like plants growing rapidly in a soil which nurtured their roots, only to find that, once above ground, the climate was so uncongenial as to make survival precarious. They might be established merely to persuade Government, if possible, to give force to old legislation which, with all its faults, had given a measure of protection to workers as well as employers, and to the community both parties were deemed to serve. Artisans of the eighteenth century often looked back longingly to State paternalism as symbolised in the Statute of Labour, and tried to have the old industrial code invoked for their protection against the raw brutality of the new, uncontrolled capitalism.

The State, on the other hand, was finding those ancient laws a positive embarrassment, although it continued to give lip-service to them. There were combinations too, which, reluctantly recognising the facts of life as they now were, wanted to make terms with, or (surprisingly often) impose them by force on employers. Their methods were often rough, as were those of the masters they dealt with. In many cases they were trying to stem the flowing tide of industrialism, as in seeking to prevent the introduction of modern methods by the destruction of new-fangled machinery. Such combinations were outside the law and could be proceeded against by special Acts of Parliament promoted by the aggrieved employers, or under the common law as conspiracies in restraint of trade. The prevalence of the combination movement is evidenced by the fact that there were some forty Acts specially directed against particular combinations by the end of the eighteenth century.

During the French Wars the State's dislike of any unofficial organisation of this sort became intensified, since quite often they might be seditious in character. The notorious Combination Act of 1779, however, did not signify a new policy, nor was it particularly vindictive in its provisions: it was 'an Act to prevent unlawful combinations of workmen', and its chief purpose was to simplify the procedure, further modified for the better in 1800, against associations whose *raison d'être* was to raise wages, regulate hours, or otherwise impose working conditions, in breach of the traditional State prerogative. The penalties imposed were not unduly severe for the times, and the Act was almost from the outset a dead letter; in Scotland it was literally so, since it did not fit into Scots law. Combinations continued to flourish openly while it was on the Statute Book, sometimes with the connivance of employers, who, for purely business reasons, were not always happy about cut-throat competition in labour costs, but more often in defiance of them, and strikes were not infrequent.

In 1813–14 the Statute of Labour was repealed, in two stages. The attitude of Parliament to combinations was, however, fairly consistent with its general policy in such matters. A Select Committee of the House of Commons in 1824 recommended 'that masters and workmen should be freed from such restrictions, as regards the rate of wages and hours of working, and be left at perfect liberty to make such agreement as they eventually think proper'. It might be observed that some employers had given evidence to the Committee in favour of the repeal of the Combination Laws on the grounds that they tended to drive proper organisation of workers under cover and so make it infinitely more dangerous. Others, like Francis Place, who largely engineered the campaign to end the Laws, advocated reform because they believed the end of repression would be the end of combination. Parliament, quite happily, if without full appreciation of the implications, accepted this view, and not only repealed the Combination Laws and all previous legislation on the subject; it also removed such associations from the long arm of the common law of conspiracy. Unfortunately for the progress of industrial relations, this coincided with a rash of violent strikes; the methods ranged from 'sending

to Coventry' to mutilation by vitriol throwing, as a subsequent
Select Committee discovered. In 1825 the law was changed, and,
while combinations for the purpose of dealing solely with wages
and hours continued to be legal, they fell again under the shadow of
the law against conspiracy. The new Act also prescribed stricter
rules to prevent violence.

Combinations now went through a somewhat curious period of
growth, in which, while local and sectional societies continued to
be the rule, large, synthetic organisations were tried, and found
wanting. John Doherty, working on the small unions in the cotton
industry, which from the start, as the embodiment of the new order,
was a natural breeding-ground for industrial conflict, started in
1829 his Grand General Union of the Operative Spinners of Great
Britain and Ireland, followed by his even more ambitious National
Association for the Protection of Labour, also with its centre in
Lancashire. There were attempts at fomenting general strikes in
1830–1. Such attempts failed, and the grandiose schemes of
Doherty and his like collapsed. The final blow to the National
Association for the Protection of Labour was the disappearance of
the secretary with most of its funds — a hazard, incidentally, to
which the early unions were peculiarly subject, in view of their
lack of systematic organisation. The goal of these ventures, and
especially of the Grand National Consolidated Trades Union,
established in 1834, was to harness the strength of the workers
to effect a complete recasting of society, and the promoters saw
themselves as reformers in much the same way as did the Chartists
or some of the leaders of the Anti-Corn-Law League. Robert
Owen, the 'father of British socialism', was associated with
the Grand National Consolidated Trades Union, which at one
time claimed half a million members. It was highly significant,
however, that very few of them had paid any subscription.
Such projects were bound to fail: they were top-heavy, flimsy
superstructures lacking sound foundations, while their methods
and nebulous aspirations were mistrusted by other reform movements. The prosecution of the six Tolpuddle Martyrs in 1834,
not under the Combination Laws, but under the much more
rigorous Act of 1797 against the taking of 'Unlawful Oaths',

merely marked the end of the movement; it did little or nothing to precipitate it.

After this combinations took on a more practical form. The desire to change society found other agencies, and combinations were directed to the more modest and practical objective of immediate improvements in working conditions. From now on it was a case of building from the localities outwards rather than in the reverse direction. The middle of the nineteenth century saw a pronounced trend towards efficiency, with the appointment of full-time trade-union organisers, working among artisans who were jealous of their skills and privileges and well enough paid to find money for their defence. This was the so-called 'new model' unionism, particularly associated with the most successful of the school, the Amalgamated Society of Engineers (1851), a national craft union, with a headquarters in London, and with large funds based on substantial subscriptions. Such unions usually had extensive friendly-society functions — it must be remembered that, apart from poor-relief, there was no help in distress except self-help — but whatever their detractors might say to the contrary they could be thoroughly militant when the occasion demanded it.

National organisation, however, was still the exception, and even a fairly loose federation like the Miners' Association of Great Britain and Ireland, which was started in 1842, lasted only five years. It was obviously even more difficult to get any sort of national co-operation between the different unions. There was established in 1845 the National Association of United Trades for the Protection of Labour, designed to bring about a wider working-relationship than local unions could (or wanted to) establish, but it won comparatively little support. It contained the germ of an idea, however; this was that trade unions must work together if they were to achieve certain industrial legislation, for instance as regards safety regulations in the mines, limitation of hours of work and so forth. It was a task of some delicacy, for local unions were frequently parochial in outlook, uninterested in their counterparts even in the same trade, and hostile to any suggestion of centralisation. Consultation between them, therefore, was developed on a local basis, through the formation of Trades' Councils, which sprang up in the forties in most of the industrial cities, the leading one naturally being in London. Nevertheless, it was from the Glasgow Trades' Council that the demand was pressed for a national front, in support of manhood suffrage, the establishment of courts of conciliation and arbitration, and, as an urgent issue, reform of the Masters and Servants Act. In 1864 it convened a conference in London, which organised political agitation on the latter two matters so effectively that both became the subject of legislation in 1867.

Then came an unexpected crisis, which confirmed the need for unity within the movement. On the whole, the attitude of government had been to leave trade unions alone, and the unions were reasonably content with the situation, although from time to time they were made all too conscious of their vulnerability, through occasional prosecution at the instance of particularly employers, in the courts. It was generally believed that they were assured of a measure of security under the Friendly Societies Acts, while the Molestation of Workmen Act of 1859 had made quite categorical their right to indulge in peaceful picketing during strikes. In 1866 came news of the 'Sheffield Outrages', instances of brutal and systematic intimidation. The revelations of the 'goings-on' in the darker corners of industry brought home to a shocked public that the 'new model' unions, led by respectable officials who talked the language of capitalism, spoke on Liberal platforms, and insisted on constitutional procedures, were not by any means wholly representative of all workers' organisations, and that the barbarities noted in 1825 were still being practised in some quarters. In the following year came the *Hornby* v. *Close* judgment, in an action by a union against its treasurer for embezzlement, which made plain that union funds were not after all protected by the Friendly Societies Acts and furthermore that unions themselves might be deemed illegal as being in restraint of trade. The furore which followed was largely responsible for a further conference of trade unions in 1867, and in 1868 the idea of an annual Congress materialised. The third Congress, which in fact did not meet until 1871, set up a Parliamentary Committee to lobby support in the Commons on behalf of trade-union interests.

The need for revision of the law was also accepted by the Government, and in 1867 there was a Royal Commission of Inquiry, which led to the Trade Union Act of 1871. It provided that trade unions should be allowed to register under the Friendly Societies Act, unless their rules were criminal; but at the same time expression was given to the fears as regards violence expressed in the majority report, and the result was the Criminal Law Amendment Act of the same year. While this measure was not aimed at trade unions in particular, it, of deliberate intent, left them liable to criminal prosecution for intimidation. This somewhat anomalous position did not last long, for, in 1875, there was passed the Combination (Conspiracy and Protection of Property) Act, which discovered a convenient formula in prescribing that collective action in trade disputes should not be subject to the law of conspiracy unless such action would be criminal if done by an individual.

Trade unions on the whole were very well satisfied with the resulting situation. As they saw it, trade unions now had legal standing as friendly societies; their property and funds enjoyed protection; contracts between a union and its members or between it and employers did not have legal force, which was as most trade-union leaders wished; and a trade union, as such, was not subject to the criminal law. The Act made a slight obeisance towards the public interest, in declaring that a person employed in a gas or water-supply undertaking who wilfully and maliciously broke his contract, knowing that such action, whether individual or collective, would deprive consumers of their supply, remained liable to prosecution. Electricity undertakings were later brought in under the Electricity (Supply) Act of 1919.

Despite their reinforced status, trade unions' strength must lie in their relationship with employers, and their leaders fully appreciated this. Their struggle for full recognition by employers was long and often bitter. A happy augury for collective bargaining had come in 1860 with the formation of the first joint conciliation board, in the hosiery industry. The inspiration here had come from an employer, A. J. Mundella, who in 1886 became President of the Board of Trade, the only Government Department with any real concern with labour. Under his aegis, the Board of Trade set up a

Bureau of Labour Statistics, which in 1893 became a branch of the ministry, with its own Commissioner for Labour — the first being Sir George Askwith — and began to publish the *Labour Gazette*.

So far the Government had stayed on the perimeter of industrial relations. In 1896 it gingerly moved inside this contentious arena. There was passed in that year the Conciliation Act, which, as recommended by a Royal Commission set up in 1891, authorised the Board of Trade not only to encourage conciliation processes generally but empowered it to hold inquiries into disputes where the public interest was involved and to arrange for conciliation at the request of either party, or arbitration at the request of both. This constituted a grudging acknowledgement which had already been made in factory legislation that *laissez-faire* did not always work to the common good.

In the last quarter of the nineteenth century, trade unions flourished, partly because of their enhanced security and recognition, and partly because of the expansion of industry and the greater political status accruing to working men through the widening of the franchise. The movement tended to open its ranks so as to embrace all classes of workers, including agricultural and unskilled industrial labour. This fresh orientation was largely the work of a few men, such as John Burns, Tom Mann and Ben Tillett, and the outcome has been dubbed the 'new' unionism. It was inclined to give trade unions a political bias, inevitably, since it represented the most depressed ranks, who, like Robert Owen's adherents, felt that society itself must be transformed; but they never became semi-political associations, in the way that unions commonly did in France, Germany and Italy. In those countries a powerful section of the movement regarded itself as the champion of Marxist socialism and, as a result, incurred the inveterate hostility of government and employers to a degree unknown in Britain.

The Taff Vale case was a set-back. There had been a strike in 1900 involving the Taff Vale Railway Company of South Wales and the Amalgamated Society of Railway Servants; the Company sued the Union for damages and ultimately was awarded them to the tune of £23,000. This decision meant that trade unions were to be held responsible for civil wrongs committed by their members in the course of trade disputes and, as a consequence, that what was considered normal strike action — which was, after all, designed to inflict injury — could put their funds in jeopardy.

Once again the trade unions awoke to the need for political backing in Parliament, but this time the situation was different from thirty years ago. Working men had the vote, and were much more aware of their rights, while socialist doctrines had been preached assiduously by some of the most influential of their spokesmen. For the first time, the leadership of the trade-union movement came to terms with the socialists, although not necessarily with socialism, and the result was the Labour Representation Committee, which ultimately became the Labour Party in 1906. There had been a Royal Commission to inquire into the situation created by the Taff Vale decision; but, although it contained people sympathetic to labour, including Sidney Webb, it confirmed the justness of the principle implicit in the Taff Vale judgment, which was that trade unions should be liable in the courts for civil wrongs committed in the course of official trade disputes. For various reasons, however, but especially because of the political content of the issue, the ultimate outcome was the Trade Disputes Act of 1906. This gave the unions all that their representatives in Parliament had asked for and much more than they had expected. It listed various important safeguards and, in one 'omnibus' clause, decreed that 'an action against a trade union, whether of workmen or masters, or against any member or officials thereof . . . in respect of any tortious act alleged to have been committed by or on behalf of the trade union, shall not be entertained by any Court'. This appeared to give complete immunity against civil liability, and an apparent loophole discovered in a recent case (*Rooke* v. *Barnard*) in the courts was promptly stopped up by the Labour Government (1965). This Act, which also applies to appropriate employers' associations, was the cornerstone of the trade-union movement, and remains so.

There was one further stage in the evolution of trade-union law. In 1909 there was yet another case before the courts. At this point it should be noted that before 1911 Members of Parliament were not paid and therefore if trade unions were to have their candidates for or representatives in Parliament, clearly the sponsoring bodies must subscribe towards their expenses and upkeep. Now, however, one Osborne challenged his union's rule requiring a subscription — quite a small one — towards its political activities. Osborne, as a Liberal, not unnaturally objected to part of his subscription being devoted to the advancement of a Party, the Labour Party, with which he had no sympathy. The case went to the House of Lords, who held that political activities were *ultra vires* to trade unions, as were indeed, by implication, other activities such as friendly-society functions. This was clearly a blow to the Labour Party, and a serious interference with what most people had come to accept as a normal trade-union service. The Labour Party and the unions naturally made common cause in this matter, but there was little doubt from the start that the Government would rectify the situation, and in due course the Trade Union Act of 1913 was passed. It provided that a trade union could use its funds for any lawful purpose, including political objects, on condition that (*a*) for the latter a majority decision of the union by secret ballot was a prerequisite and (*b*) a member of the union could refuse to contribute for this (political) purpose if he so wished; that is, he could 'contract out'.

In 1909 the Government directly intervened in the determination of wage-rates by passing the Trade Boards Act. Under this measure, which evoked little or no enthusiasm among trade unions, boards representative of workers, employers and independent members were set up to fix minimum scales in the worst of the 'sweated' industries. In general, however, it was and continued to be Government's desire to stay out of industrial relations so far as possible.

In the decade or so before the outbreak of the First World War, there was something of a reaction, especially among the general unions, against political activity as such. Partly it was a matter of disillusionment with the Labour Party, which looked as if it might prove to be little more than a splinter party or pressure group. Partly it was a matter of revolutionary feeling in favour of 'direct action' by workers, preached by trade-union leaders like Tom Mann. In any event, this period witnessed something of a reversion to the ideas of the first half of the nineteenth century; there was a renewed belief in some labour quarters that the unions could be used to change the very nature of society through industrial unionism or syndicalism or some such doctrine of workers' control. This approach, of course, particularly appealed to the new general unions of labourers. It was accompanied by an alarming increase in strikes and lock-outs, partly deriving from purely economic motives, since the cost of living was rising faster than wages. The notion of industrial action to enforce workers' demands, and if necessary to put pressure on Government, again gained ground.

The trade-union movement remained highly fragmented; there were in 1912 approximately 1,000 unions in England — and the number had fallen substantially in recent years — as against some 400 with about the same total membership in Germany, where the principle of central control and regimentation made much more appeal. The year 1913 saw a notable consolidation of the unions in the railway industry, when the National Union of Railwaymen was born, although even in this instance industrial unionism remained incomplete, since both the Associated Society of Locomotive Engineers and Firemen and the Railway Clerks' Association refused — and still refuse — to abandon their separate identities.

In 1914 there was forged the Triple Industrial Alliance, between the Miners' Federation, the National Union of Railwaymen and the Transport Workers' Federation, designed for concerted action in the event of a national dispute. Industrial unrest reached unprecedented proportions in the years immediately before the war, with the possibility of a head-on clash in which the State was bound to be involved. Lloyd George, at the Board of Trade, was well aware of the challenge of labour, much of it unofficial, which he viewed sympathetically as marking the break-up of 'the old industrial tyranny' before 'a new and hopeful spirit of justifiable discontent'. Perhaps because of this tolerance, the Government took no special action, other than to set up an Industrial Council, representative of unions and employees, to foster conciliation processes and settle disputes remitted to it.

The war might in some ways frustrate trade-union policies, but in other ways it put the movement on the map. Trade unions were

brought into the scheme of things, as never before; they were consulted by the Government and invited to be represented on all
sorts of important bodies concerned with the running of industries.
The union movement was well on the way to becoming what
Winston Churchill later called 'the Fourth Estate'. In return it
accepted certain temporary restrictions, under the Munitions of
War Act (1915), which decreed that in certain industries vital to
the war effort there was to be no recourse to strikes or lock-outs
pending reference of disputes to a Government body. Compulsory
arbitration was abandoned in 1918, but the war had given a
decided impetus to conciliation in industry. A Ministry of Labour
had been set up. The Whitley Committee had recommended that
joint consultative machinery should be instituted in most industries,
and, as a result, there was a proliferation of joint industrial councils. Industries not sufficiently well organised to accommodate such
machinery were in 1918 brought within the scope of the Trade
Boards Act. Yet another recommendation of the Whitley Committee was acted on by the Government with the passing, in 1919, of
the Industrial Courts Act. This provided for the establishment of a
permanent tribunal, which could, by consent of the parties, arbitrate in a dispute.

After the war the march of the trade unions was resumed,
facilitated by the Trade Union (Amalgamation) Act of 1917, which
made it easier to fuse unions into large units. In 1920 the Amalgamated Society of Engineers joined with others to form the
Amalgamated Engineering Union. In 1922 came the creation of
the Transport and General Workers' Union, and in 1924 the
National Union of General and Municipal Workers, both, it
should be noted, with their nucleus consisting of unskilled labour.
There was, too, a revival of militancy, encouraged by the depression
which set in in the twenties. It was proclaimed on behalf of the
movement that it was 'challenging the whole structure of capitalist
society', an end to private profit, and 'a real share in industrial
control for workers'.

This was a harking-back to pre-war aspirations, and reached its
culmination in 1926 with the General Strike. The Strike was a
failure, which brought what the Conservative Government regarded

as remedial legislation. The Trade Disputes and Trade Union Act declared that a strike was illegal if it were both sympathetic — that is, extending beyond the bounds of its own industry — and designed to coerce the Government directly or indirectly by inflicting hardship on the community. There were checks on intimidation, a limitation on the right of civil servants to join a trade union with political affiliations, and a section forbidding public authorities to make trade-union membership a condition of employment. Not the least important of its clauses was that replacing 'contracting out' by 'contracting in', which meant that a member wishing to contribute to his union's political activities should make a special declaration to that effect.

The collapse of the General Strike, the abysmal depression which followed, and the quick eclipse of the first Labour Government had a profound effect on the outlook of the trade unions. The leaders, like Ernest Bevin, were now much more inclined than they had been to find common ground with employers, as was proved by the Conference on Industrial Reorganisation and Industrial Relations of 1928. It aimed at setting up a National Industrial Council, representative of both sides of industry, which would act as industry's agent in dealings with the Government, and would at the same time be the final arbiter in industrial disputes. The plan never materialised, because of the distrust of both employers' associations and trade unions. The trade-union movement has always disliked the idea of central direction, even from within its own ranks, as indeed have employers. Then came the Second World War, which consolidated the status of the trade unions, and enhanced it to a point unknown before. Once again, but this time as a matter of course, the advice and co-operation of the trade unions was courted by the Government, and their authority recognised by their participation in the many bodies designed to promote the war effort. Once again, too, a great incentive was given to the introduction of joint negotiating machinery; no less than fifty-six joint industrial councils were set up during the war, as well as tripartite Wages Councils for industries not appropriate for cover by the Trade Boards Act.

When Ernest Bevin became Minister of Labour and National

Service, he suggested the creation of a Central Arbitration Tribunal, which would not only arbitrate in disputes but would prescribe national standards for wage-fixing. This was not palatable either to unions or employers' associations, as being too great an infringement of their long-established prerogatives, but they accepted the principle of compulsory arbitration, with a National Arbitration Tribunal, under the Conditions of Employment and National Arbitration Order (1940). This survived the war, but was replaced in 1951 by the much less stringent Industrial Disputes Order, which did not repeat the previous prohibitions of strikes and lock-outs pending arbitration. In 1958 this Order, too, was repealed, and industrial relations reverted to the well-worn procedures of private settlement — or private dispute — between the two parties directly involved. How long this would be allowed to continue, in the context of an economy which was subject to severe internal and external stresses, and which was increasingly 'managed' by Government, was a matter for speculation.

At the end of the war the Labour Party came to power. One of its first moves was to repeal in its entirety the Act of 1927, so that the position of trade unions and employers' associations was now regulated by legislation passed before 1914. It could be argued that, in the interval, the nature of industrial society had so greatly altered, and the concepts of Governmental authority with it, that, having regard to the vastly increased power of those bodies, there was need for a new prescription of obligations; and a Royal Commission to investigate the whole subject was appointed by the Labour Government in 1965.

10 The Irish Question

IT is always difficult to select a starting-point in time for the treatment of any historical topic, since the past must always cast long shadows over the present and future. The Irish Question is an exceptionally striking illustration of this. The tale has often been told of Lloyd George, during his talks with the Irish Nationalist leaders in 1921, wryly telling a confidant during an interval that the protracted negotiations had 'only got to Oliver Cromwell'. The Irish Question had deep, strong and intertwined roots, which had been thrust out over centuries, so that the cutting of one was not only difficult but had little apparent effect on the whole.

Ever since England had first taken an active interest in Ireland, back in the reign of Henry II, the problem of how to deal with Ireland presented itself to successive English governments as one of pacification and subjugation rather than one of assimilation. The differences in the make-up and environment of the two peoples were so great as to make it appear impossible to reconcile them. The Irish were regarded by the English, and not least by the governing class, as a near-savage race — as were the Scottish Highlanders — who clung obstinately to their own ancient language and traditions and to their separate identity and refused to be anglicised. They were always ready to exploit England's misfortunes and Ireland was, geographically and otherwise, a convenient base for England's foreign enemies. The Reformation greatly exacerbated the relationship: England became predominantly Protestant, while the vast majority of the Irish retained the Catholic faith.

Tudors, Stuarts and Cromwellians alike had pursued a dual approach: Ireland was to be colonised, like other overseas

possessions, by the compulsory injection of a strong element of
English and Scots. These were to be given large grants of land,
confiscated from the native proprietors, and were to be reinforced
as the dominant caste by the severest kind of military repression,
exercised on behalf of the home government when the occasion
seemed to demand it — and the occasions were frequent. The
Revolution of 1688–9 settled the pattern for well over a century to
come, but it merely re-stated and re-emphasised in the usual lurid
characters what had long been the conventional attitude of the
Government, which was to conquer and rule, not to placate. The
yoke became, if possible, heavier and more odious, for government
in Ireland became the preserve of oligarchy at its most corrupt and
inefficient. Yet without the extirpation of all things Irish — which
was not seriously attempted even if it had been practicable — the
policy could not be successful and had in it the seeds of tragedy.
It created more contradictions than it resolved. Ulster, once a
kingdom in its own right and 'the last great stronghold of Gaelic
tradition', had the main concentration of 'planters' from England
and Scotland. They often, like their Norman predecessors, became
in course of time more Irish than the Irish, for, as with British
settlers in America and other colonies, they resented their tutelage
the more, precisely because of their special relationship with the
'home country'.

A great many of them were Protestant Dissenters, but most of
the landowning class were Anglicans, even in Ulster, and they
provided the rulers in Church and State. The great submerged
Catholic majority, in common with the Protestant Dissenters, who
were the mainstay of such industry and commerce as existed, were
until the nineteenth century debarred under the Test Acts from
the privileges of citizenship — the right to vote, to hold public
office, etc. This led to an alliance in pursuit of constitutional rights
between Roman Catholics and Presbyterians, which was a curious
feature of contemporary politics, not only in Ireland but in England
and Scotland. This helps to explain why nationalism was so strong
in the late eighteenth century in Ulster, in spite of its strong Protestant ties. There were, too, many of the Anglican persuasion who
would have liked greater independence for Ireland.

There were further contradictions implicit in this situation, however. In Ireland the Protestants' constitutional aspirations were increasingly tempered by the very real fear that Catholic emancipation could mean an end to their own supremacy and even to their survival. At the same time, although the ranks of Protestants threw up doughty champions of Irish nationalism, the Protestant landlords continued to be regarded by the native Irish as of alien stock and as the protagonists and beneficiaries of economic and political exploitation.

In the eighteenth century Ireland had its own Parliament, but it was much more corrupt and inept than England's. In addition to the rottenness of its electoral system, which was 'managed' on behalf of the British Government, General Elections were something of a rarity; there was none during the thirty-three-year reign of George II. It was quite fantastically unrepresentative, by reason of the exclusion of Catholic and Protestant Dissenters. Finally, the real power lay with the Executive, whose nominee was the Lord-Lieutenant, appointed and controlled by Whitehall.

The monopoly of power enjoyed by the Anglican establishment meant that effective opposition must be extra-Parliamentary. The nearest thing to a national repository for opposition was the Catholic Church, which after the Revolution had nothing to lose and much to gain, so that anti-Government agitation was likely to be a heady mixture of religion, liberalism and politics.

Underneath all and providing the subsoil was the endemic and all-pervasive poverty of the generality of the people. 'The Irish problem, in simple terms, was the problem of a standard of life.'[1] The population of Ireland swelled with great rapidity in the eighteenth century, as did those of England and Scotland. Unlike England and Scotland, however, there was no Agricultural Revolution in the full meaning of the term. Much of the soil was poor, but, what was worse, it continued to be cultivated on primitive lines and there was no rise in food production in any way commensurate with the increase in population. For this the landlords, and the system which they symbolised, were to a large extent responsible. Many of them were absentee landlords, seeing nothing of

[1] E. L. Woodward, *The Age of Reform*, p. 315.

their estates except the revenues remitted to them in England. Thus there was no capital to fertilise agriculture, and the land was subdivided to an extent which made its cultivation completely uneconomic and kept the tenants in a state of perpetual and often desperate need. There was a great land-hunger, since the soil offered most people the sole means of even the most precarious livelihood; yet, in spite of this — and partly because of it — there was no incentive to improve holdings, for there was no security of tenure. At the best there might be a fairly short lease and, if improvements were effected, which in all the circumstances was most unlikely, either the already comparatively high rent would be raised or the tenant would be evicted without compensation. Low standards of living tended to foster large families and depress standards even further. The potato became the staple food and a failure of the crop was nothing short of catastrophic; that of 1740–1 was said to have resulted in some 400,000 deaths. Things were better in the north, where the 'plantations' had encouraged a more equitable system and the agriculturalists could afford to show greater initiative.

That agriculture was the only source of livelihood could also be blamed, in part at least, on the British Government. Until the end of the eighteenth century mercantilism in its roughest form was applied by the Government to Irish products. Ireland was a pastoral country. Indeed, again as in the Highlands of Scotland, the change-over to pastoral farming, with wholesale eviction of tenants, was almost the only manifestation of the Agricultural Revolution. Yet Irish wool had to be smuggled to France, since it could be legitimately exported only to England, where it was met with heavy duties. The export of Irish cattle and foodstuffs was forbidden until the second half of the eighteenth century. Ireland was excluded from trade with the Colonies — not that she had much to trade, except linen, whose export England tolerated since there was no competing industry there.

The aim was clearly and unashamedly to kill industrial development in Ireland. Having regard to the situation in agriculture, the only solution therefore lay in wholesale emigration and this was on a large scale. It involved both Catholics and Presbyterians, many of whom took with them a virulent hatred of Britain which was manifested in the American War of Independence and on other occasions when England was under attack, up to recent times.

The only other policy for Irishmen who resented their injustices seemed to many to lie in violence, and organised terrorism of the most brutal kind became a feature of the Irish scene. For instance, there were the 'Whiteboys', started in 1761, directed against oppression by landlords; the organisation was soon suppressed, 'but the melody lingered on'. There were very occasional revolts of the normally subservient Irish Parliament, but increasingly the view gained ground, with the qualifications already referred to among the Protestants, that an independent Irish Parliament was the only solution and that it was to be pressed on the British Government by fair means or foul. Various reliefs were granted to Ireland in 1778–82, including the removal of restrictions on Irish external trade, and a degree of legislative independence, in theory, for the Irish Parliament, but in practice the British Government could veto any Irish measure, and the Executive remained a British agency. Either the Executive or the Irish Parliament must go; and it was the Parliament that went.

Pitt had a good deal of sympathy with Irish desires, although none with that for independence. In 1792–3 Irish Roman Catholics were given the franchise, with other concessions, but could still elect to the Parliament only Protestants, which was absurd. George III was absolutely opposed to Irish reform and Pitt perforce abandoned his own more enlightened views. Protestants and Catholics had come together in a common cause in Wolfe Tone's Society of United Ireland, founded in 1791 by Protestants. The movement soon split into Roman Catholic and Orange or Protestant organisations. This was symptomatic of the underlying divisions of Irish politics. Civil war broke out in the north; Britain was at war with France and there was the possibility of French invasion through Ireland — a French expedition did in fact arrive in 1798 — and the Irish rebels were dubbed Jacobins, with justification. The outbreak was ferociously suppressed. At this stage independence for Ireland was unthinkable for the British Government and the only alternative was a closer union. Roman

Catholic leaders supported this, believing the assurances that it would be accompanied by Catholic emancipation, while the Protestant hierarchy was now convinced that union was necessary for the maintenance of their own ascendancy. The Irish Parliament, like the Scottish Parliament almost one hundred years before, was 'bribed and bullied out of existence', and the Act of Union was passed in 1800. The United Kingdom was thus created, with Irish representatives in the House of Commons and in the House of Lords, but the Irish Executive remained much as before.

The Union did not in fact bring Catholic emancipation, for the British Government went back on its undertakings. It did not greatly improve Ireland's economic position for, while free trade was good for England, it was not so good, as Scotland had previously discovered, for a country lacking in industry and in capital with which to promote it, and with a commercially aggressive neighbour possessed of both. Irish manufacturers were not strong enough to stand on their own feet and *laissez-faire* forbade the State to give any support, as was suggested in the case of the struggling Irish railways. Politically, the Union confirmed the supremacy of Protestant landlords both in national and local affairs. Ulster, always the more prosperous part, became yet more prosperous after the Union and gradually shed its late-eighteenth-century nationalism in face of the all-Ireland movement led by Daniel O'Connell (1775–1847). The Irish Question remained; but instead of being treated in comparative detachment, it became a question in the British Parliament as well as in Ireland.

The failure of the Union to remove the disabilities under which Roman Catholics suffered constituted that segment of the association which was most vulnerable to attack, because it was a sore point in Ireland and also a sensitive one in the British conscience. The Irish Question as such did not excite any great response in British public opinion or in Parliament; both were, in fact, deplorably ill-informed on the subject, while in Parliament — particularly in the House of Lords — Irish agitation, whatever its justification, was regarded as a challenge to the sacred rights of property, including those of the Anglican Church. The fact that the dignitaries of the Church, like so many of the landlords, usually fulfilled their obligations badly, if they fulfilled them at all, was glossed over. There was, however, a growing conviction that Catholic emancipation in Ireland, as elsewhere, was overdue. This, therefore, was where O'Connell, a lawyer, a landowner and a Catholic, resolved to challenge the whole Union settlement. The Treaty to him and his followers was a symbol of Irish subservience and degradation and, although he did not insist on complete separation from Britain, he did demand an Irish Parliament, for which Catholics would vote and in which they would serve. To this end he would harness the resentment against religious inequality.

The attempts, which narrowly failed, to get emancipation through Parliament, at least revealed both the strength of the opposition, in which the royal family was conspicuous, and the growing sympathy in the House of Commons. O'Connell adopted the recognised method of the times of putting pressure on the legislature by the mobilisation of mass opinion. He accordingly formed the Catholic Association, essentially a league of the common people — although some landlords were members — who, led by the priests, gave up their meagre pennies every month ('the Catholic rent') to create a sizeable fighting fund. The Association was, of course, quickly declared illegal, but O'Connell merely formed similar organisations under other names. The 40s. freeholders, who had the vote, were weaned by threats and cajolery from the traditional support of their landlords, and the climax came in 1828 when O'Connell himself was elected to Parliament. Such a startling phenomenon was a danger signal: if Catholics, legally elected, were nevertheless declared ineligible, Ireland would be aflame. Wellington and Peel accepted this, however reluctantly, and forced the Catholic Emancipation Act through in 1829.

This success took much of the steam out of O'Connell's campaign, but he was far from satisfied. The Irish group of M.P.s, whatever its composition and however influential as a 'third force', could be no more than a check on the Government, and repeal was still only a dream. O'Connell had to temporise and for the time being played politics. There were, of course, other grievances to be remedied. There was the tithe system, which bore most heavily on the small tenants, who resisted it in every possible way. Its abolition would not only be a relief to them but also a blow to the system of government and property. Just because of this, however, the Whig Government refused to tackle it and O'Connell had to be content with half-hearted reform of the municipal corporations, the introduction of elementary education and the transplantation of the grossly defective English Poor Law system.

These were mere sops, and when the Whigs fell and Peel and the Conservatives returned to power, O'Connell decided to renew all possible pressure on Parliament. He founded the Repeal Association in 1840, but this made little impact, for Peel was on much firmer ground than he had been with regard to emancipation and refused to be stampeded. Moreover, O'Connell was riding a tiger. A section of the Association called itself 'Young Ireland', in imitation of Mazzini's 'Young Italy' and, like it, was not concerned with clericalism — its leaders were in fact mostly Protestant — or with constitutional methods. O'Connell's prestige had suffered badly when Peel called his bluff by requiring him to call off a monster meeting at Clontarf and friction between him and the ardent revolutionaries was increased by Peel's measures to promote education in Ireland on undenominational lines. The divergencies between Catholicism and pure Nationalism became apparent.

Parliament had already nibbled once or twice at what was now the chief ingredient in the Irish problem, by suggesting agrarian reform, but the opposition was too great. Then the matter was thrown into high relief in startling fashion. In 1845–6 the potato blight spread from England to Ireland and the effects were disastrous. As has been said earlier, except in Ulster the economy was of the most primitive kind, with the potato the staple food, and when the crop failed there was little money to buy and little to buy with it. The Government did not come well out of the crisis. There was a grain shortage in Britain, and corn continued to be exported from a starving country, while the Corn Laws prevented the free importation of foreign supplies. The Government took emergency measures to alleviate the situation by food distribution and relief works, but these made no real impression. Hosts of people had to emigrate — the figure for 1847 was estimated at 200,000 and it did not drop for several years thereafter — while even more died of starvation. Between 1845 and 1848 Ireland lost from both causes over a million of its population, while the lot of most of those who remained was miserable in the extreme. It was a striking demonstration of the theories of Malthus: the growth of population was not merely halted but put into reverse. This harsh purge at least relieved Ireland of a great part of its redundant people, especially the poorest, and made more practicable agrarian improvement, from within and from without, but at a price both in human suffering and in political goodwill. For while systematic agitation almost collapsed for a period under the weight of economic stress, the hatred of the British Government in Ireland, America and Australia received a fresh and lasting stimulus.

It was fitting that the United States should furnish the agency for the next burst of nationalism, namely the Fenians. Backed with American finance, they proceeded to intensify the campaign of terrorism. This did little more, however, than harden opinion on both sides.

Now there appeared a British politician with the ability, courage and vision to attempt the fundamental changes the situation demanded. In his first spell as Prime Minister (1868–74) Gladstone boldly proclaimed, 'My mission is to pacify Ireland'. His chances of doing so were by no means hopeless; as time passed, in spite of terrorist excesses and Government retribution, public opinion on this issue was becoming more enlightened, in the sense of being both better informed and more tolerant, or perhaps more indifferent as regards purely sectarian issues. The Reform Act of 1867 had created a much wider spectrum of political opinion and nonconformity was increasing in influence.

In 1869 the Irish Anglican Church was disestablished — that is, it ceased to be the official Church of Ireland — and partially disendowed. That part of its revenue of which it was deprived — more than half — was diverted to secular needs, such as the relief of poverty, as Russell had suggested over thirty years before.

Gladstone then turned to agrarian reform. It was only a beginning, for what was at stake was nothing less than a system which

gave landlords as such arbitrary power and imposed no corresponding obligations. The great gulf between landlord and tenant
in Ireland derived, like so many Irish problems, from irreconcilable
attitudes: the Irish tenants continued to believe, as did their counterparts in the Highlands of Scotland, that they had a traditional
and inalienable right to the land they occupied, whereas the landlords knew that they were no more than tenants at will and a
burden to the soil. Gladstone's first Land Act (1870) merely
straightened out some of the worst kinks in the relationship. It
insisted on compensation for tenants' improvements and for their
eviction unless it were due to non-payment of rent, while they
could get loans to buy their holdings. This was unreal, for there
was no provision for security of tenure or for restraint of rents, so
that eviction without compensation was, if anything, encouraged.
Hope deferred makes the heart sick — and sour — and the long
period of procrastination and evasion had made the position even
more intractable. Yet the Act was at least a declaration of genuine
Governmental interest and good intentions.

The campaign against the Union in the same year took a new
form, with the formation by Isaac Butt, a Protestant of moderate
views, of the Home Government Association of Ireland, which
became the Home Rule League. Home Rulers quickly constituted
a sizeable block of Irish votes in the House of Commons, but their
importunity left Parliament quite unmoved. Inevitably, therefore,
the moderate Butt gave way to the much more pugnacious and
ambitious Charles Stewart Parnell (1846–91), also a Protestant,
and a landlord. His filibustering tactics sorely harassed Parliament,
but he also proceeded to exploit to the full outside the House the
poverty and insecurity of the tenantry. This was greatly aggravated
by the depression which in the seventies afflicted agriculture
throughout the United Kingdom. He became President of the
Irish Land League, formed in 1879, and supported by the Fenians.
This was a powerful combination, if an uneasy one, of all the
forces behind the desire for independence.

In 1880 Gladstone returned to power and, under pressure from
the Home Rulers, put through another Bill to compensate evicted
tenants, only to have it rejected by the Lords. He was not dismayed

and, alongside a policy of coercion forced on him by terrorism, he put through the second Land Act (1881), which gave the 'three Fs': fixity of tenure, fair rents and free sale. Parnell believed he had the Government on the run, fell foul of the authorities and was imprisoned; but Joseph Chamberlain, a member of the Cabinet, helped to negotiate the 'Kilmainham Treaty' (1882) by which, in return for a promise to cancel the vast arrears of tenants' rent due, Parnell would bring Ireland back to a realisation of the benefits conferred by the Land Act. This *entente* was destroyed at a blow by the Phoenix Park murders; Lord Frederick Cavendish, the newly-appointed Chief Secretary, and Burke, the Under-Secretary, were assassinated, and a new rash of violence broke out.

The Reform Act of 1884 further increased the Irish electorate, and with it the Home Rule Party, which, it should be noted, included a strong element from Ulster. The Irish vote in Britain and the Irish block of members were clearly factors of great portent to both Parties, but the risk in even appearing to seek electoral advantage by making concessions to them was even more cogent. Whichever Party grasped the nettle was certain to be badly stung. Gladstone had apparently hoped that a bi-partite approach might be possible but, since this did not materialise, he took the plunge. In doing so he split the country as well as his own Party.

In 1886 he introduced his Home Rule Bill, which would have given Ireland its own Parliament, with control over Ireland's affairs except where these had an 'imperial' aspect, as with defence, foreign relations and external trade. What made the measure even more explosive was that it was to be a Parliament for *all* Ireland. Ulster would have none of this, nor would the Conservative Party, nor would an influential section of the Liberals, led by Joseph Chamberlain, who had been prepared to support a form of devolution. This Bill was, in fact, defeated because of Liberal defections. Gladstone appealed to the country, which confirmed Parliament's verdict; the Conservatives were returned with a large majority, alongside which were the Liberal Unionists.

The Irish Question put the Liberals into the wilderness, and they stayed there, with one brief interlude, for nearly twenty years.

Ireland lapsed into its habitual strife, with an epidemic of evictions by the landlords and counter-measures by the tenants. The latter included the 'Plan of Campaign', which was a sort of trade union-ism of tenants against their oppressors. The Government was left with its usual thankless and unproductive task of trying to enforce a semblance of order.

Parnell was no doubt chastened by the collapse of his schemes and, like O'Connell before him, was being left behind by the swelling tide of nationalism. In 1887 *The Times* published a letter said to have been written by him five years before, which expressed some approval of the Phoenix Park murders. Accepted by the paper as genuine, it was later conclusively proved to be a forgery, and this created a revulsion of opinion in his favour which might have brought him back as a political force. Then in 1890 occurred the O'Shea divorce case, in which he figured as co-respondent; he had, in fact, been living with Mrs. O'Shea for ten years and later married her. As the case of Sir Charles Dilke had proved, this kind of affair was more than sufficient to destroy a politician. Gladstone and his Party, now out of office, disassociated themselves from him, as did the Catholics, and this, along with his own awkwardness, lost him the bulk of his following.

In 1892 Gladstone returned to power, and, undeterred by his advanced years and previous failure, renewed his attempt to secure Home Rule. It seems that he regarded the 'pacification of Ireland' as the consummation of his career but, if so, he was disappointed. His majority over the Conservatives was only four, in addition to which there were forty-six Liberal Unionists; against these could be ranged eighty-one Home Rulers. It was a precarious position from which to press so contentious a measure, but nevertheless he succeeded in forcing through the House of Commons a Bill which reiterated the principle of an all-Irish Parliament. It was a notable achievement, but it ended there, for the Bill was hopelessly de-feated by the House of Lords. Thereafter Home Rule ceased to be a live issue in Parliament until the Liberal Party came back to power in 1905.

The Conservative policy was to 'kill Home Rule by kindness'. During the Party's long spell of office, several Acts, culminating in the generous Land Purchase Act of 1903, were passed, designed to promote easier ownership of land by making available long-term loans to enable tenants to buy their holdings. Government indeed had shown much greater tenderness to Irish tenants than to Highland crofters, who also had for over a century been cruelly used by absentee and alien landlords and had in the eighties been goaded into a 'Crofters' War'; they had had to wait until 1886 for security of tenure and fair rents. If the Irish Question had been only a problem of living standards it would have been well on the way to solution, for the economic condition of the people was vastly improved. There had been first the rough surgery of famine and enforced migration, which made curative processes feasible. There had been far-reaching land reforms, from both Conservative and Liberal Governments, and an acceptance of the need for positive State assistance, as in the tenant subsidies and the support given to the fishing industry.

Unfortunately, the conviction that Ireland's ills, whatever they might be, were attributable to the British Government was now an ineradicable part of Irish thinking. The Irish Question, said Lord Rosebery,[1] 'has never passed into history for it has never passed out of politics'. However adequate material reforms might be, they would no longer satisfy the spokesmen of Ireland without a solid measure of political independence. Even so, a compromise solution appeared in some ways more hopeful than it had immediately after the Union. The nature of the demand for Home Rule was far less extreme than the republicanism and complete separation from Britain which had been demanded earlier and the official Irish spokesman were more mature and compromising. Yet in other ways the prospect of a settlement of the political issues was apparently becoming more remote than ever, and this for a complex of reasons. Frustration had, as always, bred a tradition of violence and had divided Ireland into two hostile sections. Nationalism was now becoming an end in itself and not merely a vehicle for reform. In 1892 Douglas Hyde, a Protestant, later to become the first President of Eire, founded the Gaelic League; it gave a fresh aura and glamour to Irish nationalism. In 1899 Arthur Griffith

[1] *Pitt* (1904) p. 172.

founded the *United Irishman* newspaper and in 1905 the Sinn Fein movement came into being.

What was, if possible, worse from the point of view of attaining a settlement was that the Irish Question had also split British politics. Gladstone might and did advocate a sort of Home Rule which would commend itself to the political leaders of Ireland, but he could not command the support even of all of his own party. The Liberal Party was one of the major casualties of the Irish Question, for it created a fissure in the party's ranks which damaged it almost beyond repair. Joseph Chamberlain and others insisted on the need for Britain and Ireland to remain united and attached themselves to the Conservative Party, which derived great strength from their accession. The Conservatives became 'Unionists' and ranged themselves with Ulster, where opposition to Home Rule had been growing ever since it was first mooted. Quite apart from religious considerations, with all their political undertones, Ulster was more closely linked with Britain than ever before. Any infraction of this link would be a serious matter. Outstanding personalities in the Conservative Party — Bonar Law, F. E. Smith, Sir Edward Carson and the rest — far from trying to reach an accommodation, passionately, indeed intemperately, argued that anything of the kind contemplated by Gladstone for Ireland as a whole was out of the question. They deliberately fanned the embers of insurrection in a way which was at best unstatesman-like, at worst downright irresponsible.

When in 1912 the Liberal Government, now depending for a majority on the support of the Irish group, introduced the third Home Rule Bill, a storm of opposition was evoked in Parliament and in the country. The time was propitious, however, for in the previous year the power of the House of Lords had been curbed, and the possibility of Home Rule for Scotland and Wales was receiving strong support among Liberals. The Bill passed the House of Commons. It provided for a separate Irish Parliament for domestic affairs, with continued membership, through a token representation of Irish M.P.s, of the 'Imperial' Parliament. It foreshadowed the Constitution which, after many days, was — remarkably enough — adopted for Ulster.

The fury of the opposition knew no bounds. The Ulster dissidents, with open incitement from Carson and others, formed the Ulster Volunteers, which had its inevitable counterpart in the Irish National Volunteers, a large proportion of whom were recruited in Ulster. Disaffection in the British Army was deliberately encouraged by Conservative leaders and high-ranking pro-Ulster officers, and all this at a time when industrial unrest in both Britain and Ireland had reached an unprecedented peak and a European cataclysm was threatening. However, despite the unrelenting opposition of the House of Lords, the Bill duly became law in 1914 under the provisions of the Parliament Act; but at the same time suggestions for a plebiscite in the north to determine its attitude were being widely canvassed.

Then came the outbreak of the First World War. The implementation of the Act was deferred, with the assent of Redmond, the leader of the Irish group, and his chief colleagues. The Act was to be suspended 'for the duration'. A minority of the Irish nationalists, as on previous occasions, saw in Britain's travail Ireland's opportunity. To gain their ends they were ready to use any means, including not only the usual financial support from their expatriates in the United States and elsewhere, but also whatever help could be obtained from Germany. Their intermediary in the latter case was Roger Casement. When the Easter Rebellion broke out in 1916, led by a few hotheads who proclaimed the establishment of the 'Irish Republic', it was denounced by Redmond and treated as arrant treason in war-time by the British Government. After court-martial, fifteen of the ringleaders were shot. De Valera was one of those condemned to death, but he was reprieved on the grounds that technically he was not a British subject. The executions of the rebels and of Casement created a new body of martyrs, and gave further fervour to the cause.

The organisation of Sinn Fein, although declared illegal, continued to exploit the situation, winning by-elections for, among others, de Valera, who became its President. In the General Election of 1918 no less than seventy-three out of the one hundred and five Irish seats went to his Republican Party, with only four to Home Rulers, and the rest to the Ulster Unionists. It is true that only 60% of the electorate voted, that less than half of those who did voted for Republican candidates, and that this might be construed as a dubious mandate for what followed. It was natural, however, for the nationalists to regard the result as a great triumph. Thirty-six of the successful candidates were in prison and four abroad, but the rest decided to boycott Westminster and to proclaim themselves as members of the *Dáil* (or Parliament) of an independent Ireland (1919), with de Valera its first President.

This was the beginning of the 'Troubles', a ferocious guerrilla warfare between the Irish Republican Army (I.R.A.), which did not regard itself as merely the instrument of the Irish 'Government', and, on the other hand, the Royal Irish Constabulary. In 1920, in complete accordance with the paradoxical nature of Irish politics, the six counties of Ulster were accorded Home Rule, and a similar dispensation was made for the rest of Ireland, under the Government of Ireland Act. There was to be a Council of Ireland to deal with matters common to both territories, not unlike the Parliament of Ireland envisaged in the 1914 Act.

Ulster became the State of Northern Ireland in 1921; but the rest of Ireland was no longer interested in such compromise — partition of the country was anathema to them. The Civil War was renewed with brutalities on both sides; the reinforcement of the Royal Irish Constabulary from outside (the 'Black and Tans') was held to have made the atmosphere, if possible, worse. In 1921 Lloyd George invited the Irish leaders to negotiate and the outcome was a reasonable settlement, to those interested in reason, and certainly at this stage the only possible settlement. The Treaty of that year set up the Irish Free State, exclusive of Ulster, which was acknowledged to be a part of Great Britain, while the Irish Free State pledged itself to remain in the British Commonwealth and to allow Britain to maintain naval establishments in peace-time in certain designated ports. There were suggestions that the boundaries of Northern Ireland might be adjusted to the advantage of the south, but nothing ever came of this.

The settlement was promptly repudiated by de Valera, who was particularly irked by the idea of Dominion status and the oath of allegiance required of Irish M.P.s. His Party continued to resist the Government of the Irish Free State in the barbarous fashion of the past, and was counter-attacked by the Irish Government with the utmost severity. Finally de Valera abandoned open resistance in favour of constitutional action; his followers provided the opposition party in the *Dáil*, and in 1932 became strong enough to form the Government. Still they chafed under the nominal allegiance to the British Crown which was now all that remained of the former links between Britain and her Dominions, and de Valera signalised his return to power by formally abolishing it. In 1937 his Government promulgated a new Constitution, which eliminated the last vestiges of the monarchical bond, and the Irish Free State was proclaimed Eire. The name meant, and was intended to mean, all Ireland and not merely the southern part.

In 1938 the British Government agreed to give up its rights in the 'Treaty ports', much to the disgust of Winston Churchill, who disliked the concession in principle and was apprehensive of the potential military threat to Britain which might accrue; this, after all, had been one of the original ingredients of the Irish Question. His fears were justified, but, in the Second World War, Eire's neutrality was respected.

De Valera's Government fell in 1948, after a run of sixteen years, and the Costello Government provided the epilogue to the long story of Anglo-Irish relations. It passed in that year the Republic of Ireland Act, which completely severed the connection with Britain. It did not necessarily dispose for ever of the Irish Question. It could be held that in a sense it perpetuated it, for it also in effect confirmed the partition of the country, which many Irish on both sides of the border would continue to lament.

11 Britain and the Empire

THE expansion of Britain overseas in the sixteenth, seventeenth and, more especially, the eighteenth centuries was
motivated not so much by considerations of national prestige,
although these were present, as by the desire to get a share of the
growing trade with the West and with the East. This ambition
was given a sharper edge by the strength of mercantilism, in
accordance with whose dictates nations set out to acquire and
so far as possible reserve for their own exclusive use, supplies of
needful primary products, including precious metals, together with a
submissive market for their manufactures, the traffic to be borne in
their own ships. This meant colonisation. Britain, in common with
Spain, Portugal, France and Holland — the other maritime nations
of Western Europe — subscribed to the doctrine of mercantilism,
and enshrined in it her Navigation Laws of 1651 and 1660, although
in her interpretation of it she was rather more generous than the
rest, more as a matter of realism than as one of policy. While emphasis
on the doctrine was to the advantage of the mother country, it was
by no means unfavourable to the colonies. In return for channelling
their products to Britain, in British ships, they enjoyed a preferential market and might even have their exports subsidised by the
British Government. Thus it was a feature of colonial preference,
then and since, that the British consumer might in some cases have
to pay more for colonial goods than if they had been bought in a
free market. And it seemed natural in the development of virgin
territories that they should concentrate on indigenous products,
always provided that this did not threaten home producers, while
Britain supplied their more sophisticated requirements in the
way of manufactures. The system was never as rigid as it appeared:

commodities not 'enumerated' might be traded in freely, and, furthermore, inevitably the Navigation Laws were evaded extensively and often openly. It should be noted, too, that Britain, through her fleet and garrisons, provided at her own expense protection for the colonies against foreign interference and native hostility.

On the other hand, it was galling, more particularly for British expatriates or, worse, as in Quebec, another white people under British rule, to be denied the right to develop their resources as they thought best, as well as to endure constitutional restrictions exercised on behalf of a far-away country, with whose political system they might have little sympathy, and which they might have set out in the first place to escape. It was frustration, not flagrant oppression, that drove the thirteen American colonies to revolt in 1775.

Before 1763 the Empire was regarded at home as little more than a miscellaneous collection of trading bases situated on coastal strips in America, India, West Africa and the West Indies. They had been established, in most cases, by private enterprise, as with the East India Company, the Hudson's Bay Company, the South Sea Company, the Levant Company and the African Company, operating with the blessing of the home Government in the form of monopolistic privileges. The British colonies were looked on by most people at home as appendages, not as an integral part of the national structure. There was, of course, political and economic control from the centre, but little material assistance. Emigration of men and money was considerable, but it was not officially promoted, except in rare cases, and then indirectly, as with James I's offer of baronetcies to those who took up land in Nova Scotia; neither population nor capital was regarded as an excess commodity for export. West Africa was looked on as the base for the lucrative slave-trade and a convenient station for ships going around the Cape of Good Hope to and from India.

All this is not to say that the Government was not interested in the Empire. It appreciated full well that trade meant national prosperity. As industrial expansion quickened, so did the need for colonies increase, and Britain's wars in the eighteenth century

were at least as much concerned with this desideratum as with the
balance of power in Europe, although the distinction is a fine one,
since commerce was strength. Her navy was developed to enable
her both to defend her shores and to consolidate and enlarge her
overseas trade, of which the colonies were a part. The seizure of
territory from France and Spain was for her a most important
element in the Treaty of Utrecht (1713), which gave a foothold in
Canada and the *entrée* into South American commerce, while the
Peace of Paris (1763) finally drove France out of the greater part
of North America — and incidentally left Britain with the legacy
of a predominantly French colony in Quebec — as well as out of
India, except for a few trading posts, while it also established her
in the West Indies.

The loss of the American colonies in 1783 was a blow to
Britain, since, even if they were still essentially coastal settle-
ments, they had been by far the largest aggregation of her colonial
possessions, and the damage to national prestige was serious. The
blow, however, was less severe than has sometimes been suggested.
It was highly significant that Britain's chief preoccupation — and
America's — in the negotiations which concluded the War of
Independence was to maintain the closest possible trading relations.
There were politicians in Britain who nursed the idea of a
British-American *entente* which would encourage America to
expand geographically westwards, thus providing a wonderful
market for British goods. This idea did not materialise, and the
immediate political reaction took a mercantilist form, in the attempt to stop the West Indies and Canada from trading with
America; but the long-term results were to loosen the bonds of
empire. The rupture was regarded in Britain by Adam Smith and
many others as conclusive proof of the evils of mercantilism, if
not of the whole colonial system, as well as a demonstration of
governmental ineptitude, and the belief grew that, with Britain's
economic superiority, all the advantages of colonies could be available to her without the expense and friction involved in sustaining
an empire.

There were other important consequences. About 30,000
Loyalists streamed northwards, with help from the British Govern-

ment, to settle in Nova Scotia, then including New Brunswick, and in what became Ontario, thus initiating the first stage of the opening-up of Canada as it is known today. Population from the mother country continued to flow to Canada — as it did to America — but it owed little or nothing to State policy, except in so far as it was an exodus inspired by depression and misgovernment at home. There was an exception. The southern states of America had been a dumping-ground for convicted felons; now that they were barred, another site was perforce opened up, in Australia, and the possibilities of this great continent slowly and dimly dawned on Britain.

The international settlement of 1814–15, following the French Wars, demonstrated the character of British colonialism. In 1814 a Cabinet minute recorded that the Government 'do not desire to retain any of those colonies' (won during the war) 'for their mere commercial value . . . too happy if by their restoration they could give other states an additional motive to cultivate the arts of peace'. That this was not pious posturing was proved conclusively by the restitution of most of the territories in question. The Cape of Good Hope, captured from Holland, was retained, at the cost of £2 million compensation to the Dutch, as was Ceylon, together with Malta and Mauritius and British Guiana. These were not large gains, but they were of great strategic importance for the protection of Britain's trade routes in the Mediterranean and the road to India. They do not suggest that imperialism for its own sake was a factor; otherwise the Dutch would not have been handed back the East Indies, nor the French most of their West Indian losses. It is a remarkable fact that Singapore, destined to become one of the great entrepôts of the world, and the naval base for the Far East, was taken over, most reluctantly, in 1819, as a result of the unauthorised initiative of one man, Sir Stamford Raffles. Foreign policy entered into those dispositions, since Britain needed a strong Holland in Europe, and, even a reasonably strong France.

The attitude to Empire on the part of the Government was a mixture of different and sometimes ill-assorted factors. From early in the nineteenth century, the philosophy of free trade was a constant influence and remained so for over a hundred years. Huskisson, in pursuance of a policy inherited from his immediate predecessor at the Board of Trade, completely freed trade between the West Indies on the one hand and the United States on the other, with certain reservations regarding the use of British shipping and the principle of mutual reciprocity. His work was completed by Peel and Russell in the 1840s, culminating in the repeal of the last of the Navigation Acts in 1849. The Manchester school of political economists was determined to eliminate the last remnants of mercantilism, including colonial preference, and they could support their case, not only with abstract arguments for *laissez-faire*, but with statistics which were bound to make an impression on any government, notably the high cost of colonial defence, running to perhaps £4 million a year, and the fact that trade with the United States, after its defection, was greater than trade with the whole of the Empire.

This *laissez-faire* policy was regarded with misgivings in the colonies themselves. They might, like Canada, proceed to erect their own tariff barriers, as soon as they had responsible government — Canada did so in 1859 and Victoria in 1865 set a similar pattern for the rest of the Australian provinces — but they also wanted free access to the enormously valuable market in Britain. Canada strongly resented the loss of the preferential market in corn, while the West Indies were crippled by the final abandonment of the sugar preference in 1854, which exposed them to competition from the cheaper, slave-produced article in Brazil, and from sugar-beet grown in Europe. The West Indies was perhaps an exceptional case, since, until the late nineteenth century, it remained a one-product economy. Britain was not above exerting pressure on colonial industry to suit her own selfish ends, as in the case of Indian cotton goods, but, even in this apparent exception to her rule, the competition from other countries was the main cause of the decline of Indian exports. In general, Britain remained adamant in her pursuit of free trade, regardless of the unfavourable impressions it might arouse in the colonies, and even when late in the century she granted charters to the private companies which had been exploiting the resources of Africa and the Far East, she normally attached the condition that a monopoly of trade should not be operated — a far cry from the policy towards the chartered companies of the sixteenth and seventeenth centuries.

Certainly, in the first half of the nineteenth century, there was another school, with which Edward Gibbon Wakefield, Lord Durham, Charles Buller and others were associated — Radical Imperialists, who, as their designation suggests, were anxious to preserve the Empire by a combination of systematic British colonisation and a devolution of responsible government. The two provinces of Upper and Lower Canada had in 1791 been given their own Legislative Councils, but with the Governor and Executive responsible not to the Legislatures but to the home Government. This unsatisfactory duality was rendered the more unpalatable and unworkable by the fact that Lower Canada had a powerful French settlement which did not take kindly to British rule. Following a rebellion in 1837, Lord Durham — one of the architects of the 1832 Reform Act — was sent out as Governor. He was a man of vision, although not a successful administrator, with associates like Wakefield and Buller, who saw in the Empire much more than a collection of satellites which would soon find their own separate orbits. In 1839 appeared the Durham Report, which has been called the 'Magna Carta of colonial self-government', and rightly, since it marks a turning-point not for Canada alone, but for the Empire. It recommended autonomy for the Provinces, with some important but, for the times, not very objectionable qualifications in regard to control of foreign policy, international trade, and the wastelands. The crux of the Constitution was to be that not only was the Legislature to be independent within the stated limits, but the Executive was to be responsible to it. It was appreciated that this would tend towards separatism, but this, it was advocated, should be countered by the continuance of the monarchical link and of British institutions, which would be consolidated by large-scale immigration from Great Britain.

The Report did not evoke any enthusiasm in Britain, but neither did it meet with hostility, and in 1847 its policy began to be implemented; a start had been made with an Act of 1840 uniting the Provinces. Canadian independence could not come too soon for the British Government: a visiting Canadian politician in 1866 reported that 'the leaders on both sides, Gladstone and Disraeli included, would have been much more pleased if we had asked for our independence at once'. This was no exaggeration. Disraeli had in 1852 declared that 'these wretched colonies will all be independent in a few years and are a millstone round our necks'. In 1867 there was passed the British North America Act, which paved the way for a confederation of all the Canadian Provinces except Newfoundland, which always retained its distinct identity. The grouping was to comprise Upper and Lower Canada, Nova Scotia and New Brunswick, which together became the Dominion of Canada. It was to have a bicameral Federal Parliament and provincial Legislatures. The link with the Crown was to continue, for 'the Sovereign of Great Britain' was to remain the titular head of the executive power and to be represented by a governor-general. Other provinces came in in due course, helped by a growing awareness of mutual interests, which itself received a special stimulus from the construction of the Canadian Pacific Railway. Indeed, the accession of British Columbia in 1871, which followed on that of Manitoba in the previous year, was made conditional on the creation of a railway link between British Columbia and the east. The railway was started in 1880 and opened in 1886. Prince Edward Island joined the confederation in 1873 and Saskatchewan and Alberta came in in 1905.

The trend was not confined to Canada. In 1850 the Australian Colonies Government Act, passed after consultation with the colonies, permitted them to establish their own Constitutions, and in 1856–7 New South Wales — the original settlement — Victoria, South Australia, Tasmania and Queensland reaped the benefits. New Zealand, whose systematic colonisation had begun with Wakefield's New Zealand Company, chartered in 1841 and dissolved ten years later, had gone the same way in 1854. It was typical of the British Government's pragmatic approach that in 1865 the Colonial Laws Validity Act in effect put the imprimatur on *faits accomplis*. One of its clauses read: 'Every colonial Legislature shall have, and be deemed at all times to have had, full power within its jurisdiction to establish courts of judicature, and to abolish and reconstitute the same, and to alter the constitution thereof, and to make provision for the administration of justice therein: and every Representative Legislature shall, in respect to the colony under its jurisdiction have, and be deemed at all times to have had, full power to make laws respecting the constitution powers and procedure of such Legislature, provided that such laws shall have been passed in such manner and form as may from time to time be required, by any Act of Parliament, Letters Patent, Order in Council, or colonial law for the time being in force in the said colony.' The colonies were free to make their own laws so long as these did not conflict with imperial statutes. This was not in practice a burdensome reservation, and it survived until 1931.

It is clear that the relaxation of political control was not an abdication of responsibilities on the part of the home Government, inspired by colonial discontent on the one hand and lack of interest on the other. The Colonial Office genuinely believed that the deliberate extension of self-government was the only constructive approach to colonial development.

The Cape of Good Hope presented a special problem. It had been taken over as a tiny enclave in 1795, and was treated as a Crown Colony, retaining the institutions of government established by the Dutch. However, it was ominous that, from the start, the British Government had very different ideas from the Boers as regards treatment of the native races. The situation was exacerbated by the fact that the Boers, with their strong disposition towards pastoral farming, wanted to spread into the interior and, of course, to occupy farming land. This raised an issue which was inherent in other white settlements, including the American colonies before their breakaway, but it was peculiarly intractable in this instance, partly because of the incompatibility of the two white peoples. Britain sought to change the situation by increasing the proportion of British settlers, and in 1820 some 5,000 were sent there. The Boers, who were highly developed in the tradition of independence, did not take kindly to such infiltration and their resentment sent them on their Great Trek, literally in search of new pastures, which started in 1835 and went on for years, inland beyond the Orange and Vaal rivers and into Natal. The British Government was not prepared to leave them to their isolation and in 1843 annexed Natal. In spite of all the difficulties, which would not be resolved merely by constitutional changes, Cape Colony got responsible government in 1872.

In India things went differently. A distinction, and a reasonable one, was made between those territories where a white population had settled and the other territories where the whites were little more than a ruling caste, holding native races in subjection. Pitt's India Act of 1784, which set up a Board of Control to supervise the administration of the East India Company, lasted until 1858. The joint rule of the British Government and the East India Company had many beneficial effects, not least the restoration and maintenance of order between the various races and States, but the administration, semi-detached as it was, became ever more bureaucratic and insular. It was modified for the better by the institution in 1853 of competitive examinations for entry into the Indian Civil Service. Then in 1857 came the Indian Mutiny and in the next year the Company's powers and land were transferred to the Crown. Direction was exercised through a Secretary of State for India, working through a Council appointed by him.

Yet another doctrine of empire was voiced by the humanitarian reformers like the Clapham Sect. They preached that white interference with native races was bound to lead to the exploitation and degradation of the latter, and their views carried weight in Whitehall. The abolition of slavery was unquestionably one of the motives behind the British penetration of Africa. The Arab traders had always carried on this nefarious traffic, with or without the connivance of native chiefs, and it could be stopped only by controlling the territories. The British Government's attitude to native races was generally surprisingly enlightened for the times, as the records of the Colonial Office show, and its insistence on the emancipation of slaves and on native rights was a cause of friction with the white settlers not solely in the West Indies, but in South Africa, Australia and New Zealand as well. This same paternalism had fretted Americans before they asserted their independence. Relations with the colonies were not infrequently strained for one reason or another, and, as late as 1870, in New Zealand, which has at all times been perhaps the most consistently loyal to the British Crown of all the colonies, there was talk of breaking away from the Empire and joining the United States.

Influences like those of the Clapham Sect were the more powerful because the Government only very slowly built up an effective Civil Service to administer the colonies. Imperial policy, so far as it could be said to exist at all, derived its shape and continuity from administrators rather than from ministers. An organisation was evolved very gradually and almost fortuitously. In 1801 responsibility for the colonies was transferred from the Home Office to the War Office, but it was not until Lord Bathurst became Secretary of State for War and the Colonies that real progress was made, as might have been expected in the circumstances. He held office from 1812 to 1827 and had as his Under-Secretary a man who also took a great interest in colonial affairs, Henry Goulburn. As the pressure of military matters began to abate, they created a Colonial Office which, working on a shoe-string, built up a cadre of experienced officials. Those individuals wielded much authority, for the Colonial Office was not highly regarded in parliamentary circles until Joseph Chamberlain gave it a new *cachet*, and debates were sparsely attended. Both ministers and the highest civil servants were often under the influence of humanitarian reformers; Bathurst himself was, and so was Sir James Stephen, who was finally elevated to the rank of Permanent Under-Secretary and wielded great power from 1836–47, as was his successor, Herman Merivale, and Sir Frank Rogers (1860–71). It is interesting that Rogers, before he became Permanent Under-Secretary, had referred to the 'eventual parting on good terms' with the colonies. There were, too, ministers who were conscious of the Government's obligations to subject races, such as Lord Glenelg and W. E. Gladstone; the latter, of course, was not only in charge of the Colonial Office for a year, but influenced policy throughout his long spells of office as Prime Minister.

The criticism made of the officials was that, in the absence of a strong lead from the Government, they arrogated to themselves an undue degree of power and that that power was not always wisely exercised, as witness certain unfortunate appointments to offices in the colonies. The fact, however, that the Empire not only survived but moved fairly steadily along a well-defined path was largely due to their good sense, high degree of impartiality and devotion.

It would be wrong to assume that the Empire remained static, either in size or form, in the period between 1815 and 1870, or that the British Government abandoned interest in it. The impression that nothing much happened derives from the fact that, by contrast with the last quarter of the nineteenth century, there was little or no public sentiment in favour of imperialism and no dramatisation of the concept. It was also partly due to the fact that too deep a distinction has been drawn between political and economic motives in Empire-building. Both were present in the seventeenth and eighteenth centuries and continued throughout the nineteenth. The fact is that British imperialism was, at root, a manifestation of metropolitan growth; the surplus energy of a booming economy was finding outlets in the export of population and finance, and in the provision of shipping and other services which in turn made possible the imports which an industrial nation needed. Free trade, affected the situation but the motives fundamentally did not alter. Britain's interests, it was hoped, could be safeguarded by a blending of Empire-building and trading opportunities, which might have to be asserted, as in China, by force, or might flow from commercial understandings, and by the influence which accrued from investment. From early in the nineteenth century the search for new markets, whether in South America or the East, had been actively prosecuted and an 'Informal Empire' of trading and political influence had been established without the need to take over territory.

As things worked out, there was no hiatus in the growth of the British Empire in the first three-quarters of the nineteenth century, but the growth was not achieved by any policy of systematic conquest. Between 1841 and 1851 Britain annexed New Zealand, the Gold Coast, Natal, the Punjab and Hong Kong, and in the next twenty years she took control of Lower Burma, Lagos, Basutoland, Griqualand and the Transvaal, and set up the flag in Queensland

and British Columbia. These gains were usually dictated by fairly simple and practical motives: there was the need to round off frontiers, for reasons of security, or efficiency in administration, or the protection of indigenous peoples, or their might be an organic growth as in Australia or in South Africa. Finally, and always pre-eminent in the minds of the Government, there was the need to protect existing possessions and trading routes; thus the incorporation of British Columbia (1858) was due to rivalry in that area with the United States.

It has become a stock thesis that Britain in the 1870s suddenly experienced a conversion to out-and-out imperialism. This is not so. The conviction that the colonies were something of a luxury, which the country did not want and could not afford, never became extinct, and was especially deeply rooted in the Treasury. The Foreign Office, too, was suspicious of fresh territorial annexations. When the 'scramble' was under way, the Foreign Office decided, as regards West Africa, 'to confine ourselves to securing the utmost freedom of trade on that coast, yielding to others the territorial responsibility . . . and seeking compensation on the east coast . . . where the political future of the country is of real importance to India and imperial interests'.[1] Like the Cabinet minute of 1814 quoted earlier, this was not a pronouncement designed to impress the outside world with British magnanimity; it was a statement of policy.

It has been contended that the main force in British expansion in the last quarter of the nineteenth century and after was the potency of British investment, which demanded Government intervention for its protection. That the need to protect investment entered into politics there can be no doubt; that it was the prime motive is a contention clearly impossible to sustain since the same equally applied in the periods before. British investment was well entrenched in the most profitable places before 1870, through strong companies which, generally speaking, were safe enough. Of the 20 million people who emigrated from Britain in the century before the First World War, nearly three-quarters went outside

[1] Quoted by Gallagher and Robinson, *The Imperialism of Free Trade*, in Nadle and Curtis, *Imperialism and Colonialism*.

the Empire, as did one-half the capital invested overseas. Even after 1870 Africa, for obvious reasons, was relatively unattractive to the average investor.

The fact remains that after 1870 there were new forces at work or old forces in a slightly different guise. The opening of the Suez Canal created a new route to India, which must at all costs be safeguarded against foreign interference, and this appeared most likely to come from France or Russia. It was more, however, than a matter of merely securing the Canal zone; it implied a complete assurance of Egyptian co-operation. Britain was already involved there financially, but the decisive factor in Britain's taking over the domination of Egypt was not to protect British capital investment as such, although this certainly counted, but to preserve the route.

The international situation, too, in both its diplomatic and commercial aspects, was deteriorating. Power politics and considerations of international prestige were keeping Europe in a ferment, and with them went economic nationalism, which also dominated the thinking of the United States and Japan, as well as of some of the Dominions, such as Canada. All this made it necessary to be strong both militarily and economically and to preserve the Empire as a force in world politics. It gave new emphasis to world strategy, which was also apparent in diplomatic relations and was leading to alliances and counter-alliances. It also made it more necessary than ever to ensure the flow of old raw materials and some new ones, and if possible fresh markets; for, at the same time as the erosion of free trade was taking place, the needs of Britain's expanding population and of her mass-produced manufactures were becoming larger. Industrial chemistry was giving a new value to all sorts of products, like rubber (which had its repercussions in Ceylon and Malaya) and in new uses for metals, like tungsten, asbestos, nickel, etc. (which increased the potential of places like Nigeria, Burma, Australia and Canada). It was possible to penetrate into the interior of Africa and the Far East because of railways and the advance in the knowledge of tropical diseases; Schools of Tropical Medicine were established in London and Liverpool at the end of the nineteenth century.

There were spasms of public interest, which Disraeli, having recanted his earlier views, did his best to foment. He saw the Crown as the symbol of a great and glittering constellation and, following his purchase in 1875 of a large interest in the Suez Canal, had the Queen dubbed the following year Empress of India. He talked of imperial preference and trusteeship, and his foreign policy developed a pronounced imperialist tinge. He accused the Liberals of 'a deliberate and sinister attempt to effect the disintegration of the British Empire', ignoring the fact that the apathy in regard to colonies had been shared by both Parties. Certainly, however, it fitted better into the Liberals' philosophy, and a reaction against their *laissez-faire* attitude in this direction may have helped in a small way to return the Conservative Government in 1874. Ten years later Gladstone was still quite impenitent, although his Party now contained outspoken imperialists. He had condemned the methods of annexation of the Transvaal in 1877, and committed Britain to the evacuation of the Sudan, which had been regarded as within the Egyptian sphere; the outcome was the siege of Khartoum and the death of General Gordon (1885). The public response to this tragic event, at home, was violent but this was as much a matter of simple patriotism as of imperialism; what was called 'jingoism' was a kind of chauvinism stemming partly from the public consciousness that Britain now, and for the first time since 1815, was internationally vulnerable and was being roughly jostled by other countries. Yet the expansion of the Empire went on and, oddly enough, some of the most conspicuous acquisitions were made under Gladstone's auspices. It was a Liberal Government that in 1881 incorporated the British North Borneo Company, forced to recognise that, without such sanctions, British commercial interests in that region would be overrun by Dutch and Spanish, who would not brook competition. Partly Gladstone's hands were forced by events, but there was also a strong feeling, especially among Liberals, that it was Britain's lot — the white man's burden, which destiny compelled it to bear — to protect the more backward races from themselves, from each other, and from external oppression, and to bring them the benefits of civilisation. To this theme Kipling gave a new lustre and popularity. It was in

no way incompatible with economic development; Dr. Livingstone
had earlier declared that his mission in Africa was to open a path
for 'commerce and Christianity'.

Africa offers the classic illustration of British imperialism as it
worked in the late nineteenth and early twentieth centuries. The
West African footholds on the coast seemed of little commercial
value after the abolition of slavery, nor were the South African
settlements, taken over from Holland, deemed of much account,
until the last quarter of the nineteenth century. Then, as already
stated, the economic potentialities of the hinterland were becoming
more apparent and their exploitation more feasible. The initiative
came not from the Government but from private enterprise. The
National Africa Company received its Charter in 1886, with a
restriction on monopolistic trade, as in the case of the North
Borneo Company. It was bought out by the Government in 1899–
1900 and the opening up of Nigeria began. With the encouragement and help of the Government in the promotion of railways
and port facilities, the territories took the form of Northern and
Southern Nigeria, which in 1912–14 were united as the Colony
and Protectorate of Nigeria. It was in Nigeria that Sir Frederick
(later Lord) Lugard introduced the policy of indirect rule, through
native institutions, which came to be regarded as the model for
British administration in Africa in the twentieth century.[1] In 1887
the British East African Association received concessions from the
Government and a Charter in the following year. Its sphere of
operations was Uganda and this territory was incorporated in the
Empire in 1893 by Gladstone — reluctantly, and no doubt influenced by the blunt assertion of his Scottish agent that, if he
abandoned Uganda, he might as well abandon his constituency.
The Uganda Railway was completed in 1901.

South Africa presented the most complex problem of all. The
vacuum left in the Cape and Natal by the exodus of Boers was
filled by British colonists, and the net result was a period of
uneasy stability in South Africa, during which the Cape
was accorded responsible government. In the seventies the
British Government was converted to the idea of a federation of

[1] See Lord Lugard, *The Dual Mandate in British Tropical Africa* (1922).

South African States, which, as had happened with other white colonies, would form a Dominion. This solution of a Federation has always been something of an *idée fixe* for Britain and there has been a tendency to disregard the natural differences between the component parts in the anxiety to achieve some sort of unity. Federation under British control was repugnant to the Boers, but the Transvaal was formally annexed in 1877, and Gladstone, on his return to office in 1880, refused to revoke this decision, partly, at least, because of his dislike of the Boers' racialist policies. Kruger asserted the Republic's independence, and a short war in 1880–1 ended with a patched-up compromise. In 1884 the Transvaal became the South African Republic. Meanwhile Cecil Rhodes had built up wealth and power and taken over the concept of a Federation, seeing it, however, in a different guise from that envisaged by the British Government, as the one thing which might reconcile settlers of British and Dutch stock by imposing a white supremacy, rooted in Africa and becoming nothing short of an Empire in its own right. In 1889 his British South Africa Company received a Charter for the opening up of the country which in 1895 was named Rhodesia, and continued to administer it until 1923, when it became a Crown Colony. 'Here, but nowhere else in all the territories acquired by European powers during the great imperial scramble, a considerable white population took root in the soil.'[1]

In 1895 Joseph Chamberlain was appointed Colonial Secretary, a post he preferred to that of Chancellor of the Exchequer, and found full scope for his doctrine — which the Conservative Party, of which he was now an associate, had still to accept — of strengthening the imperial connections. During his period of office, which lasted until 1903, much was done. For instance, a sorely needed diversity was introduced into the economy of the West Indies. The Colonial Office backed up the task of developing West Africa, the Sudan, Malaya, etc., especially through the construction of railways. This worked well with the more passive tropical territories, but South Africa remained a problem. The British settlers in the Transvaal — the Uitlanders — were denied full citizenship

[1] Burt, *The British Empire and Commonwealth*, p. 527.

by the Boer Administration, and a conspiracy against the Republic culminated in the misconceived and ill-starred Jameson Raid, 1895–6, to which Rhodes, now Prime Minister of the Cape, was party, and of which Chamberlain was certainly cognisant. Three years of negotiation with President Kruger followed, with failure well-nigh certain, since the real issue was not one of domestic reform but one of Dutch or British hegemony. Sir Alfred Milner, who had gone out as High Commissioner in 1897, made little impression on the President, and the South African War broke out in 1899. It ended in 1902 with the Boers' acceptance of British suzerainty but with a promise of responsible government, which was implemented in 1907–8. It might be noted in passing that New Zealand, which had enjoyed responsible government since 1856, now became a Dominion. Milner, who had become Governor of the Transvaal and Orange River Colony, laboured to restore stability, and in 1909 there was passed the Act for the Union of South Africa, which became effective the following year, and which instituted a central Parliament, with General Botha as the first Prime Minister.

Chamberlain had been working in other directions to consolidate the Empire. The idea of some form of consultation between the white colonies had been mooted as early as 1869, but had been lukewarmly received both at home and overseas. In 1887 the mood was more congenial, for this was the year of Queen Victoria's Golden Jubilee and a gesture of imperial kinship seemed specially appropriate. A Colonial Conference was called in that year in London which, while almost casual in its organisation and agenda, provided a forum for mutual discussion of, in particular, imperial defence. The next Conference was in Ottawa in 1894 and it was perhaps a portent that this should be the venue for an affirmation by the colonies concerned, but not by Britain, of the principle of imperial trade preference. This seemed to Chamberlain, when he took office, a propitious time to press the gospel and he made the most of it. In 1897, the year of Queen Victoria's Diamond Jubilee, the third Conference met. There were no less then eleven self-governing colonies, including the Australian States, represented, and imperial preference was again debated.

This was never a question of imperial free trade, for the colonies themselves, each with its tariff system, would have none of it. The idea was that Britain should erect tariffs against foreign imports, thus making possible a reciprocal modification of protection within the Empire. A fourth Conference was held in 1902 and agreed to meet every four years; but it should be noted that the possibility of a federation, or even any permanent organisation, was never a practical proposition. Canada in particular opposed the very suggestion, and was determined to set up its own navy, a line Australia was soon to follow. On the other hand, Canada argued strongly for imperial preference. Chamberlain failed to convince his own Government and in 1903 resigned to conduct a free-lance agitation for the cause. He failed to win the country to it, and the spectre of 'dear food', which was implicit in imperial preference, helped to defeat his Party in 1906. In the next Conference of 1907, the Liberal Government recorded its dissent from the principle and thereafter the exchanges were mainly concerned with matters of defence. While the proposal that there should be some sort of central Commission was rejected by Canada in 1907, the British Government set up a separate Dominions Department of the Colonial Office.

The Empire contributed its full quota of support in the First World War. South Africa showed some internal dissension in the matter, as, to a minor extent, did Canada, but General Botha, with the support of General Smuts, rallied his country behind Britain. When the Imperial War Conference, whose representatives also sat in the Imperial War Cabinet, met in 1917, the principle of imperial preference was affirmed, this time unanimously.

The war added to the territorial scope of the Empire as a whole. The Union of South Africa acquired German colonies, as did Australia and New Zealand in the Pacific, while there were also mandated territories in Africa and the Near East which came under Britain's tutelage. At Versailles the Dominions signed the peace treaties as Britain's full equals and became independent members of the League of Nations, ready to express policies differing markedly from those of Britain.

The Imperial Economic Conference which met in 1923 pledged

all its members to imperial preference, but the Conservative Party then suffered electoral defeat on this issue. It was returned to power again in 1924, and the gradual implementation of the policy was started in 1925. In 1924 the Dominions Department became the Dominions Office, under its own Secretary of State, and in 1926 the Imperial Conference stated categorically that Britain and the Dominions were autonomous countries within the Empire, completely independent in regard to both their domestic and external affairs.

Developments in one of the Dominions suggested that even the now tenuous bond of Empire might be found too onerous by some members. The unity achieved in South Africa between Botha's and Smuts's parties was broken in 1924, when the Nationalist Party came to power under its new leader, General Hertzog. There was little warmth towards Britain and the old explosive factor was still all too evident, for the Nationalist Party's approach to the native question was through segregation, including the defranchisement of the natives in the Cape.

Among the colonies still lacking Dominion status, and chafing under British control, India was far and away the greatest and most difficult case. The Liberal Government had passed the Indian Councils Act (1909), which provided for the appointment of Indian representatives to the Councils of the Secretary of State and Viceroy and the provincial Councils. While the First World War was in progress, the Government declared its intention to give India responsible government, and in 1919 the Government of India Act set up a bicameral legislature, but the executive power remained with the Viceroy and his Executive Council. Nationalist feeling found an unofficial vent through the Congress Party and, perhaps more effectively, through Gandhi, who preached non-co-operation and then mass civil disobedience and became a symbol of India's aspirations. There was a growing division, however, between the Hindus and the Moslems, the latter working through the Moslem League. The idea of a separate State of Pakistan was already in the air. In 1935 Burma, which had been linked with India, as an administrative convenience, was detached from it and given its own Constitution.

So far as the white Dominions were concerned, there were still some legal anachronisms in the imperial relationship, and in 1930 the Imperial Conference recommended legislation to eliminate them. The recommendation was given effect in the Statute of Westminster (1931). This put beyond question in law, what was already true in practice, the recognition of the Dominions as sovereign States. In 1931 Britain finally abandoned free trade, and an Imperial Conference meeting in Ottawa in the following year established a system of imperial preference.

The Second World War was a severe test of the Dominions' attachment, but, to the surprise of some observers, they promptly joined in on Britain's side, although there was a strong section of opinion in South Africa which opposed this course. In 1933 Smuts and Hertzog had formed a coalition Government and fused their parties into one United Party, but on the question of entering the war there was a split. Smuts, who advocated support of Britain, won the struggle, carrying Parliament with him, and became Prime Minister.

There could be little doubt that the war would greatly accelerate the process of devolution, if not separation, which had been a feature of British policy, even if Winston Churchill protested that he had not become Prime Minister in order to preside over the liquidation of the Empire. The declaration of good intentions towards the underdeveloped territories in the Colonial Development and Welfare Act (1940), reasserted at the end of the war, could not assuage the hunger for independence. In 1947 the Labour Government not merely agreed that India should become independent, but set a time-limit of eighteen months for this undertaking to be given effect. In fact, it was achieved in the same year. One of the biggest problems was the bitterness of the differences between the spokesmen of Hindus and Moslems. By a judgment of Solomon, it was decreed that India and Pakistan should be separated, although the operation involved much shedding of blood. India chose to become from the outset a Republic, the first within the Empire to do so, and Pakistan followed its example later. Ceylon became independent in 1948, as did Burma, which elected to leave the Commonwealth. In the same momentous year the Federation of Malaya was formed, comprising the nine Malay protectorates and the settlements of Penang and Malacca; and in 1957 it was accorded full sovereignty within the Commonwealth. In 1963 it was enlarged by the inclusion of Singapore, North Borneo, Sarawak — where the Brooke family had abdicated their century-old dominion in 1946 — and Brunei. A ten-year period of gestation saw the birth of a West Indian Federation in 1958, which, however, soon disintegrated with the secession of Jamaica.

Tropical Africa was a complex of territories and races whose path to autonomy was bound, in the natural course of events, to present many hazards, demanding slow and careful guidance. It had been under British dominion for little more than the space of a lifetime, and there had not been time, even if there had been the will, for the phased evolution towards self-government which Britain had always favoured. Indirect rule, admirable as it was in many respects, was a form of administration by remote control, not a preparation for the assumption of power by its subjects. Yet the agitation of the nationalists would not tolerate delay; the gradual approach must be replaced by a short cut. The number of educated Africans was few, and those who graduated to politics were thus invested with a prestige among their countrymen which conferred extraordinary influence.

This was well shown in the case of the Gold Coast. A Constitution of a comparatively liberal character was introduced in 1946, but, although it was soon improved on, it was no more than a stop-gap to the nationalist leader Nkrumah and his Convention People's Party. In 1957 the Gold Coast became Ghana, independent but with a Constitution reflecting British conceptions of democracy adjusted to African circumstances. In 1960 it was replaced by a Republican, one-party form of government.

Nigeria took a more deliberate course and in 1960 became an independent Federation. In 1961 Sierra Leone became independent. East Africa was less advanced, but there too events followed the same pattern. Tanganyika became independent in 1961, Uganda in 1962, and Kenya emerged from the struggle with Mau Mau terrorism as a sovereign state in 1963. In Central Africa the Federation of Rhodesia and Nyasaland was effected in 1953, but broke up ten years later when Northern Rhodesia became Zambia and Nyasaland Malawi, leaving Southern Rhodesia still to work out, under the supervision of the British Government, the explosive question of how the transition from white supremacy to majority rule was to be effected. In 1965 the Government of Southern Rhodesia evaded the issue, and in effect repudiated the conception of colonial evolution on which British policy was based, by unilaterally declaring its independence of British tutelage. This action created a crisis between the countries and dramatically heightened racial tensions within the Commonwealth.

12   Foreign Policy

(1) BALANCE OF POWER

IT is a profound mistake, which is liable dangerously to distort current views on Britain's relationship with the Continent, to believe that each has traditionally regarded the other as alien, with little or no community of interest. On the contrary, she has always been deeply involved in Continental affairs, both diplomatically, militarily and economically, although to a fluctuating degree. England, as distinct from Scotland, had for centuries asserted rights in Europe, and the dynastic ties with the House of Orange and later with the Hanoverians strengthened this attitude. Throughout the eighteenth century, France was her chief antagonist, partly because France threatened to dominate Europe and partly because French possessions overseas were an obstacle to the expansion of Britain's Empire. The climax came with the long-drawn-out 'French Wars'; in these Britain played a dominating part — she was the instigator and the inspiration of the coalition which finally defeated Napoleon, and she had a correspondingly important role in the making of peace.

As an island nation whose strength and scope for development lay in overseas trade Britain had built up her navy to the point where, after the French and Spanish defeat at Trafalgar, she was undisputed mistress of the seven seas. Her army was not outstandingly massive or efficient, compared with those of other countries; but, thanks to her sea power, she could deploy her forces swiftly and effectively in any corner of the globe where her interests were threatened, and as a trading nation her interests were world-wide. Her acquisitions from the post-war settlement were relatively modest, but they were of immense importance strategically. She was rich compared with continental powers, not in natural resources, although these were substantial, but in the exploitation of her potential at home and abroad. She had other intangible assets. She was immensely strong in the stability of her government and the unity of her people. Certainly she was far from being a democracy but she came closer to it than any other nation in Europe, and was thereby the more sympathetic to the liberal impulses which were to convulse Europe in the nineteenth century. Finally, as was natural with a régime which was throwing up new political and economic philosophies, she produced, as well as thrusting entrepreneurs, statesmen, who for all their shortcomings, were more realistic than most of their contemporaries in their appreciation of events. Realism is sometimes interpreted as a kind of shortsightedness, producing policies of expediency. Britain had her share of such thinking in the nineteenth century, and in the twentieth; but the tenor of British foreign policy, at least in the fifty years following Waterloo, when Britain was at the zenith of her diplomatic power, suggests that it was generally conducted, sometimes with wisdom, almost always with an intelligent regard for Britain's long-term interest, spiced from time to time with a more than perfunctory consideration for the well-being of Europe at large.

This is not to be unctuous about the country's foreign policy; the simple and fundamental fact was that it was in Britain's own interest to have peace. She needed no more territory and indeed, in the early nineteenth century, was undergoing a period of disillusionment about imperialism as such. On the other hand, she wished to develop her industry and trade, and the Empire offered benefits as well as burdens in this regard. It was plainly to her advantage for the promotion of her prosperity as a trading nation to have world peace and free access to sources and markets. The formula for securing this desirable state of affairs was the 'balance of power'. It had become fashionable in the eighteenth century but was, in fact, very old and elementary. On the continent of Europe equilibrium was to be maintained between the differing

States so that no one could be supreme or a threat to the rest. This was patently easier of achievement when, as for most of the nineteenth century, the main concentration of world power was in Europe and was there divided between a few nations.

The menace to Europe in general and to Britain in particular had been for over a century, and still remained, France. As a fomenter of revolution and an insatiable aggressor she had kept Europe in turmoil continuously for over twenty years. Britain had been at war with her off and on for over a century and had profited largely from the contest, gaining the bulk of her possessions in Canada and the East. Smarting from her losses, France might recover to renew her long campaign for the hegemony of Europe and to regain her lost possessions beyond the seas. She stood uncomfortably close to England across the Channel. On these and other grounds her containment was a first priority.

Italy in 1815 was merely a collection of States, with one, Piedmont, forging to the front, but the paramount influence there was Austria. The Austro-Hungarian Empire was vast: a hybrid aggregation of races, almost impregnable, as it might seem on the map, but a prey to internal stresses and strains which might rend her asunder unless nationalism could be curbed. Nationalism was one of the great forces at work in the nineteenth century, encouraged by the desire to escape oppression and to secure free institutions, which governments intent on unity at all costs and fearful of liberalism as such dared not give voluntarily.

Russia had been edging into Europe since Peter the Great built his 'window on the Baltic' — St. Petersburg, now Leningrad. She had made large encroachments at the expense of her Western neighbour, Poland — in collaboration with Prussia and Austria, who shared in the spoil — and southwards to the Black Sea at the expense of the ramshackle Turkish Empire. Her more far-seeing rulers had long realised that, if she were to attain the status of a true world power, she must have intercourse with the West and outlets for her latent and still untapped energy, including a geographical outlet through the Bosporus into the warm waters of the Mediterranean or perhaps in the Persian Gulf. She therefore represented a possible threat to British trading communications.

She was of enormous size, with a despotic Government, and was looked at askance by Western Europe, partly because her very bulk inspired apprehension, partly because of her ambitions, and partly because she was something of an enigma. She was deemed to be Asiatic rather than European, and hardly a natural member of the family of Western nations, but the French Wars had forced her into an uneasy alliance with the West and she was therefore accepted as a partner in making and keeping the peace.

Finally there was Prussia, which had since the time of Frederick the Great, or earlier, been building herself up, both militarily and territorially, with substantial gains from Austria and Poland. She was still, however, only the foremost of the German States and her ambitions lay primarily in Germany.

Perhaps there is no department of State activity which is more influenced by the prejudices of particular ministers than foreign policy; nevertheless it is possible to detect, against this background, certain themes in Britain's relations with her neighbours.

The Foreign Secretary in the immediate post-war years was Castlereagh. Despite his detractors — and they were and are many and vicious — both Britain and Europe were fortunate that he held office in this period. Certainly he was a pragmatist, and none the worse for that, since Europe, thrown into disarray by the whirlwind of revolutionary doctrine and Napoleonic conquest, had to be reconstructed, without any well-defined precedents to guide the builders. His first concern was that the foundations should be solid and enduring; his aim, he said, was not to collect trophies but to bring back the world to peaceful habits. The materials he favoured were often old-fashioned, and in this Castlereagh no doubt revealed his own political sympathies as well as the mood of his Government. The tides of nationalism and liberalism were rising in Europe and were to find their only means of expression in revolution; but revolution was a fearful word to Castlereagh and his contemporaries, the more so because of the French Revolution and its long and bloody aftermath. In any case, Castlereagh, like his Cabinet colleagues, was suspicious of 'liberalism' and it was only grudgingly and for fear of worse that Parliament relaxed the oligarchy under which Britain had operated since 1688. They were equally suspicious of nationalism, where it had appeared to threaten the unity of their own country, as in Ireland. Besides, a Foreign Secretary must perforce work with foreigners, and Castlereagh's European counterparts to a man (including Frenchmen) were utterly convinced that the well-worn — often out-worn — accoutrements of government were still the best. The sacred word was 'legitimism', the restoration of the *anciens régimes*. How else could the Tsar, although curiously impregnated with a tincture of liberalism, or Metternich as the representative of the Habsburg Empire, have thought? For them nationalism was synonymous with fragmentation, and liberalism with anarchy; and the rulers of Prussia were of the same mind. So tyranny was reinstated in Italy, Spain and Portugal, and even in France, which was all the harder to bear because of the comparatively enlightened systems they displaced.

There was a latent contradiction here. Britain's was a constitutional parliamentary system and she was proud, perhaps overproud, of it. She knew that evolution is a condition of survival. How long could she continue to work in harmony with the autocrats of Austria, Prussia and Russia? This was not a moral issue. Britain's attitude to post-war challenges was bound to be at variance with that of the others. This fact was to become all too apparent very soon. Castlereagh had shown great tact and shrewdness in forging the Grand Alliance which succeeded in toppling Napoleon from his pedestal. For the rest of his short life he devoted himself, single-mindedly and dispassionately, to the exclusion of other considerations, to the task of shaping a system, of which Britain would be a part, to keep the peace. Co-operation between the Great Powers was the keystone of his design, with reasonable regard to the susceptibilities of the smaller States. The responsibility and the authority would, however, be vested in Britain, Austria, Russia and Prussia. He worked assiduously, therefore, towards a new conception of international relations by which, even before the war was ended, these four pledged themselves to maintain the peace. They agreed not merely to guarantee the settlement, but to consult regularly 'for the consideration of the measures which at each of these periods should be considered the most salutary for the repose and prosperity of Nations and for the maintenance of the Peace of Europe'. It was not a grandiose conception, like the Holy Alliance, founded on Christian principles, advocated by the Tsar; it was merely a system of 'summit conferences'. Yet it was a recognition of the principle of collective security and, as such, an advance in international thinking.

As for the settlement itself, the first essential was to ensure the proper balance, with such checks for the future as seemed necessary. France was therefore treated with magnanimity, and soon admitted to the Concert of Europe.

The settlement seemed even to contemporaries and much more to those equipped with hindsight a cynical disregard of popular aspirations. In fact, in many cases these were yet no more than embryonic, the cause of uneasy stirrings from time to time. It has been denounced as a surrender to 'power politics'; and the cession of the Duchy of Warsaw to Russia, the restoration of Austrian dominance in Italy, the absorption by Prussia of part of Saxony, the enforced unification of Belgium and Holland, and so on, was nothing less, although Britain successfully resisted other extreme demands. Castlereagh and the statesmen of his time took 'power politics' for granted, and the end, to ensure a proper balance and safeguard it by a complex of checks, was held to justify the means.

Revolutions in Spain, Italy and Portugal quickly threatened the principle of 'legitimism', and Castlereagh proclaimed, with little effect, the doctrine of non-intervention in the internal affairs of the other States — a doctrine which was to be repeated time and again on Britain's behalf. Then arose an issue pregnant with even greater hazards for future international collaboration and one which was to bedevil international diplomacy for the rest of the century. This was the future of Turkey, the so-called Eastern Question. It posed a dilemma for all the Western Powers, not least Britain. The Turkish Empire sprawled its decaying limbs across south-eastern Europe and the Middle East, and so covered Britain's trading routes to the wealthiest part of her Empire. It must at all costs be protected. At the same time, it had been a cardinal feature of Russian policy to develop southwards at the cost of Turkey and to secure entry into the Mediterranean. Further,

Russia had a special interest, formally acknowledged by Turkey, in the protection of the latter's countless Christian subjects. France, too, had for centuries maintained close relations with Turkey and she also claimed to be a guardian of Christian interests in the Holy Land. Austria was bound to be concerned with the Balkans. Finally, a rebellion of Christians against Moslems, such as occurred in Greece in 1821, could be regarded as a Crusade, as well as an eruption of liberalism against despotism.

Canning, who succeeded Castlereagh in 1822, more accurately reflected the prevailing British temper. He was less internationally-minded; he wished 'for Europe now and then to read England'. He was also less committed to the *status quo* and warned that 'those who have checked improvement because it is innovation will one day or another be compelled to accept innovation when it has ceased to be improvement'. He reiterated the doctrine of non-intervention in regard to Spain where, paradoxically, France, which had not so long ago lit the fires of revolution, now wished to quench the flames. Britain's protests were ignored and a French force restored despotism. Canning had a brilliant revenge and one very much in accord with Britain's particular interests. He took the initiative in resisting the plan to force Spain's American colonies, which had broken away, back into their former allegiance. Britain had her purely selfish motives; she wished to build up her already lucrative trade with the South American countries, and in 1824, to the disgust of some of his British colleagues as well as of the king, Canning gave formal recognition to the South American Republics. In a resounding phrase he declared that 'he called the New World into existence to redress the balance of the old'.

The paramount consideration for Britain in regard to Turkey was that Russia must be contained; this should be done, if possible, by agreement — Russia was not the kind of power to be coerced easily — but the issues for Britain were deemed so important that force could not be ruled out. Increasingly, account had also to be taken of public opinion at home, which was deeply imbued with religious and political antipathies and recked little of strategic matters. When the Eastern Question flared up again, therefore, it was agreed between Britain and Russia, and confirmed by the Treaty of London (1827), to which France also was party, that a settlement should be imposed on the contestants by these Powers. The approach and the method were in accord with the diplomatic thinking of the times. The formula in this case was severely practical, and evaded, so far as possible, the larger problems of Turkey's future. Turkish sovereignty over Greece was to continue, but Greece was accorded a measure of autonomy. Like all succeeding attempts to deal with the Eastern Question, this was an essay in procrastination.

In the same year, after a brief spell as Prime Minister, Canning died. As Foreign Secretary he had, interpreting correctly the mood of his country, adopted a more insular policy than that of his predecessor, savouring and taking full advantage of the differences in outlook which existed between Britain and her European allies. He saw Britain's position as 'one of neutrality, not only between contending nations but between contending principles', from which she could hold those nations in a state of equipoise. In taking this stand, he set an example which most of his successors were happy to follow. The danger was that such neutrality might go so far as to suggest that Britain was no longer interested in Europe, beyond making diplomatic utterances.

The sequel to the Treaty of London was dramatic but, having regard to the make-up of Turkey, not surprising. The Sultan, reinforced by his nominal vassal, Mehemet Ali of Egypt, objected to its terms and showed fight. The outcome, which neither Britain nor France had sought or anticipated, was the destruction of the Turco-Egyptian fleet by the combined French and British squadrons in the battle of Navarino (1827). There followed a brief and, for Turkey, an inglorious war with Russia, ending with Russia dictating the Treaty of Adrianople; but finally, under pressure from Britain and Austria, the small but wholly independent monarchy of Greece emerged.

Nearer home, another facet in the long-term evolution of British foreign policy was highlighted. In 1830 the enforced and artificial union of Belgium and Holland split; both as a revolution and as an infraction of the peace settlement, this was a matter of great moment to all the Powers, but especially to Britain and to France,

where the July Revolution had enthroned Louis-Philippe. He was
bound, for reasons of personal and national prestige, to play a part,
but he could not afford, as a *bourgeois* king distasteful to the hereditary monarchs of Europe, to alienate Britain. Lord Aberdeen
arranged a conference of the Five Powers in London to settle the
affair and at this point was succeeded by Palmerston. Palmerston
made no secret of his views, then or afterwards: France in general
was to be distrusted, and above all must be kept out of Belgium.
Finally, after recriminations and many set-backs, Belgium was
established as an independent nation with, as in the case of Greece,
a German princeling for its king, and a guarantee of its neutrality
from the Five Powers. This guarantee was the treaty to be dismissed by the German Chancellor in 1914 as a 'scrap of paper'.

Palmerston showed in this affair both the strength and the weakness which stamped his long dominance of British foreign policy.
He had inherited the suspicion of France, and was to demonstrate
it time and again, but his deliberate neglect of the subtleties of
successful diplomacy needlessly exacerbated national sensitivities
here, as elsewhere. He believed not merely in showing the flag but
in brandishing it in other people's faces. He was determined that
Britain should assert herself in Europe and rightly recognised that
she must negotiate from strength, but he was apt to confuse strength
with belligerence. This was a kind of diplomacy which rested
entirely on British prestige. So long as Britain's right to interfere
and her willingness to exercise it were accepted, such displays
might suffice.

Again like his predecessors and successors, although he was
suspicious of France he was even more suspicious of the Eastern
Powers and particularly Russia; because, apart from purely diplomatic considerations, he was sympathetic to liberalism and
nationalism abroad. There was nothing really new in his policy;
what was new was his technique, which upset his fellow ministers
and his monarch almost as much as it annoyed foreign statesmen,
but his very 'John Bull-ishness' appealed enormously to the public
at home.

Once again the Eastern Question forced itself on Europe. The
Sultan of Turkey, now assailed by his former coadjutor, Mehemet

Ali, in 1831 appealed to Britain for help and Britain ignored the plea. Turkey in desperation went straight into the arms of Russia. The upshot was the Treaty of Unkiar-Skelessi (1833), which, to the dismay of Britain and of the rest of Europe, seemed to turn Turkey into a Russian satellite. Whatever Palmerston's views on the viability of Turkey had been hitherto, this denouement convinced him finally that Turkey had to be saved from herself, and, more especially, from Russia, and that the situation could be retrieved only by a resumption of co-operation with the latter. This would inevitably precipitate a rupture with France, then nursing a liaison with Mehemet Ali in furtherance of her own designs, but Palmerston was not unduly perturbed by this possibility. It suited the Tsar Nicholas to have an understanding with Britain, for he detested Louis-Philippe and relished the idea of estranging the two countries. After all, an alliance between them might conceivably be directed against his own country — as indeed happened in due course. Besides, he had come to the conclusion that Turkey might be taken, as Palmerston put it, rather 'by sap than by storm'.

A renewal of the war between the Sultan and Mehemet Ali in 1839 gave the opportunity for a new initiative. Britain, with Russia, Austria and Prussia — but not with France, which had her reservations and so was by-passed — forced Mehemet Ali to disgorge his Turkish gains; and finally the Five Powers — for France belatedly jumped on the bandwagon — restored the *status quo*, with the Bosporus closed to all foreign warships while Turkey was at peace (1841). The Russian route to the Mediterranean was once again blocked and Britain was almost irrevocably committed to propping up the Turkish Empire.

Needless to say, this did not dispose of the underlying tension. Russia reverted to the idea of carving up Turkey and began to build up Sevastopol as a naval base. Any chance of *rapprochement* between Britain and France seemed more remote than ever, and it seemed to be finally destroyed with the unpleasant incident of the 'Spanish marriages'. Not the least unsavoury feature of this sordid episode was that it left Prussia and Austria free to gobble up all that remained of Poland, the Republic of Cracow. The omens for Franco-British friendship were worsened by the accession to

power of Louis-Napoleon. His very name and his assumption of
the imperial title in 1852 were ominous reminders of the past, as
for France they were meant to be.

Events were, however, unexpectedly to draw Britain and France
into a short-lived partnership. Turkey had once again failed to use
the respite given to her in 1841 to put her house in order, and there
were suggestions that she should be partitioned. Russia was genuinely perturbed at this time by Napoleon III's pretensions in the
Near East. Such ambitions had marked France's foreign policy
since the first Napoleon, but they fitted in extremely well with
the new Emperor's views. He renewed France's claim to guardian-
ship of the Holy Places, thus inviting a conflict with Russia, and
Turkey's acceptance of the claim and its rejection of Russia's
counter-claim sparked off an explosion.

The British Cabinet was weakly led by the Prime Minister,
Lord Aberdeen, but opinion was bound in any case to be divided.
Palmerston, then Home Secretary, and others saw in this the
Russian menace, and public opinion, disgusted by Russia's action
in helping to crush revolution in Hungary (1849), was behind them.
Not for the first or last time, Britain, at a vital juncture, let matters
drift, but when Russia invaded the Danubian Principalities, once
again British and French squadrons patrolled the Eastern Mediterranean and once again what was intended to be a deterrent action
'escalated'. War broke out between Russia and Turkey, and the
latter's fleet was destroyed at Sinope in the Black Sea; but both
parties showed themselves impervious to suggestions of a truce
and Britain had to make up her mind quickly. Britain and France
sent Russia an ultimatum, backed up by the threat of their joint
fleet before Sevastopol, and, when Russia inevitably rejected
negotiation under such duress, they formally allied themselves with
Turkey and the Crimean War began (1854). It was a war which
no one had wanted or anticipated, but it once again served notice
on Russia that Britain would oppose her entry into the Mediterranean over the body of Turkey. It also showed that Britain's
organisation for war was by no means as efficient for the times as
had been generally believed.

The nominal *casus belli* was dealt with in the peace by making the European Powers, including Turkey, and not just Russia, the guardian of the Principalities and of Turkish Christian subjects. The fate of the Principalities was symptomatic of the trend in the Balkans; the two came together to form a semi-independent unit, still officially subject to Turkey, and called Rumania.

The year 1848 had been one of revolutions against established régimes. One had been in Italy and, like the rest, it had failed in its purpose. Nevertheless the germ of liberalism remained and Piedmont was to be its forcing ground. The problem was how to get rid of Austrian tutelage. France was Austria's ancient rival in Italy, and Napoleon, like his famous uncle, saw here the opportunity to support liberalism and win prestige and territory for France, all at the same time. He and Count Cavour of Piedmont came to an understanding in the matter and the brief Franco-Austrian war ensued in 1859, ending with the Truce of Villafranca.

Palmerston was sympathetic to the idea of Italian liberation from oppression and in this he had the powerful support of Gladstone and others, and of the great body of public opinion, though not of Queen Victoria. On the other hand, he thoroughly disapproved of the acquisition by Napoleon III, through the Peace, of Nice and Savoy. 'The whole drift of our policy', he wrote in 1861, 'is to prevent France from realising her vast schemes of expansion and aggression.' When Garibaldi attacked and overthrew the Bourbons in the south, Britain, although by no means unenthusiastic about Italian unification, made a stand for non-intervention which cost her nothing and gained her Italian goodwill. In the event, the unification of Italy achieved, in another way, one of her basic aims, the establishment of a barrier to French ambitions in the peninsula.

Hitherto, in British eyes the menace to European peace had come from France and Russia. In 1862 Bismarck became Minister-President of Prussia and a new phase of expansion in that quarter began. He quickly showed his hand over the twin Duchies of Schleswig-Holstein, long linked with Denmark. A problem of succession there had been settled by the Five Powers by the Treaty of London (1852), but Prussia would not let such a trifle stand in the way of her aspirations. She coveted the Duchies and dynastic squabbles following the death of Frederick VII of Denmark gave her her opportunity. Britain was very much interested, for Edward, Prince of Wales, in 1863 married Princess Alexandra of Denmark. Palmerston followed his stock method of making warning noises directed against outside interference; but this time the method did not work. Prussia, jointly with Austria, occupied the Duchies, and presented Palmerston with a *fait accompli*. Palmerston shrank from recourse to war as he had shrunk in 1863 when, despite his protests, Russia had subjugated a Polish rebellion. There was little likelihood at this time of co-operation between Britain and France, and Bismarck was always ready to exploit and enlarge the differences already existing between them, as part of his long-term policy. In any event, intervention would have meant a war against the combination of Austria and Prussia, possibly allied with Russia, for Prussia had gone out of her way to show friendliness to Russia in the affair of Poland. The fact was that against Prussian technique bluster served no purpose, and in any case Britain failed to appreciate that Prussia was again on the march. In the short, sharp Austro-Prussian war of 1866 Prussia finally achieved the ambition she had long entertained of driving Austria out of Germany. Indirectly, the war also lost Austria her last Italian foothold, Venetia. Prussia then, in 1870, led Germany against France, beat her to her knees, and seized Alsace-Lorraine, and in 1871 proclaimed the German Empire. Britain had attempted conciliation between the parties, but not in any determined fashion and not because of any sympathy with France. Gladstone had insisted that the neutrality of Belgium should be respected, but in this matter he was, with reason, even more suspicious of French than of Prussian ambitions.

Even if Britain had had the will, she had not the means to compel a withdrawal on the combatants. She had an army — on paper — of perhaps 100,000 men, while Germany could muster close on half a million. True, Edward Cardwell, Gladstone's Secretary for War from 1868 to 1874, was working miracles of reform in the Army, in face of military conservatism and aristocratic reaction, and he was helped by the shock to public opinion of the Franco-Prussian War. He transformed its organisation and increased its size, and this on the shoe-string budget on which his leader insisted. The Navy, to which at this juncture the French Navy was the nearest rival, fared rather better, since even the Admiralty had, grudgingly, to recognise the transition from wood and sail to iron and steam; but here, too, progress was slow and haphazard, partly because of administrative ineptitude, partly because of Governmental parsimony. Ships and especially artillery had an inbuilt obsolescence, because of the rate of technical advance, which demanded heavy and recurrent expenditure, and this was anathema to the economically-minded Gladstone. It took his resignation, and the creation of a new direct tax, death-duties, to allow of a serious programme of replacement and expansion in the 1890s.

To the major Powers was now added a kingdom of Italy and a German Empire and, young and virile as they were, they were not likely to be quiescent. Italy for the time being had quite enough to do welding herself into a proper unit, but Germany had all the makings, not only of an aggressive military nation, but of an equally aggressive industrial State. The 'take-over' by Prussia of the rest of Germany permitted, as in a business enterprise, a co-ordination and central direction, which, taking into account the German character, was bound to force Germany into the foreground of the industrial Powers. In both capacities, she was also almost bound to be a rival of Britain, especially if, as a corollary of industrial expansion, she began to think in terms of Empire and naval prestige. The only real question was whether she would be a friendly rival. Britain was slow to realise that the balance of power in Europe had been transformed and that France, for the first time in two centuries, was no longer the force she had been on the Continent. Bismarck, the arch-statesman of the new Germany, systematically did his best to delay realisation.

Britain was even less concerned than she would have been a decade or so earlier. It was true, and plain to see, that she had no dependable allies in Europe, but she had no desire for such. The long process of disassociation from the Continent, which had started in Castlereagh's time, and had been given new impetus by the Crimean War, was now reaching its farthest point, for, apart from the diminished interest in Europe, she was now becoming increasingly preoccupied in other parts of the world. Hitherto she had tended to regard her Empire as at best a useful adjunct, at worst a positive embarrassment, involving a degree of responsibility out of proportion to the corresponding advantage. Disraeli had become an ardent imperialist and, as was natural to one of his race and temperament, he looked to the East. India was the brightest jewel in the Imperial Crown and the policy of safeguarding and improving the routes to it must be continued and strengthened. This did nothing to assuage Britain's traditional suspicions of Russia.

Like Palmerston, Disraeli would have liked spectacular successes achieved through adroitness, with which he was richly equipped, rather than through force. On the other hand he lacked Palmerston's liberal sympathies. In 1875 he brought off a *coup*, although it was not recognised as such by his colleagues at the time, by the purchase, entirely on his own initiative, of a 44% interest in the Suez Canal. This cost £4 million, and the finance had to be provided privately by the Rothschilds. It was a shrewd and splendid investment, since from the date of the Canal's opening in 1869, over three-quarters of the traffic passing through it was Britain's. This committed Britain even more deeply to participation in Middle East affairs, and to the support of Turkey. Disraeli accepted it as the price of Empire. In this he differed radically from Gladstone, who would have happily written off Turkey as an offence to liberalism and to Christianity.

In 1875–6 the Balkans were aflame, as the embers of nationalism burned more fiercely. Russia, no doubt encouraged by the vociferousness of anti-Turkish sentiments in Britain, declared war on Turkey. As on previous occasions, when the 'crunch' came there were divided opinions in Britain as regards the comparative merits, or, perhaps better, the demerits of the contestants, but the usual collapse of Turkey stimulated the usual anti-Russian revulsion, together with an outburst of 'jingoism'.

The Treaty of San Stefano (1878) between Russia and Turkey practically eliminated the latter from Europe, and both Britain and Austria refused to accept it. Once again the issue was referred to a Congress of the Powers, which produced the Treaty of Berlin. The Balkans were recarved to prevent Russia from establishing a sphere of influence, but the resulting fragmentation created an area of friction and of weakness which not only Austria and Russia, but also Germany, could exploit to their own advantage. Austria was given control — not outright possession — of Bosnia-Herzo-govina and thus was embroiled to a greater extent than ever before in Balkan politics; shows she was almost certain to run foul of the new Serbia, which had ethnic claims in Bosnia-Herzogovina, and also of Russia. Britain took over Cyprus, ostensibly to help her fulfil her guarantees to Turkey in Asia. This was the settlement which Disraeli dubbed 'Peace with Honour', a description which another Prime Minister sixty years later was to apply to another Treaty with even less appositeness.

Bismarck dominated European politics until his fall in 1890. The central motif of his complex diplomacy was to isolate France. It was not very difficult for him to keep Britain at loggerheads with her; the two continued to squabble, as they had done in the past, in the Middle East, particularly Egypt.

It looked more likely that Britain would find a *modus vivendi* with Germany, and there were statesmen on both sides who desired this. The stumbling-block was Germany's insistence, both under Bismarck and afterwards, that an alliance between them should be directed against France, whereas Britain was more concerned at this stage with the Russian threat in the Far East. Britain made overtures in 1898 and 1901 for an understanding with Germany, but these proved abortive, mainly because each country had different interests, Germany being preoccupied with France, while Britain was concerned with Russian encroachments in China.

The Continental Powers were divided into two camps: Germany, Austria and Italy united in the Triple Alliance on the one hand, and Russia and France in the Dual Alliance on the other. As regards the Middle East, a new complication had been introduced, for Germany was now insinuating herself into Turkish affairs, in furtherance of her own commercial and imperial ambitions, and displacing Britain as the patron of that distressful nation. In that capacity she must also be regarded as an obstacle by Russia.

It was the Boer War (1899–1902) which forcibly brought home to Britain that her position of 'splendid isolation' could and did mean simply a total lack of friends. The growing divisions between Britain and Germany, however, had positive causes. It was not a matter of economic rivalry; each was a very substantial trading customer of the other. The trouble lay elsewhere. Kaiser Wilhelm II not only aroused Britain's suspicions by proclaiming his desire for the extension of German influence in Turkey and the Middle East, by infiltration through a network of railways (the Berlin–Baghdad line); he challenged Britain in the sphere where she was most sensitive and where she would not brook a rival — that of maritime supremacy. With the German Navy Law of 1898, Germany officially declared her intentions.

In 1902 Britain found an ally in an unexpected quarter. Japan had been forging ahead fast since the mid-fifties, when she had been compelled, like China, to open her frontiers to traders from the Occident. Britain's alliance with Japan had a European angle, since it was inspired by her apprehensions about Russian designs on China and the threat to the British market there. Russia had occupied Manchuria in 1900 and was now facing Japan, and it was the impending conflict between them that prompted France, which was allied with Russia, to seek Britain's friendship.

The death of Queen Victoria (1901) facilitated, although it was not responsible for, a reappraisal of British foreign policy and Edward VII's visit to France in 1903 at least served to create a friendlier public opinion on both sides of the Channel. In the following year the *Entente Cordiale* was confirmed; among other provisions it included secret recognition of the British position in Egypt and French claims to Morocco.

Here was what the Kaiser might well take as an affront, for not only were Germany and France acting as allies, whereas it had been Germany's policy to keep them apart, but they were doing so in disregard of Germany's views on a specific issue. Even Italy had been placated by recognition of her claims to Tripoli, but Germany's belated imperial pretensions were simply ignored.

Germany, accordingly, and using her well-tried tactics, made minatory gestures which the German General Staff was quite prepared to translate into full-blooded action. It was a propitious moment for such a move, for Russia, the bogy of Germany and the ally of France, had been devastatingly defeated by Japan in 1905. It was a delicate situation, for Russia was also the bogy of Britain, and the ridiculous Dogger Bank episode (1904), when the Russian Baltic fleet on the way to its débâcle in the Far East had mistakenly fired on British trawlers in the North Sea, had nearly precipitated open rupture. So the Kaiser went in his yacht to Tangier to announce that Morocco must be free and Germany's rights there respected.

In the event, the Kaiser miscalculated Britain's reaction — not for the last time — for the incident served to bring Britain and France closer together. It was not that Britain had any desire to break with Germany; on the contrary, she had made and kept on making sporadic efforts to come to an understanding with her. At the same time the British Government was by no means won over to the idea of an alliance with France, but the Foreign Secretary, Sir Edward Grey, without the Cabinet's authority, but with the foreknowledge of some of his colleagues, including the Prime Minister, Sir Henry Campbell-Bannerman, authorised the initiation of military consultations with France in 1906. There were also conversations with the Belgian General Staff, with particular reference to a possible German attack through that country, a contingency which was in fact an integral part of the military Schlieffen Plan adopted formally by Germany in the previous year.

In practice, therefore, although not officially, an understanding with France was well on the way to becoming a firm alliance. The British Admiralty, under Sir John Fisher, was authorised to accelerate its programme of construction, as a counterpoise to growing German strength. Now came the most remarkable volte-face of all in the realignment of the Powers. Russia, following the pattern of France, and disheartened by her defeat at Japan's hands, went far to disarming British suspicions by joining in a Convention in 1907, which disposed of the issues between them in Afghanistan,

Tibet and Persia. This was an unpopular *détente* in Britain; the Tsar had just crushed, in bloody fashion, a popular revolution in his own country. From the point of view of Britain's long-term policy, however, it was a considerable achievement. It meant that Russia, already stopped in the East by Japan, was now also blocked in the Persian Gulf. Her only chance of access to the much-desired warm-water port was in the Mediterranean. Here she could still entertain hopes, for the Turkish Empire was beyond redemption, and Russia, posing as the champion of 'pan-Slavism', could exploit the explosive forces of nationalism to her own ends. She was now, however, faced not only by Austria but by Austria's close ally, Germany.

In spite of tensions elsewhere, the Balkans remained the powder-magazine of Europe, with all the great Powers involved to a hitherto unprecedented degree. Austria in 1908 annexed Bosnia-Herzo-govina, in flagrant breach of treaty, and without the prior know-ledge even of Germany. This was a grievous blow to the up-and-coming Serbia, which had hoped to incorporate these territories into a larger union. It was also a sore insult to Russia. Germany, whatever her misgivings, backed up Austria in menacing fashion and Russia had to give way. In the following year Germany and Austria concluded a military pact by which the former undertook to support the latter, in the event of Russian intervention in an Austro-Serbian war.

Yet another Morocco crisis occurred in 1911, when Germany sent a gunboat to Agadir in protest against French military action in protection of the Sultan's — and her own — interests. It also blew over, largely because Britain stood by France; but the chain reaction was setting in. Italy took advantage of the affair to seize Tripoli, Rhodes and the Dodecanese Islands from Turkey. The four Balkan states — Bulgaria, Serbia, Greece and Montenegro — with Russia's connivance, now renewed in concert the attack which was designed to complete the final dismemberment of Turkey in Europe (1912). This might suit Russia; it certainly did not suit Austria, whose integrity and ambitions might be jeopardised if Balkan nationalism went unchecked. Neither did it suit Germany, whose own designs would be thwarted by a strong Balkan bloc.

Sir Edward Grey sought to keep things within bounds through the usual medium of a conference, which was held in London (1912–13). Round-table discussions might reconcile the interests of the Great Powers, but they could no longer repress the bounding and conflicting ambitions of the Balkan Powers themselves. The Second Balkan War broke out in 1913. From it Serbia emerged more powerful and ambitious than ever, to the fury of Austria. Yet the near-certainty of an open quarrel between the two did not dismay Germany; it is clear that the German General Staff, which was in control, was more than prepared for such an eventuality. It would have preferred Britain to remain neutral when it came, but this was not regarded as a decisive consideration.

Once again Britain, this time through Winston Churchill, First Lord of the Admiralty, proposed to Germany a 'Naval Holiday'; the Kaiser dismissed the approach as 'mere humbug'. As with France previously, so now with Russia, Britain entered into naval conversations, which Germany denounced as part of a deliberate policy for her own encirclement.

Britain remained reluctant to transmute the understandings with France or Russia into full-bodied alliances; there were many in Government circles who remained distrustful of both and would have preferred friendship with Germany. Events, not diplomacy, were to decide the issue. In June 1914 Archduke Francis Ferdinand, heir to the Austrian throne, was assassinated at Sarajevo. Neither Austria nor Germany would accept anything less than the humiliation of Serbia and dismissed the idea of an international conference. Serbia rejected an ultimatum from Austria and the latter declared war; Russia mobilised her army; Germany demanded Russian demobilisation in the most uncompromising terms and, when this was not forthcoming, declared war on Russia. She then demanded a passage through Belgium for her army and when this was refused, she invaded that country. Britain had no option but to take up the gauntlet and declare war on Germany. It was the beginning of the First World War and the official closure of an era in British foreign policy, although the portents had been apparent for the past thirty years.

(2) BRITAIN UNDER STRAIN

From the ruins of the First World War emerged a new Europe. Out of the debris of former governments and empires new nations were constructed and old ones rebuilt. Russia, Austria-Hungary, Germany and Turkey had collapsed under the external and internal stresses, and the victorious Powers in the peace settlement had again to face the task of reshaping national boundaries, this time with due and perhaps over-much regard for 'self-determination'.

Germany was naturally expected to make restitution. Alsace-Lorraine reverted to France; the Rhineland was occupied; the coal-mines of the Saar were transferred for fifteen years to France as some recompense for the damage she had sustained at German hands; and German colonies were confiscated, to be administered under mandate, mainly by Britain and France. Finally, heavy financial reparations were to be exacted from her.

Poland was re-created as an independent State, regaining lost possessions from Germany — including the Polish corridor, separating East Prussia from the rest of Germany, with Danzig declared an international city — and from Austria. Hungary was broken off from the old Habsburg Empire, as was the new Czechoslovakia. Italy and Rumania, too, shared in the spoils. Germany, Austria, Hungary and Bulgaria had strict limitations imposed on their military strength; this was to be the prelude to general disarmament.

There was an impressive array of new or enlarged States. Particular mention should be made of Yugoslavia, the old Serbia writ large. Turkey was, in effect, to be written off, and its Arab colonies, including Palestine, were taken over in trust by Britain and France.

There was also established a system of international government, the League of Nations, Article X of which bound the signatory Powers 'to respect and preserve as against external aggression the territorial integrity and existing political independence of all members'. The wording was somewhat reminiscent of the Holy Alliance.

The non-participation of the United States meant that it was essentially a European organisation, although Japan was a member;

it was regarded as such by the non-European members, and notably by the British Dominions. Russia was also outside it.

Britain's gains from the war were exiguous — indeed, almost unreal — in relation to the magnitude of her effort and her losses. She had been impelled to fight Germany, in the first instance, because of the clash over sea-power. German sea-power was now destroyed — her fleet had been scuttled in Scapa Flow — but the stark fact remained that the era of Britain's sea-supremacy was over. The Dominions still relied on her for sea-defence and she could not escape her commitments in the Far East, because of her interests in India and beyond. The attenuation of her resources, however, and the rise of other naval Powers made it impossible for her to exert a decisive influence alone. This was quickly recognised in 1922 when, under the Washington Agreement, she accepted naval parity with the United States, with Japan not far behind; the ratios were 5:5:3. Under pressure from the United States and her own Dominions she also broke off her alliance with Japan, and undertook not to build up her naval bases in the Far East, except for Singapore.

The balance of power in Europe nevertheless remained a guiding principle, but here too she was powerless to enforce it except in co-operation with others, as indeed had always been the case. She could to this end either operate through the League of Nations — and clearly a great responsibility devolved on her to make its concept, to which she had contributed so much, a reality — or she could resort to a policy of expediency, operating through alliances with like-minded nations.

The sad reality from Britain's point of view was that the war had debilitated her to an extent which left her at best only marginally a first-class power. Her strength derived from commerce, and even before the war she was being strongly challenged in this department by other States. The war itself had inflicted enormous losses on her both in man-power and in material resources. In the fight for existence she not only had been forced to neglect peace-time functions, thus creating opportunities of which other countries were not slow to take advantage, but she also had had to dispose of much of her investments overseas to pay for war material. She could no longer sustain the burdens she had been able, if not always willing, to carry before 1914.

The links with her Empire had been stretched until the Dominions could properly claim independent representation at the peace conferences and could assert their separate interest in regard to preservation of peace. There were stirrings in her colonial dependencies, notably India. In the immediate post-war period Ireland, too, was a great distraction.

There was nothing inherently new in this picture; it was only that the lines were more clearly etched. Yet it was a situation the implications of which Britain herself was reluctant to accept and some of her allies slow to understand.

The classic elements in her foreign policy were still the same as before. Russia was again the bogy. She had undergone a great revolution in 1917, and had defected from the ranks of the Allies. Her internal workings were if anything more mysterious than they had been before and this invested her with an aura of fearfulness. There was now an additional cause for suspicion; the Government was Communist and openly proclaimed its mission to propagate the gospel throughout the capitalist world, to its eventual destruction. The country was, however, greatly weakened as a result of the war and the Revolution, and was reckoned by Britain and others to be of comparatively little military significance. Russia, for her part, above all wanted peace in which to rebuild. She was profoundly sceptical of the good intentions of the West, as the West was of hers, and sought to secure her frontiers by direct alliances. She quickly, therefore, came to an understanding with Germany, which was an ill omen for Poland.

Ironically and tragically, a good deal of friction developed between Britain and France in the post-war era. France had been dreadfully mauled by Germany for the second time in half a century, and she could ill afford the ruinous sacrifice of men and resources, for, in terms both of population and industry, she had lagged behind Britain and Germany. It was natural in these circumstances that she should insist on security, in particular against German aggression. Britain, on the other hand, while anxious to preserve peace, did not long retain any marked animus to Germany;

indeed, the view quickly gained strength in political circles that Germany had been harshly treated at Versailles, and Germany did her best to encourage this attitude.

Almost from the start, therefore, Britain and France had differing approaches to international relations. Britain was much readier to make modifications of the peace treaties in favour of Germany; the burden of reparations was scaled down until by 1932 it was virtually eliminated. Britain would have written off entirely the debts owed to her by Germany and other European Powers if the United States had done half as much for her, but the United States refused. Russia had already repudiated her debts to Britain and France. In the outcome Germany paid, and could afford to pay, only a tithe of the amounts originally prescribed, and that largely by means of borrowing. France was so incensed by German evasion of her reparations that she invaded the Ruhr in 1923, an action which evoked no sympathy in Britain.

Britain, in fact, passionately wanted peace but would go to great lengths to avoid the use of force to compel it. After the war she underwent the usual revulsion against European entanglements and tended to concentrate on what she regarded as her own business. The Dominions, too, were downright opposed to any policy which might involve them afresh in European quarrels.

These considerations and others dictated Britain's attitude to the League of Nations. The net effect was that, as after 1815, she evinced a preference for a system of balances in Europe and beyond rather than for an international agency committing all its members, in theory, to a common course of action against an aggressor.

Lloyd George, returned as Prime Minister in the General Election of 1918, was for all practical purposes in charge of foreign affairs during the four years remaining to him of effective political life, with Balfour and then Lord Curzon Foreign Secretaries. His Coalition Government broke up in 1922 and it was perhaps significant that one of the reasons for his unpopularity with the Conservatives, who overthrew him, was his determined stand against a resurgent Turkey's threat to Greece. The Conservative Government, first under Bonar Law and then under Baldwin, was replaced in 1924 by a short-lived Labour Administration, headed by Ramsay MacDonald. He, like most of his party, was a convinced internationalist, and one of his first actions was to resume diplomatic relations with Russia. His main aim was to inject greater life into the League of Nations, whose prestige had already suffered when it permitted, by default, the bombardment of Corfu (1923) by the new Italian dictator, Mussolini. He welcomed the Geneva Protocol of that year, by which war between member-states was outlawed and arbitration in disputes was made mandatory under threat of sanctions against an offender.

The Conservatives returned to power in the same year, and the new Foreign Secretary, Austen Chamberlain, lost no time in disowning the Geneva Protocol, mainly because of its implication that force could be used, which was particularly repugnant to the Dominions. On the other hand, he appreciated that positive and specific safeguards were needed to assuage French misgivings. The result was the Locarno Pact (1925) by which, among other things, Britain joined with Italy, France and Germany in guaranteeing Franco-German and Belgo-German frontiers. It was noteworthy that the Dominions and India were not party to the Pact and also that it was left to France to promise assistance against German aggression to Poland and Czechoslovakia. The various treaties helped to relax tension by creating 'a most effective and formidable looking scarecrow'. In 1926 Germany was admitted to the League and in the same year renewed her understanding with Russia, which was still outside it.

The international climate seemed to be improving. The Kellogg Pact (1928–9), ultimately signed even by the U.S.S.R. and the U.S.A., renounced wars of aggression, and in 1929 the French Foreign Minister, Briand, floated the idea of 'a United States of Europe'; but there was no progress in general disarmament. In 1929 the Conservative Government fell, and with it a Foreign Secretary who was far more European-minded than his Cabinet or Party. Labour returned to office, with Arthur Henderson as Foreign Secretary, and Britain restored diplomatic relations with Russia[1]. She also made a gesture to Germany, which France en-

---

[1] They had been broken off by the previous Government, after the Arcos affair.

dorsed, by instigating the withdrawal of the Allied forces of occupation from the Rhineland, five years in advance of the prescribed date. Briand coined the word 'appeasement', then lacking the derogatory connotation it acquired later.

The deterioration in international relations which marked the thirties derived from frictions inherent in the post-war situation, but it was precipitated by one factor more than any other, namely, the terrible industrial depression which, starting in the United States, rapidly overwhelmed Europe. Its onset unseated the Labour Government in 1931, and promoted the formation of a National Government, which was predominantly Conservative. The Foreign Secretary was Sir John Simon, a man of brilliant intellect but narrow vision. The depression aggravated Britain's economic inadequacies and made her Government even more anxious to avoid dissipating her resources in hazardous adventures. A dramatic illustration of her difficulties was provided by a mutiny in the Fleet (1931).

It was no accident that Japan should choose this juncture for her invasion of Manchuria. Effective action by Britain against Japan would have been difficult as well as dangerous, unless the other Western Power in that area, the United States, was also prepared to risk war by imposing sanctions, which she was not. The United States even refused to be associated with the Lytton Commission of Investigation, which was the League's response to China's appeal for help. By the time the Commission reported, Japan had established her puppet State of Manchukuo (1932), and her retort to the strictures of the Commission was to resign from the League.

Britain continued to profess allegiance to the League, but attached less and less importance to it, while France's faith in collective security, never very strong, was shaken. The 'Manchurian Incident' had demonstrated that Britain was unable to protect her own interests in the Far East, still less those of the League; it brought Japan into open enmity; it increased the coolness between Britain and the United States; and, worst of all, it encouraged other would-be aggressors.

In 1933 Hitler, the product of the economic and political miasma into which Germany had descended, took over as Chancellor and in 1934 he became President. He fully appreciated, as had earlier German leaders, that France was the arch-enemy, and that Franco-British collaboration would be the main obstacle to German ambitions. In 1935, with great acumen, he concluded a Naval Agreement with Britain which disarmed British suspicions while, at the same time, allowing him to concentrate on his main objective, the build-up of his land forces: He was little concerned with the platitudious exchanges of Britain, Italy and France at their Stresa Conference earlier in the year.

In 1935 Germany annexed the Saar, and France drew closer to Russia, now in the League, and to Italy. This *rapprochement* was used by Hitler as an excuse for remilitarisation of the Rhineland (1936). It was a 'try-on', and a successful one, and it dealt French prestige a damaging blow. It was, of course, also a triumph for *machtpolitik*. Many observers believed that the occasion had offered the last chance of stopping the Nazi programme without involvement in all-out war.[1] Britain herself had announced in 1935 her intention of rearming and Hitler reacted by reintroducing conscription.

The precedents set by Japan and Germany were not lost on Mussolini. In threatening Abyssinia he also threatened British interests in the Mediterranean and the Middle East but, on the other hand, Britain was unwilling to forfeit Italian friendship, and so was France. The Government was faced with a public — and this was largely the Government's own fault — which was ignorant of the realities of the situation and, while pro-League in sentiment, was also pacifist to the point of weakness. The same was true of the Labour Opposition. When the Italian attack on Abyssinia was launched in 1935, Britain successfully advocated a policy of sanctions through the League, but this was half-heartedly applied; oil was not included. The British Foreign Secretary, Sir Samuel Hoare, agreed with Laval, his French opposite number, that part of Abyssinia should be ceded to Italy, but the public outcry forced the resignation of Hoare and Anthony Eden replaced him. In 1936 Abyssinia collapsed.

[1] Cf. A. J. P. Taylor, *English History 1914–1945*, pp. 387–8.

Again Britain had refused to face realities; but it should be remembered in her defence that the realities were grim and that she got little support even in her half-measures. Yet again her interference only strengthened the hostility of the aggressor; Italy turned to Germany — collusion between the two Dictators was in any case natural — and in 1937 joined her and Japan in their Anti-Comintern Pact against Russia, and abandoned the League.

The harsh lesson was being taught that, as Litvinov, the Russian Foreign Minister said, 'peace is indivisible', but the lesson was not yet complete. In 1936 the Spanish Civil War broke out. The Axis Powers, Germany and Italy, made little secret of their predilection and gave active support to General Franco, while Russia and France were sympathetic to the Republican Government, and Britain proclaimed her traditional policy of non-intervention in domestic conflicts. The policy, however, was little more than a façade, behind which other, bolder Powers tried out their military strength.

The British Prime Minister, Neville Chamberlain, was still determined to restore friendly relations with Italy, while Anthony Eden was equally insistent that Britain at least should not appear to condone the designs of the Axis Powers, and ultimately resigned in protest against his Government's attitude. The U.S.S.R., whose earlier fervour for collective security had been viewed with strong reservations in British quarters, was now clearly disposed to resort to other means to safeguard her own interests.

It was in this atmosphere of general disillusionment and cynicism that Germany proceeded to deal the final hammer-blows to the ramshackle structure of international organisation, in Austria and Czechoslovakia. The British Government was certainly becoming wary of German declarations but does not seem to have appreciated the extent of Hitler's ambitions or the audacity with which he would pursue them. Chamberlain was still confident of his own ability to find common ground with the Dictators and so avert the war he greatly feared. He distrusted Russia and was impatient of French nervousness.

In 1938 Hitler used the alleged oppression of German subjects in Austria as an excuse for an ultimatum and quickly brought about the *Anschluss* by which Austria was brought within the German Reich. Hitler then turned against Czechoslovakia on the same grounds. Chamberlain called this 'a quarrel in a far-away country between people of whom we know nothing', and the British Dominions felt the same way. Britain refused to take any positive action of her own or to back up France's somewhat diffident protests. Instead, the British Government put pressure on Czechoslovakia to make a sacrifice for peace and France was ready to be persuaded to acquiesce. Chamberlain thrice visited Hitler in September 1938 and brought back from the third meeting in Munich what he called, after Disraeli, 'Peace with Honour'. Winston Churchill took a different view: 'The Government', he said, 'had to choose between shame and war. They chose shame and will get war.' It was all of no avail except perhaps to give Britain time in which to accelerate her rearmament. In 1939 Hitler swallowed up what little had been left of Czechoslovakia and turned east against Poland, which also had a German minority. Britain finally committed herself: she gave a guarantee against aggression to Poland, which was already allied with France. Undoubtedly Hitler believed, and no doubt with justification, that Britain would not go to war over the issue of Poland, but he cautiously made a pact with Russia in August 1939, which envisaged the repartition of Polish territory between them. He then sent his armies against Poland and Britain declared war on Germany on 3 September 1939. The Second World War had begun.

Britain had never thought of herself as simply, or even mainly, a European Power. In Canning's time she had 'brought in the New World to redress the balance of the Old', with an eye on her own global interests, and, with the same motives, had struck up an alliance with Japan at the beginning of the twentieth century. The independence of her Dominions alone would have compelled her, and did compel her between the World Wars, to put her foreign policy in a world-wide context; and the strength of the United States, as exerted during and after the first war, was a potent influence in her diplomacy. After 1945, Europe, war-ravaged and poverty-stricken, was dependent as never before on American help for its resuscitation. Britain herself was drained of resources, at home and abroad, and was faced now with a struggle for economic survival.

Even so, the same basic motives that had dictated her foreign policy before the second war were still at work after it. Russia had been an ally, but the common war-effort had not eliminated the mutual distrust. Russia's ambitions in Europe continued to be a cause of deep concern, including her search for a Mediterranean outlet. She might achieve these, not through conquest but, more easily, having regard to the breakdown of Germany and the weakness of France, by an extension of the Communist bloc. She still apparently entertained her aspirations in the Persian Gulf area, and she had again resumed a cherished role in the Far East, abandoned as a result of her defeat in 1904–5 by Japan. She could be kept in check only with the help of the United States, and Winston Churchill had, even before the war ended, tried to alert that country to the danger, in vain. So the sphere of Russian influence moved westwards in Europe, engulfing a large part of Germany, the traditional bastion against it.

Britain was more than ever driven, by events and by her own weakness, to seek ways of preserving peace, without further attrition of the frontiers of Western Europe. She must to this end ensure the support of the Commonwealth, but especially of the United States, the only single nation powerful enough to act as a counterpoise to the U.S.S.R. The United States was intensely concerned with Western Europe as an obstacle to Communist expansion; some of the newly-independent Commonwealth States, like India, were at best lukewarm, inclining towards what became known as 'a policy of non-alignment'.

It quickly became apparent that the hopes of international cooperation embodied in 1945 in the Charter of the United Nations — the organisation to replace the League — were not to be realised. Russia, under Stalin, proceeded to erect an 'iron curtain' between herself and her satellites, including Poland, Hungary, Rumania, Yugoslavia, Bulgaria and Albania, constituting an Eastern Communist bloc, and, on the other side, the Western democratic Powers. The partition of Berlin was a symbol of this barrier. International relations became the battle-ground for a 'cold war' of conflicting ideologies and ambitions. A Communist 'take-over' in Czecho-slovakia in 1948 and the creation of the 'People's Republic' in China in 1949, tilted the balance further against the West and made it inevitable that Britain would be drawn into the American orbit. At the same time she was bound in the cause of defence to maintain an association with likeminded countries in Europe; the only question was how close the association should be.

If Western Europe achieved some sort of unity, it could rank as a 'third world force', both economically and militarily speaking. Most British politicians, however, were not enamoured of the concept of a European union, and Winston Churchill's support of it did nothing to recommend it to the Labour Government which took office in 1945, nor did American pressure in the same direc-tion. It was true that the Labour Party had always professed sup-port for federalism, but 'federalism in the British Labour Move-ment, like socialism, has generally been a flexible need, splendidly evocative, but practically circumspect'.[1] Both Labour and Con-servative Governments in the post-war years were equally reluc-tant to merge the national identity in a supra-national structure, even in such a limited agency as the European Coal and Steel Community, set up in 1951, and much more in a complete customs-union (the European Economic Community), envisaging a measure of political integration, such as other nations accepted by the Treaty of Rome (1957).

Britain, therefore, followed her usual policy of compromise. In 1949 she helped to set up the North Atlantic Treaty Organisation (NATO), which embraced, in addition to herself and France, Italy, Norway, Denmark, Iceland, Portugal and the Benelux countries (Belgium, Holland and Luxembourg), along with the United States and Canada, for their mutual defence. Later, West Germany, Greece and Turkey were enrolled. She also joined in 1954 a similar grouping, the South-East Asia Treaty Organisation (SEATO), which included the United States, France, Australia, New Zealand and Pakistan. In those groupings the United States was dominant, by virtue of her strength, and Britain leant heavily on her. This did not prevent divergencies of policy. The most

[1] F. S. Northedge, *British Foreign Policy, 1945–1961*, p. 136.

disastrous of those, for Britain, concerned the Suez Canal. In 1954 Britain had abandoned her military base there, in deference to Egyptian nationalism, and in 1956 President Nasser nationalised the Canal. Britain and France, already alarmed by the increasing influence of Russia in the Middle East, and believing that their vital interests were threatened by this unilateral action, sent troops to take and occupy the Canal Zone. This action aroused so much hostility, and markedly from the United States, that there had to be an ignominious withdrawal. The Atlantic Alliance has survived this and other less critical differences of approach mainly because Britain has perforce recognised that the maintenance of her own security, as well as the fulfilment of obligations still remaining to her in other parts of the world, involve a burden quite beyond her individual capacity to sustain.

Further Reading

GENERAL

The standard work is the *Oxford History of England*, the relevant volumes being J. Steven Watson, *The Reign of George III, 1760–1815* (1960); E. L. Woodward, *The Age of Reform, 1815–1870* (1962); R. C. K. Ensor, *England 1870–1910* (1936); and A. J. P. Taylor, *English History 1914–1945* (1965). G. D. H. Cole and R. Postgate, *The Common People, 1746–1946* (1946), is a wide-ranging and readable narrative. É. Halévy, *A History of the English People in the Nineteenth Century*, running to six volumes (paperback edition, 1961) is an illuminating interpretation of that age, to which D. Thomson, *England in the Nineteenth Century* (1950), is an attractive introduction. Asa Briggs, *The Age of Improvement, 1783–1867* (1959), is packed with information, while the latter part of the period is the subject of H. M. Pelling, *Modern Britain, 1885–1955* (1960); A. V. Havighurst, *Twentieth Century Britain* (1962), and D. Thomson, *England in the Twentieth Century* (1964). For the nineteen-twenties and nineteen-thirties, much the best book is C. L. Mowat, *Britain Between the Wars* (1955). Scotland has not been well served; J. Pryde, *Scotland from 1603 to the Present Day* (1962) is a somewhat colourless chronicle.

For modern social and economic history, the bible remains J. H. Clapham's three-volume *History of Modern Britain* (1924–38). P. Deane and W. A. Cole, *British Economic Growth, 1688–1959* (1964), is necessarily selective but admirable within its limits. W. H. B. Court, *A Concise Economic History of England* (1958), is perhaps the best general textbook, and Jones and Pool, *A Hundred Years of Economic Development* (1940), commencing at 1840, is a reliable source of facts and figures, as is S. G. Checkland, *The Rise of Industrial Society in England, 1815-1885* (1964). Part III of E. Lipson, *The Growth of English Society* (1954), is a skilful synthesis of a great deal of knowledge, and L. C. A. Knowles, *Industrial and Commercial Revolutions in Great Britain during the Nineteenth Century* (1933), a scholarly assessment of the chief factors in the changing economy. For the latter part of the period, the student should refer to W. Ashworth, *An Economic History of England, 1870-1935* (1960), A. W. Lewis, *An Economic Survey, 1919-1939* (1949) and S. Pollard, *The Development of the British Economy, 1914-1950* (1962).

Basic information, including contemporary material, can be found in W. H. B. Court, *British Economic History, 1870-1914: Commentary and Documents* (1965); J. F. C. Harrison, *Society and Politics in England, 1780-1960* (1965); B. R. Mitchell, *Abstract of British Historical Statistics* (1962); and D. Butler and J. Freeman, *British Political Facts 1900-1960* (1963).

THE EXPANSION OF INDUSTRY

T. S. Ashton, *Industrial Revolution, 1760-1830* (1948), is a brilliant short study, which should be supplemented by M. W. Flinn, *Origins of the Industrial Revolution* (1966) and by P. Deane, *The First Industrial Revolution* (1965), covering the period 1750-1850. J. D. Chambers, *The Workshop of the World* (1961), is a brief but illuminating economic history from 1820 to 1880. Industrial expansion in Scotland is treated in H. Hamilton, *The Industrial Revolution in Scotland* (1932); R. H. Campbell, *Scotland since 1707* (1965); and W. H. Marwick, *Economic Developments in Victorian Scotland* (1936). The classic account of agricultural development is by Lord Ernle, *English Farming Past and Present* (1961); and there is also a *History of British Agriculture, 1846-1914* (1964), by C. S. Orwin and E. H.

Whetham. The social implications of industrialisation are brought out in L. G. Johnston, *The Social Evolution of Industrial Britain* (1959); E. P. Thomson, *The Making of the English Working Class* (1963); and B. L. Hutchins and A. Harrison, *A History of Factory Legislation* (1926).

POPULATION

The best guide to the study of population is in the increasingly elaborate decennial Census Reports. *The Report of the Royal Commission on the Distribution of the Industrial Population* (1940) and *The Report of the Royal Commission on Population* (1949) set the position in historical perspective. G. Kitson Clark, in chapter iii of his *Making of Victorian England* (1962), makes a critical assessment of the various theories of growth, and a summing-up of the latest state of knowledge is found in D. V. Glass and D. E. C. Eversley (eds.), *Population in History* (1965). Scotland's special problems are examined in A. M. Struthers (ed.), *Scotland's Changing Population* (Scottish Council of Social Service, 1948), and J. G. Kyd (ed.), *Scottish Population Statistics* (Scottish History Society, 43, 1952).

THE BEGINNINGS OF REFORM
and
THE TRIUMPH OF FREE TRADE

These aspects are dealt with extensively, as an integral part of the history of the times, in a number of the authorities already listed. The constitutional factors can be studied separately in D. L. Keir, *A Constitutional History of Modern Britain* (1938); K. B. Smellie, *A Hundred Years of English Government* (1950); and Sir Ivor Jennings, *Party Politics* (1961). The best explanation of the Parliamentary system before and after the first Reform Act is in N. Gash, *Politics in the Age of Peel* (1953); and D. G. Southgate, *The Passing of the Whigs* (1962), throws light on the period 1832–86. A valuable article, quoted in the text, is G. Bartlett Brebner, '*Laissez-faire* and State Intervention in Nineteenth Century Britain', reprinted in E. M. Carus Wilson (ed.), *Essays in Economic History*, iii (1962). The significance of international trade is considered in A. L. Bowlay, *England's Foreign Trade in the Nineteenth Century* (1905); A. M. Imlah, *Economic Elements in the Pax Britannica* (1958); and J. H. Richardson, *British Economic Foreign Policy* (1936).

THE FINANCIAL STRUCTURE

The growth of investment at home and overseas is described in J. F. Rees, *A Short Fiscal and Financial History of England, 1815–1918* (1952); W. O. Henderson, *Britain and Industrial Europe, 1750–1850* (1954); and A. K. Cairncross, *Home and Foreign Investment, 1870–1913* (1953); and the development of financial institutions in J. H. Clapham, *The Bank of England: A History* (1944); W. F. Crick and J. E. Wadsworth, *A Hundred Years of Joint Stock Banking* (1936); and A. W. Keir, *History of Banking in Scotland* (ed. Allan, 1926). Two articles by H. A. Shannon, entitled 'The Coming of General Limited Liability' and 'The Limited Companies of 1866–1883' are reprinted in E. M. Carus Wilson (ed.), *Essays in Economic History*, i (1954).

THE DEVELOPMENT OF TRANSPORT

The most comprehensive history is W. T. Jackman, *The Development of Transportation in Modern England* (2 vols., 1962). There is a short sketch by C. I. Savage, *An Economic History of Transport* (1961); and a more concentrated study by C. E. R. Sherrington,

A Hundred Years of Inland Transport, 1830–1933 (1934). L. C. A. Knowles, *Industrial and Commercial Revolutions* (1933), already listed, assesses the economic and social repercussions. There is an interesting article by H. Pollins, 'Railway Contractors and Finance of Railway Development in Britain' (*Journal of Transport History*, iii. 1, and 2, 1957–8), and one by A. J. Quin-Harkins on 'Imperial Airways, 1924–40', in the same periodical (i. 4, 1954).

THE GROWTH OF SOCIALISM
and
TOWARDS A PLANNED ECONOMY

The best survey of socialist and trade-union development is G. D. H. Cole, *A Short History of the British Working-Class Movement, 1789–1907* (1948), which, on the political side, can be supplemented by the same author's *History of the Labour Party from 1914* (1948). H. M. Pelling has written *A Short History of the Labour Party* (1961), as well as *The Origins of the Labour Party, 1880–1900* (1954). M. Beer, *A History of British Socialism* (1929), gives a clear account, and G. Dangerfield, *The Strange Death of Liberal England* (1961), is stimulating. Section x of H. A. Clegg, A. Fox and A. F. Thomson, *A History of British Trade Unions since 1889* (1964), gives a good picture of politics in a crucial period, 1900–10. The transition in industrial organisation and State policy is described in J. H. Dunning and C. J. Thomas, *British Industry: Change and Development in the Twentieth Century* (1961).

INDUSTRIAL RELATIONS

S. and B. Webb, *A History of Trade Unionism* (1956 edn.), retains its pre-eminence, despite some errors. The first volume of an exhaustive history since 1889 by Clegg, Fox and Thomson has been noted above. A. Bullock, *The Life and Times of Ernest Bevin* (vol. i, 1960), covers the period 1881 to 1940. The *Industrial Relations Handbook*, issued by H.M. Stationery Office, is a succinct work of reference; a fuller account is given in A. Flanders and H. A. Clegg, *The System of Industrial Relations in Great Britain* (1954); and the historical relationship between the Government and the trade-union movement is traced in D. F. Macdonald, *The State and the Trade Unions* (1960). Trade-union law can be followed in R. Y. Hedges and A. Winterbottom, *The Legal History of Trade Unionism* (1930). A serious gap has been well filled by S. Pollard, *The Genesis of Modern Management* (1965).

THE IRISH QUESTION

The problem of Ireland bulked so large in the politics of the period that it is dealt with adequately in most of the standard histories. There is a good sketch in J. C. Beckett, *A Short History of Ireland* (1958), and the issues are well brought out in N. Mansergh, *The Irish Question, 1840–1921* (1965). J. L. Hammond has written on *Gladstone and the Irish Nation* (1938), while the background is described in J. E. Pomfret, *The Struggle for the Land in Ireland, 1800–1923* (1903).

BRITAIN AND THE EMPIRE

The last three volumes of the Cambridge History of the British Empire bring the general history up to 1919. J. A. Williamson, *A Short History of British Expansion* (vol. ii, 1947), compresses a vast amount of information into comparatively short compass, and A. L. Burt, *The Evolution of the British Empire and Commonwealth from the American Revolution* (1956), is a careful and impartial account, less successful in the treatment of British domestic politics. L. C. A.

Knowles, *Economic Development of the Overseas Empire* (1928), is a searching analysis of economic factors, and for a summary of historial interpretations there is a collection of essays, edited by G. H. Nadel and P. Curtis, entitled *Imperialism and Colonialism* (1964). C. E. Carrington, *The Liquidation of the British Empire* (1961), and M. Perham, *The Colonial Reckoning* (1961), review the influences in the break-up of the Empire. An article by R. Pares, 'Economic Factors in the History of the Empire' is reprinted in E. M. Carus Wilson (ed.), *Essays in Economic History*, i (1954).

FOREIGN POLICY

Temperley and Penson, *Foundations of British Foreign Policy from Pitt to Salisbury* (1938), gives a scholarly selection of documents, and J. Joll (ed.), *Britain and Europe: Pitt to Churchill, 1783–1940* (1950), is a more modest compendium of contemporary sources. A. B. Keith (ed.), *Speeches and Documents on International Affairs* (1938), refers to the period 1918–37. There are two booklets published by the Historical Association dealing with the background to the two World Wars, the first by B. E. Schmitt, *The Origins of the First World War* (1958), and the other by W. N. Medlicott, *The Coming of War in 1939* (1963). For the nineteenth century, there is R. W. Seton Watson, *Britain in Europe, 1789–1914* (1938), and for the twentieth M. R. D. Foot, *British Foreign Policy since 1896* (1948), P. A. Reynolds, *British Foreign Policy in the Inter-War Years* (1954), and an excellent survey by F. S. Northedge, *British Foreign Policy, 1905–1961* (1962).

List of Dates

ECONOMIC AND SOCIAL

1776   Publication of Adam Smith, *An Inquiry into the Nature and Causes of the Wealth of Nations.*

1781   Steam-engine with rotary movement patented by James Watt.

1785   The first effective power-loom patented by Edmund Cartwright.

1798   Publication of Thomas Malthus, *Essay on the Principle of Population.*

1799   Income tax introduced by William Pitt.

1799–1800   The Combination Acts.

1801   First Census of Population.

1802   Health and Morals of Apprentices Act.

1807   Prohibition of slave trade.

1813–14   Repeal of the Statute of Labour (1563).

1815   Corn Law.

1824–5   Repeal of Combination Acts.

1825   Opening of Stockton–Darlington Railway; repeal of 'Bubble' Act.

1829   Establishment of Metropolitan Police.

1833   First effective Factory Act.

1834   Poor Law Amendment Act.

1835   Municipal Corporations Act.

1838   Anti-Corn-Law League founded; 'People's Charter' proclaimed.

1840 Introduction of penny post.

1844 Bank Charter Act; Factory Act; establishment of co-operative Rochdale Pioneers; Cheap Trains Act.

1846 Potato blight in Ireland; repeal of Corn Laws.

1847 Ten Hours Factory Act.

1848 Public Health Act.

1851 Amalgamated Society of Engineers formed.

1855 Civil Service Commission established.

1856 Henry Bessemer's converter steel process; Joint Stock Companies Act (Limited Liability).

1863 Co-operative Wholesale Society founded.

1866 William Siemens's open-hearth steel process.

1867 Royal Commission on Trade Unions appointed; *Hornby* v. *Close* judgment.

1868 First regular Trades Union Congress.

1896 Opening of Suez Canal.

1870 Education Act, creating local School Boards with power to levy rates for elementary education; competitive examination for entry to Civil Service.

1871 Trade Union Act; Criminal Law Amendment Act; University Tests Act.

1875 Conspiracy and Protection of Property Act; Employers and Workmen Act.

1876 Trade Union Amendment Act.

1879 Gilchrist–Thomas steel process.

1880 Employers' Liability Act.

1881 (Social) Democratic Federation founded.

1884 Fabian Society established.

1887 Tea-Porters' and General Labourers' Union formed by Ben Tillett.

1889 London Dock Strike; publication of first instalment of Charles Booth, *Life and Labour of the People of London.*

1896 Conciliation Act.

1901 Taff Vale judgment; Seebohm Rowntree publishes *Poverty: A Study of Town Life* (York).

1905 Unemployed Workmen Act.

1906   Trade Disputes Act; Workmen's Compensation Act.

1908   Old Age Pensions Act; Coal Mines Regulation Act.

1909   Osborne judgment; Labour Exchanges Act; Trade Boards Act.

1911   National Insurance Act.

1912   Coal Mines (Minimum Wage) Act; *Daily Herald* founded.

1913   Trade Union Act.

1914   Triple Alliance.

1916   Ministry of Labour established.

1917   Whitley Committee Reports; formation of Federation of British Industries.

1919   Ministry of Transport established; Industrial Courts Act; Sankey Coal Commission Report.

1920   Amalgamated Engineering Union formed.

1921   Safeguarding of Industries Act.

1922   Transport and General Workers' Union formed.

1924   Imperial Airways Corporation established.

1925   Return to Gold Standard.

1926   General Strike; Central Electricity Board created; Imperial Chemical Industries formed.

1927   Trade Disputes and Trade Union Act.

1928   Mond–Turner discussions on industrial relations.

1929   Unilever and Lancashire Cotton Corporation formed.

1931   Gold Standard abandoned.

1932   Import Duties Act imposes tariff on wide range of manufactures; Ottawa Agreements.

1934   Special Areas (Development and Improvement) Act; Unemployment Act.

1940   (Barlow) Report of the Royal Commission on the Distribution of the Industrial Population.

1942   Beveridge Report on Social Insurance.

1945   Distribution of Industry Act.

1946   Nationalisation of Bank of England, coal industry, civil aviation and communications; National Health Service and National Insurance Acts; repeal of Trade Disputes and Trade Union Act.

1947   Nationalisation of public (and some private) transport and electricity supply; Ministry of Economic Affairs established.

1948   Nationalisation of gas supply; Monopolies and Restrictive Practices Act.

1949   Iron and Steel Act for nationalisation of the industry.

1953   Iron and steel industry and road haulage denationalised.

1956   Restrictive Trade Practices Act.

1962   National Economic Development Council; National Incomes Commission.

1965   Appointment of Royal Commission on Trade Unions and Employers' Associations; Prices and Incomes Board set up.

POLITICAL AND CONSTITUTIONAL

1783   First Pitt Administration.

1800   Act of Union with Ireland.

1801   Addington Administration.

1804   Second Pitt Administration.

1806   Death of Pitt; Grenville Administration.

1807   Portland Administration.

1809   Perceval Administration.

1812   Liverpool Administration.

1816   Spa Fields Riot.

1819   'Peterloo Massacre' and the Six Acts.

1820   Accession of George IV.

1827   Canning Administration; Goderich Administration.

1828   Wellington Administration; repeal of Test and Corporation Acts.

1829   Catholic Emancipation Act.

1830   Accession of William IV; Grey Administration.

1832   First Reform Act.

1834   First Melbourne Administration; first Peel Administration and Tamworth Manifesto.

1835   Second Melbourne Administration.

1837   Accession of Queen Victoria.

1841   Second Peel Administration.

1846   First Russell Administration.

1852   First Derby Administration; Aberdeen Administration.

1854   Corrupt Practices Act.

1855   First Palmerston Administration; abolition of newspaper tax.

1858   Second Derby Administration.

1859   Second Palmerston Administration.

1860   Gladstone's Free Trade Budget.

1865   Death of Palmerston; second Russell Administration; Fenian movement in Ireland; National Reform League.

1866   Third Derby Administration.

1867   Second Reform Act.

1868   First Disraeli Administration; first Gladstone Administration.

1869   Disestablishment of Anglican Church in Ireland; Labour Representation League.

1870   Isaac Butt launches Home Rule movement.

1871   Cardwell's Army Regulation Act abolishes purchase of commissions; Local Government Act.

1872   (Secret) Ballot Act; Licensing Act.

1874   Second Disraeli Administration.

1877   National Liberal Federation formed.

1879   Irish Land League started.

1880   Second Gladstone Administration.

1881   Death of Disraeli; Irish Land Reform Act.

1882   Phoenix Park Murders.

1884   Third Reform Act.

1885   First Salisbury Administration.

1886   Third Gladstone Administration; second Salisbury Administration.

1891   Death of Parnell; Liberal's 'Newcastle Programme'.

1892   Fourth Gladstone Administration.

1892   Independent Labour Party founded; second Home Rule Bill.

1894   Rosebery Administration; Local (Parish Councils) Government Act.

1895   Third Salisbury Administration.

1898   Death of Gladstone.

1900   Labour Representation Committee created.

1901   Accession of Edward VII.

1902   Balfour Administration.

1903   Women's Social and Political Union founded by Mrs. Pankhurst; Wyndham's Irish Land Purchase Act.

1905   Campbell-Bannerman Administration.

1906   L.R.C. becomes Labour Party.

1907   Qualification of Women Act.

1908   First Asquith Administration.

1909   Lloyd George's Budget rejected by House of Lords.

1910   Accession of George V.

1911   Parliament Act.

1914   Third Home Rule Bill receives royal assent, but operation suspended

1915   Asquith Coalition Administration.

1916   Lloyd George Coalition Administration; Easter Rebellion.

1918   Representation of the People Act.

1920   Emergency Powers Act; Government of Ireland Act.

1921   Recognition of Irish Free State with Dominion status.

1922   Bonar Law Administration.

1923   First Baldwin Administration.

1924   First Ramsay MacDonald Labour Administration; second Baldwin Administration.

1928   Franchise Act giving equal voting rights to women.

1929   Local Government Act; second Ramsay MacDonald Labour Administration

1931   First and second Ramsay MacDonald National Administrations.

1935   Baldwin National Administration.

1936   Accession and abdication of Edward VIII.

1937   Accession of George VI; Chamberlain National Administration; Ministers of the Crown Act gives statutory recognition to leader of the Opposition and Cabinet.

1940   Winston Churchill Coalition Administration.
1945   Attlee Administration; Representation of the People Act.
1947   Parliament Act, further limiting delaying power of House
           of Lords.
1949   Legal Aid and Advice Act.
1951   Churchill Conservative Administration.
1952   Accession of Queen Elizabeth II.
1955   Eden Administration.
1957   Macmillan Administration.
1959   Second Macmillan Administration.
1963   Douglas-Home Administration.
1964   First Wilson Administration.
1966   Second Wilson Administration.

FOREIGN AND IMPERIAL

1783   Peace of Versailles, ending American War of Independence.
1784   Pitt's India Act establishes Board of Control.
1788   Establishment of convict colony in New South Wales.
1791   Canada Act creating Provinces of Upper and Lower Canada.
1801   Secretaryship for War and Colonies created.
1815   Congress of Vienna.
1819   Annexation of Singapore.
1823   Declaration of Monroe Doctrine.
1824   Recognition by Britain of South American Republics.
1827   Battle of Navarino.
1830   Britain, Russia and France recognise an independent
           Greece.
1833   Abolition of slavery throughout the Empire.
1836   First British settlement in South Australia.
1839   Durham Report.
1840   Canada Act uniting Upper and Lower Canada; annexation
           of New Zealand
1843   Natal declared a British colony.
1846   Sugar Duties Act.
1849   Repeal of Navigation Acts; annexation of Punjab.

1854   Outbreak of Crimean War; Colonial Office established as separate Department.

1856   Peace of Paris ends Crimean War.

1857   Indian Mutiny.

1858   Government of India Act.

1864   Annexation of Schleswig-Holstein by Prussia and Austria.

1865   Colonial Laws Validity Act.

1866   Austro-Prussian War.

1867   British North America Act makes Canada first Dominion.

1870   Franco-Prussian War; completion of Italian unification.

1871   Proclamation of German Empire.

1875   Disraeli acquires share-holding in Suez Canal.

1876   Queen Victoria becomes Empress of India.

1877   Annexation of the Transvaal.

1878   Congress of Berlin.

1885   Fall of Khartoum and death of General Gordon.

1886   Royal Niger Company receives Charter.

1887   First Colonial Conference.

1888   British East Africa Company receives Charter.

1895–6   Jameson Raid.

1899–1902   Boer War.

1901   Commonwealth of Australia formed.

1904   Anglo-French *Entente Cordiale*.

1907   Anglo-Russian *Entente*; Dominion of New Zealand established.

1910   Union of South Africa.

1914   Outbreak of First World War.

1919   Treaty of Versailles; Government of India Act.

1922   Washington Conference; Egypt becomes sovereign State.

1923   Southern Rhodesia becomes colony.

1925   Locarno Agreements.

1931   Japan attacks Manchuria; Statute of Westminister.

1932   Ottawa Economic Conference.

1933   Hitler becomes Chancellor.

1935   Reoccupation of Rhineland; Anglo-German Naval Agreement; Italian invasion of Abyssinia; Hoare–Laval Agreement; Government of India Act.

1936   Outbreak of Spanish Civil War.

1938   German annexation of Austria; Munich Agreement.

1939   German annexation of Czechoslovakia; German–Russian
       Pact; Anglo-Polish Agreement; German invasion of
       Poland and outbreak of Second World War.

1945   Yalta Conference.

1947   Indian Independence Act.

1948   Organisation for European Economic Co-operation set up
       to supervise allocation of American assistance; Brussels
       Treaty Organisation; Ceylon and Burma become inde-
       pendent; Federation of Malaya created.

1949   NATO set up.

1957   Ghana (Gold Coast) becomes independent.

1960   Nigeria becomes independent.

1961   Sierra Leone and Tanganyika become independent.

1962   Uganda becomes independent.

1963   Kenya becomes independent; break-up of Central African
       Federation.

1965   Southern Rhodesia makes unilateral declaration of inde-
       pendence (U.D.I.).

1966   Guyana (British Guiana) becomes independent.

Index